900 Sentences of Situational English
in Transportation Engineering

交通工程情景英语 900句

魏永幸 刘彦琳 张红英 白雪 苏玲梅 等 编著

人民交通出版社股份有限公司
China Communications Press Co.,Ltd.

内 容 提 要

本书的编写旨在满足海外工程技术人员的业务沟通需要。书中内容取材于海外专业技术人员在实际工作中经常使用的语言,涵盖铁路交通工程领域20多个专业的业务场景对话、核心词汇及术语。本书突出"业务情景"的设置,以及"典型对话"句型和专业"替换单词",采用中英文对照典型对话的形式呈现,以便于工程技术人员备考查用。

本书可供涉外工程的工程技术人员、商务人士参考使用。

图书在版编目(CIP)数据

交通工程情景英语900句 / 魏永幸,刘彦琳,张红英编著. — 北京:人民交通出版社股份有限公司,2017.2
 ISBN 978-7-114-12927-8

Ⅰ.①交… Ⅱ.①魏… ②刘… ③张… Ⅲ.①交通工程—英语—口语—教材 Ⅳ.①H319.9

中国版本图书馆CIP数据核字(2016)第072870号

```
书    名:交通工程情景英语900句
著 作 者:魏永幸  刘彦琳  张红英  白 雪  苏玲梅  等
责任编辑:王 霞(wxccpress@126.com)
出版发行:人民交通出版社股份有限公司
地    址:(100011)北京市朝阳区安定门外外馆斜街3号
网    址:http://www.ccpress.com.cn
销售电话:(010)59757973
总 经 销:人民交通出版社股份有限公司发行部
经    销:各地新华书店
印    刷:北京市密东印刷有限公司
开    本:720×960  1/16
印    张:25
字    数:480千
版    次:2017年3月  第1版
印    次:2017年3月  第1次印刷
书    号:ISBN 978-7-114-12927-8
定    价:86.00元
```

(有印刷、装订质量问题的图书由本公司负责调换)

编审委员会

顾　　　问：朱　颖　　许佑顶　　张雪才　　秦小林　　王国良
主 任 委 员：魏永幸　　刘彦琳
副主任委员：张红英　　白　雪　　苏玲梅
编　　　委：李　佳　　柏飞标　　黄华平　　吴彦格　　江　凯　　龙宗明
　　　　　　常　啸　　杨　昉　　付　刚　　罗仁立　　徐锡江　　吴建明
　　　　　　王利军　　林绍平　　郭建文　　张　维　　韦道准　　袁　蕾
　　　　　　严　瑾　　高　宏　　邓云川　　汪秋宾　　陈纪纲　　唐　伟
　　　　　　李　洪　　李佳妮　　谷学东　　马　捷　　熊　琪　　甘　源
　　　　　　张利明　　林　波　　程良爽　　陈　峰　　杨　柳　　刘鸿旭
翻　　　译：刘　珊　　贾燕玲　　郑志刚　　任　玲　　王　斌　　张月祎
　　　　　　何　叶　　胡桂芳　　陈庆博　　朱　欣　　赵文佳　　李　明
　　　　　　蒙　婷　　向　宇　　宋方方　　孟　鑫
审　　　校：王　建　　胡新明　　王锡根　　张　桓　　戴若愚　　魏春予
校　　　阅：David Mikhail　　包　慧
英 文 朗 读：Andrew GEE　　Rhys　　Amanda Harrold
主 编 单 位：中铁二院工程集团有限责任公司

前言

中铁二院工程集团有限责任公司是中国陆地交通领域大型勘察设计企业之一,近年来发展迅速,业务已扩展到东南亚、非洲、南美和欧洲等地区。但在实践中,涉外工程业务人员深感语言障碍造成业务交流困难,迫切需要进一步提高应用外语进行业务沟通、交流的能力。为此,中铁二院技术中心策划并组织相关业务人员编写了《交通工程情景英语900句》。

本书内容包括交通工程20多个专业的业务情景典型对话,专业常用或核心单词、术语,以及商务旅行常用口语和备查的通用常识图表。

本书内容主要取材于相关专业业务人员在实际工作中经常遇到的问题,具有很强的针对性和实用性;在内容编排上,突出"业务情景"的设置,结合业务情景的"典型对话"句型和专业"替换单词",最终形成覆盖陆地交通工程主要专业的"业务情景"+"典型对话"+"替换单词"的中、英文对照典型对话的汇编。同时,邀请外籍专家为本书录制了对话同步音频(可扫描二维码播放)。本书可供涉外工程的工程技术人员、商务人员等参考使用。

本书的编写是一种新的尝试,难免存在疏漏和不当之处,诚望广大读者不吝指正,以期逐渐完善。

编者

2016年7月

目 录

第一部分　交通工程情景会话 ·· 1

第一章　经调 ·· 2
Chapter 1　Economy Investigation

第二章　行车 ·· 6
Chapter 2　Organization of Train Operation

第三章　测量 ·· 23
Chapter 3　Survey

第四章　地质 ·· 33
Chapter 4　Geology

第五章　线路 ·· 48
Chapter 5　Route

第六章　路基 ·· 69
Chapter 6　Subgrade

第七章　桥梁 ·· 80
Chapter 7　Bridge

第八章　隧道 ·· 87
Chapter 8　Tunnel

第九章　站场 ·· 101
Chapter 9　Station and Yard

第十章　轨道 ·· 110
Chapter 10　Track

第十一章　机务车辆 ··· 120
Chapter 11　Locomotive & Rolling Stock

第十二章　机械 135
Chapter 12　Mechanics

第十三章　信号 167
Chapter 13　Signal

第十四章　通信 177
Chapter 14　Communication

第十五章　信息 195
Chapter 15　Information

第十六章　牵引供电 216
Chapter 16　Tractive Power Supply

第十七章　牵引变电 236
Chapter 17　Traction Substation

第十八章　接触网 264
Chapter 18　Overhead Catenary System

第十九章　供电段 279
Chapter 19　Power Supply Section

第二十章　建筑 292
Chapter 20　Architecture

第二十一章　结构 307
Chapter 21　Structure

第二十二章　电力 314
Chapter 22　Electric Power

第二十三章　暖通 321
Chapter 23　Heating & Ventilation

第二十四章　给排水 333
Chapter 24　Water Supply & Drainage

第二十五章　环评 343
Chapter 25　Environment Assessment

第二十六章　环保·· 347
Chapter 26　Environment Protection

第二十七章　施预·· 354
Chapter 27　Construction Estimate

第二十八章　城市轨道交通······································ 358
Chapter 28　Urban Rail Transit

第二部分　商务旅行情景会话·································· 371

第三部分　常用信息附图附表·································· 383

第一部分

交通工程情景会话

第一章 经调
Chapter 1　Economy Investigation

业务情景：中方王工程师与外方工程师Jones交流，收集资料。
Scene: Mr Wang, the engineer from Chinese side, is communicating with Jones, the foreign engineer, for data collection.

典型对话 Conversation

王工程师：我们需要贵方提供一些基础资料，用作运量需求预测①的依据。

Jones：好的，请问需要哪些资料？

王工程师：主要包括社会经济、交通量、规划等，我们有一个详细的资料清单，请您过目。（给对方资料清单）

Jones：对应的统计数据是按清单上的表格填报吗？

王工程师：是的。

Jones：您要求的一些规划资料目前尚处于编制阶段，没有最终成果，怎么办？

王工程师：能否请您提供中间成果②？以便我们设计时与贵方的相关规划衔接一致。

Mr Wang: We need you to provide some basic data as the basis for traffic volume demand prediction①.

Jones: Fine, what kind of data do you need?

Mr Wang: We need social economy, traffic volume and planning data. We have one specific data list for your reference. (Hand over the data list)

Jones: As for the corresponding statistical data, can we complete it in the form on that list?

Mr Wang: Yes, please.

Jones: The planning data you want is still being compiled. We don't have the final results yet. What shall we do?

Mr Wang: Can you provide the intermediate outcomes②, so that our design can be consistent with your relevant planning?

第一部分　交通工程情景会话

Jones：没问题。
王工程师：如果资料收集过程中有什么问题，请随时与我方联系。

Jones：好的，谢谢。

Jones: No problem.
Mr Wang: If any questions arise in the process of data collection, please contact us at your time.

Jones: Ok. Thanks.

替换单词 Alternative terms

① 综合交通规划
　公路网规划
　铁路网规划
② 最终成果

① comprehensive transportation planning
　highway network planning
　rail network planning
② final results

业务情景：中方王工程师与外方工程师 Jones 讨论路网规划。
Scene: Mr Wang is discussing with Jones about the road network planning.

典型对话 Conversation

王工程师：我们希望同贵方讨论一下路网规划的相关问题。

Jones：好的，请说。
王工程师：从既有资料分析，贵方做过铁路网规划①，但是完成时间相对较早。请问在本次项目设计中，是否需要严格执行既有的路网规划？

Mr Wang: We'd like to discuss the road network planning and other relevant matters with you.

Jones: Ok, Please.
Mr Wang: According to the analysis on the existing data, you have done the rail network planning① before, but that was completed a long time ago. So, for the project design, is it necessary to carry out the existing road network planning stringently?

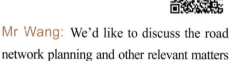

Jones: 原则上执行既有规划，但是如果你们有更好的建议，也可以在本次设计中反映出来，但调整前请先与我方沟通。

Jones: Essentially, we will follow the existing planning. If you have a better idea, you can reflect that in the design, but please discuss with us before doing so.

替换单词 Alternative terms

① 综合交通规划
　 公路网规划
　 城际铁路网规划

① comprehensive transportation planning
　 highway network planning
　 intercity rail network planning

业务情景：中方王工程师与外方工程师 Jones 讨论运量设计。
Scene: Mr Wang is discussing the traffic volume design with Jones.

典型对话 Conversation

王工程师：我们希望同贵方讨论一下运量设计的相关问题。

Jones：好的。

王工程师：沿线的工矿企业规划①对项目运量水平影响较大，请问这些规划是否能按时实施呢？

Jones：可以按时实施。

王工程师：可否请贵方提供相应的书面材料作为设计依据？

Jones：没问题。

Mr Wang: We'd like to talk about the traffic volume design and relevant matters with you.

Jones: Sure.

Mr Wang: The Industry and Mining Enterprises Planning① along the line could affect the project traffic volume level a lot, so we are wondering whether this planning can be carried out on time.

Jones: Certainly. It will be carried out on time.

Mr Wang: Can you provide such paperwork as the design basis?

Jones: Sure.

第一部分　交通工程情景会话

> **替换单词 Alternative terms**
>
> ① 矿产开发规划　　　① mining development planning
>   旅游发展规划　　　 tourism development planning
>   城镇体系规划　　　 urban system planning

业务情景：中方王工程师与外方工程师 Jones 讨论运量设计。
Scene: Mr Wang is discussing about the traffic volume with Jones.

典型对话 Conversation

王工程师：我们希望同贵方讨论一下运量①设计的相关问题。

Jones：好的。

王工程师：请问贵方的运量审批是独立的，还是含在项目审查中一并进行？

Jones：针对具体项目有所不同。

王工程师：能否请贵方落实一下本项目的运量审批流程？

Jones：可以，落实后告知你。

Mr Wang: We'd like to talk about the traffic volume① design and relevant matters with you.

Jones: Ok.

Mr Wang: About the approval of traffic volume, is it separated or included in the program review?

Jones: That depends.

Mr Wang: Would you please confirm the traffic volume approval procedure for this project?

Jones: Ok, I will tell you after confirmation.

> **替换单词 Alternative terms**
>
> ① 客运量　　　　　　① passenger volume
>   货运量　　　　　　 freight volume

第二章 行车
Chapter 2　Organization of Train Operation

业务情景：中方余工程师向外方业主代表 Sandy 索要设计资料。
Scene: Mr Yu, the engineer from Chinese side, is asking for design data from Sandy, the Employer's Representative.

典型对话 Conversation

余工程师：我们希望贵方运营管理部门提供列车运行图等技术资料，包括列车等级与种类、货物列车牵引质量①、列车对数、列车间隔时间标准②、综合维修天窗③、线路允许速度④、车站到发线有效长、列车时刻表等。

Mr Yu: We hope your operations management department can provide us with train working diagrams and other technical information, including train class and type, freight train tractive mass①, train pairs, train interval time standards②, comprehensive maintenance "gap"③, allowable speed of line④, effective length of station's arrival and departure track, timetable for trains, etc.

Sandy：还有其他可以帮助您的吗？

Sandy: Is there anything else that I can help with?

余工程师：我们还需得到贵地区运营收入与成本的相关资料，包括运营企业的收费标准和运量，当地平均人员工资与福利⑤、原材料、电力与燃油价格、企业管理费用、企业财务报表等。

Mr Yu: We also need relevant information on operating incomes and costs in the region, including charge standards and traffic volumes of operating enterprises, average local salaries and welfare⑤, prices of raw materials, electricity and fuel, overhead expenses and corporate financial statements.

第一部分　交通工程情景会话

Sandy：好的，我们会按照贵方要求将资料准备齐全。

余工程师：为了更好地完成项目，我们需要贵方价格管理部门提供缅甸中部地区铁路、公路、航空的市场运价与管制运价。

Sandy：好的，查询后会回复您。

余工程师：此外，我们还需要了解运输企业相关的<u>税收法律与制度</u>⑥，特别是营业税、增值税、企业所得税的税基与税率。

Sandy：我方财税部门将于15日内将资料的纸质及电子文件交予贵方。

Sandy: Well, we will prepare the materials as requested.

Mr Yu: In order to complete the project, we need your price management department to provide marketing and regulatory freight rates of railway, highway and air in the central region of Myanmar.

Sandy: Fine, I will reply to you when I have the relevant information.

Mr Yu: In addition, we also need to know the transport related <u>tax laws and system</u>⑥, especially the tax base and rate of business tax, value-added tax and corporate income tax.

Sandy: Our revenue department will submit the paper and electronic documents to you within 15 days.

替换单词 Alternative terms

① 牵引机型
② 追踪间隔
　 连发间隔
③ 施工天窗
④ 设计最高时速
　 速度目标值
⑤ 各部门定员
⑥ 税收优惠政策

① traction locomotive type
② tracing headway
　 successive headway
③ construction "gap"
④ designed maximum speed per hour
　 target speed value
⑤ personnel quota of various departments
⑥ preferential tax policy

业务情景：中方余工程师与外方工程师 James 讨论技术标准制订。
Scene: Mr Yu is discussing technical standards with James, the engineer from foreign side.

典型对话 Conversation

余工程师：我认为我们应该对本项目的技术标准达成共识。

James：是的。

余工程师：根据运量预测，本线各区段远期客货流密度为 1500 万 t/年，采用单线就能够满足运输需求。

James：本线建成后将在我国路网中发挥重要的骨干作用，而且客货运量的增长潜力很大，我们希望按一次建成双线①考虑。

余工程师：单线即可满足本线初近期的运量，一次建成双线将会造成资源浪费，我们建议按预留双线考虑。

James：这个问题先搁置，我们下一轮再讨论。

Mr Yu: I think we should reach a consensus on the technical standards of the project.

James: Yes, I agree.

Mr Yu: According to transport volume forecasts, the density of freight and passenger flow on sections of this line is 15 million tons per year in the long term and it can be satisfied by a single track.

James: The line will play a key role in our rail network after it is built, and it will bring great growth in passenger and freight traffic volume. Therefore, we hope it can be completed as double tracks①.

Mr Yu: Since a single track can satisfy the transportation volume of this line in initial and short terms, to complete double tracks will result in a waste of resources. We propose to reserve conditions for double tracks.

James: Let's put this issue aside and discuss it in the next round.

余工程师： 本线以长途客流为主，铁路建成后主要的竞争对手是高速公路。根据对本线时间目标值的研究，考虑与既有交通方式相协调，满足沿线居民出行需求，本线速度至少需要达到120km/h。

Mr Yu: As this line mainly targets long distance passenger flow, its major competitor will be expressway after construction. In order to meet the requirement of resident trips along the line, the line speed should at least reach 120km/h according to studies on the time target for this line as well as taking coordination with existing traffic modes into consideration.

James: 本线位处高原，地形起伏较大，希望贵方在设计时对速度目标值的可行性进行论证。

James: This line is located on the plateau with great topographic relief, so you need to demonstrate the feasibility of target speed value in design.

余工程师： 我方在设计中已考虑此因素。本线A站至B站间有较长的24‰紧坡地段，普通旅客列车本坡度最高速度低于100km/h，因此该段我方考虑在紧坡地段采用120km/h设计速度，自由坡地段线路平纵面预留160km/h条件。

Mr Yu: We have taken account of that factor in design. There is a long section of 24‰(24 permil) sufficient grade between Station A and Station B, and the maximum speed of an ordinary passenger train is less than 100km/h on this section. Therefore, with respect to this section, we plan to adopt the design speed of 120km/h for sections of sufficient grade while reserving conditions of 160km/h in both plan and profile for sections of insufficient grade.

James: 还有考虑了其他影响因素吗？

James: Have you taken other influence factors into consideration?

余工程师：此外，我们也考虑了相邻路网的情况，目前与本线密切相关的既有及规划铁路，其速度目标值都在120km/h 及以上，从相邻路网匹配和运输组织上分析，本线推荐旅客列车最高行车速度 120km/h、部分路段线路平纵断面预留 160km/h 条件是合适的。

James：请问贵方选定的限制坡度为多少？我方希望尽量缩短线路长度。

余工程师：限制坡度的确定应结合工程可实施性、工程风险及工程投资综合考虑，并与相邻线路相适应。本线限制坡度采用 12‰，加力坡采用 24‰，便于进行运输组织，减少列车换装作业、提高运输效率、提高运输质量。

James：请问本线推荐何种牵引方式？

Mr Yu: We also considered the situation of the adjacent railway network. Currently the target speeds of both the existing and planned railway lines closely related with this line are 120km/h and above. From the analyses of matching with the adjacent railway network and transportation organization, the recommended maximum running speed of a passenger train is 120km/h for this line, and it is appropriate to reserve conditions for 160km/h in both plan and profile for some sections in this line.

James: What's your selected ruling grade? We hope to minimize the length of the line.

Mr Yu: Ruling grade must be determined comprehensively in accordance with engineering feasibility, engineering risks and project investment, and it should be compatible with adjacent lines. The ruling grade is 12‰(12 permil) and the pusher grade is 24‰(24 permil) for this line, which will facilitate transportation organization, reduce train transshipment operations, raise transport efficiency and enhance transport quality.

James: What's the recommended mode of traction for this line?

余工程师: 受地形限制,本线必须采用连续的长大坡道和长隧道,若采用内燃牵引,速度和牵引质量都会受到很大的影响,所以我方考虑采用电力牵引。另外从对环境的影响考虑,电力牵引也更加节能环保。

James: 我国电力资源缺乏,前期外部电力接入困难,所以我建议初期还是考虑内燃牵引过渡。

余工程师: 好的。我们在设计中会考虑这一点。对于机型的选择,根据我国的经验,本线内燃过渡期建议采用内燃六轴机型双机牵引,牵引质量为1800t。近远期采用电力六轴机型牵引,牵引质量近期3000t、远期4000t。

James: 请为我介绍本线车站分布情况?

Mr Yu: As the line is limited by topography, there must be continuous long steep grades and long tunnels. If diesel traction is used, the speed and tractive tonnage will be greatly affected, so we are considering adopting electric traction. Besides, electric traction is also more energy-efficient and environmentally friendly.

James: Electric power resources are insufficient in our country, and it is difficult to introduce external power in the preliminary stage, so I would suggest using diesel traction in the initial phase for transition.

Mr Yu: Fine, we will consider it in the design. For locomotive type selection, based on our experience in China, we recommend double locomotive traction with six-axle diesel locomotives and tractive tonnage of 1800t for the diesel transitional period, and use locomotive traction with six-axle electric locomotives, in both the short and the long term, whose tractive tonnage is 3000t in the short term and 4000t in long term.

James: Could you please show me the distribution of stations along the line?

余工程师：为了满足远期输送能力，本线车站的最大站间距离不能超过20km。结合沿线城市布局与运量分布情况，我方建议初期开放南帕卡等20个车站，近期开放淡罢亚等3个车站，远期开放剩余缓开站。其中木姐等5个车站为办理客货运作业的中间站，其他车站为会让站。

James：请问贵方推荐何种运营管理方式？

余工程师：本项目由中缅两国合作建设及运营②，我方建议成立缅中合资铁路公司，负责项目建设及资产管理。未来根据双方运营技术力量，充分利用既有设备资源、人力资源、运营经验等，通过合同委托方式，将部分运营业务，如维修养护等，委托给有实力的运营公司。

Mr Yu: In order to meet the requirement of long-term transportation capacity, the maximum interval between stations along the line should not exceed 20km. Considering the city layout and traffic volume distribution along the line, we suggest opening twenty stations such as Nam hpak ka in the initial stage, three stations such as Than pa ya in short term and the remaining stations in long term. Five stations among them including Muse are intermediate stations where passenger and freight operations are handled, and the rest of stations are passing stations.

James: What's your recommended operation management mode?

Mr Yu: As this project is jointly constructed and operated② by China and Myanmar, we propose to establish Myanmar-China Joint Venture Railway Company which takes charge of project construction and assets management. In the future, according to the operation technology strength of both parties, the company can make full use of existing equipment resources, human resources, operational experience, etc., and commission some operations, such as repair and maintenance, to powerful operating companies by commission contracts.

第一部分　交通工程情景会话

James: 贵国与我国间存在大量的物资交流,请问贵方推荐哪种通关模式?

James: There are a large number of goods exchanges between your country and our country, which mode of customs clearance do you recommend?

余工程师: 为了简化运输作业流程,提高国境口岸站的作业效率,缩短通关时间,我们建议采用"一地两检"的通关模式,在木姐站设置边检场。

Mr Yu: In order to simplify the process of transportation operations, improve operational efficiency of frontier port stations and shorten the time of customs clearance, we suggest adopting the customs clearance mode of "two inspections at one site" and set one border inspection field at Muse station.

James: 贵国与我国的边检、监管方式有很大区别,此外一地两检需要较大的查验用地,木姐站无法提供足够空间。我方认为"两地两检"更为可行。

James: Your methods of border inspection and supervision are quite different from those of our country. Besides, "two inspections at one site" requires a large inspection site, which cannot be provided at Muse station. We believe that "two inspections at two sites" is more feasible.

余工程师: 通关模式的设定涉及两国的政策与司法管辖问题,我方认为还需进一步协商方可确定。

Mr Yu: As the customs clearance mode is related with the policies and jurisdictional issues of both countries, we believe that further consultations are needed prior to the final decision.

James: 请为我介绍本项目的旅客运输组织方案。

James: Could you please show me the passenger transport organization plan for the project.

余工程师：本线的客流主要以贵国首都、经济发达城市与边境、邻国重点城市间商务出行为主。旅客运输组织的首要目标是提高旅行速度，满足通道快速交通需求。本线考虑组织开行中国昆明至缅甸内比都的国际列车，以及木姐至曼德勒的城际列车。

James：修建本线的另一个主要目的是为了运送煤炭、金属、矿石等大宗货物，以及沿线零星货物，请在设计货车开行方案时考虑我方货运需求。

余工程师：对于大宗货流，我方建议尽量组织装车地直达或技术直达列车，其余车流则组织直通、区段货物列车通过本段铁路。此外本段铁路地方运量占比比例较大，对地方经济发展很重要，设计时考虑开行直达及摘挂列车满足地方需要。

Mr Yu: Main passenger flows of this line are business trips between your capital, economically developed cities and borders, and important cities in neighboring countries. The top goal of passenger transport organization is to improve travelling speed and to meet the requirement of rapid transit passage. It is being considered to organising and running international trains between Kunming, China and Naypyidaw, Myanmar and intercity trains between Muse and Mandalay on this line.

James: Another major objective for building the line is to transport coal, metal, ore and other bulk cargo, as well as odd-lot goods along the line. Please consider our requirement for freight transportation when you design the freight train operation scheme.

Mr Yu: For bulk cargo flow, we recommend through or technical through trains originated from loading points as practical as possible. The other freight flows can pass this railway by transit or district freight trains. In addition, as local traffic volume accounts for a large proportion of the railway, and it is important for local economic development, it is being considered running through trains and pick-up and drop trains in design in order to meet local needs.

James: 请告诉我本项目各研究年度的行车量与车站工作量。

余工程师：根据运量及客货列车开行方案，本线开行客车 5 对、货车 11 对。本线主要货运站为腊戍西，运量主要以发送③为主。根据运量，木姐站初期④装车数为货场 3 车/d、专用线 11 车/d，卸车数为货场 7 车/d、专用线 2 车/d。

James: 本线维修天窗时间有多长？

余工程师：在内燃过渡期，本线综合维修天窗时间考虑 60min，近远期考虑 90min。

James: 设计的线路输送能力能否满足运输需求？

余工程师：本线初、近、远期设计输送能力分别为 888 万 t/年、1832 万 t/年、2223 万 t/年，能够满足各研究年度的运输需求。

James: Please tell me the traffic throughputs and station workloads of the project in the study years.

Mr Yu: According to the traffic volume and passenger and freight train operation plans, five pairs of passenger trains and eleven pairs of freight trains will run on this line. Lashio West is the major freight station of this line, whose traffic volume is mainly origination③. According to the traffic volume, the quantity of car loadings of Muse station in the initial stage④ is three cars per day for freight yard and eleven cars per day for private siding, and the number of car unloading is seven cars per day for freight yard and two cars per day for private siding.

James: How long is the maintenance gap for this line?

Mr Yu: The maintenance gap for this line is planned as 60min for the diesel transitional period and 90min in both the short and the long term.

James: Can the design capacity for transportation satisfy the transportation demand?

Mr Yu: The design capacity is 8.88, 18.32 and 22.23 million tons per year respectively for the initial stage, short term and long term of this line, which can satisfy the transportation demands in the study years.

James: 本线需新配几台调机？设于何处？

余工程师: 我方考虑曼德勒东站增设调机1台，其他各站不考虑新增调机，货场取送作业由本务机车担当。

James: 我想了解调度区划分情况。

余工程师: 本线建成后在曼德勒新设两个行车调度台[5]，分别管辖木姐—曼德勒段以及曼德勒—皎漂段。

James: How many shunting engines should be added for this line? And where are they located?

Mr Yu: We plan to add one shunting engine for Mandalay East station, but no additional shunting engines for other stations. Leading locomotives will be responsible for taking-out and placing-in operations in freight yard.

James: I'd like to know about the train control sections.

Mr Yu: Two traffic control panels[5] will be established at Mandalay after the line is constructed to control Muse-Mandalay section and Mandalay-Kyauk Pyu section respectively.

替换单词 Alternative terms

① 单线
　　增建二线
② 委托运营
　　自管自营
③ 到达
④ 近期
　　远期
⑤ 客运调度台
　　货运调度台
　　综合调度台

① single line
　　additional second line
② entrusted for operation
　　self-administered and self-operated
③ destination
④ short term
　　long term
⑤ passenger traffic control panels
　　freight traffic control panels
　　comprehensive control panels

业务情景：中方余工程师与外方工程师 James 讨论项目财务分析。
Scene: Mr Yu is discussing the financial analysis of the project with James.

典型对话 Conversation

James: 请问本项目经济评价的计算期按几年计算？

余工程师：本次经济评价是以中缅铁路合资公司为评价主体。根据前期协商，建设期为6年，特许经营期60年，计算期采用66年。

James: 请说明一下本项目的投资情况。

余工程师：本项目建设期静态投资[①] 794.08亿元，不含建设期利息投资总额总计905.43亿元。此外，本项目运营期需要进行电气化改造，届时需追加投资额77.91亿元。

James: 本项目投资巨大，投资回收期较长，风险较高，请问贵方将采用哪些方式进行资金筹措？

James: How long is the calculation period for the economic evaluation of this project?

Mr Yu: China-Myanmar railway joint-venture company is taken as the subject for this economic evaluation. According to previous consultations, the construction period is 6 years and the concession period is 60 years, so the calculation period is 66 years.

James: Please can you explain the project investment.

Mr Yu: The static investment[①] for the construction period of the project is 79.408 billion yuan, and the total investment is 90.543 billion yuan, excluding interests incurred during construction period. Moreover, this project will be electrified during the operation period, and an additional investment of 7.791 billion yuan is required then.

James: For the huge investment, long payback period and high risks of the project, how will you raise funds?

余工程师：本项目资本金比例为30%，债务资金来源计划由中方国家开发银行、中国进出口银行和中国银行等组成的银团贷款和少量缅方贷款，贷款比例占总投资的70%。

Mr Yu: The project capital funds account for 30%. Debt capitals are planned to be provided by Chinese loans from bank consortia such as China Development Bank, Export-Import Bank of China and Bank of China and some Burmese loans, which account for 70% of the total investment.

James：考虑本项目实际情况，本着实事求是的原则，从紧从严控制，本次测算成本时请不要考虑通胀因素。

James: The cost must be estimated strictly in accordance with the actual situation of the project, practically and realistically, without taking inflation into account.

余工程师：根据贵方要求，本次测算营运成本初期、近期、远期分别为14.9亿元、21.1亿元、30.9亿元，按运营成本要素分为工资及福利、材料、修理费、燃料、电力及其他费用②。

Mr Yu: Following your requirement, the operation costs estimated this time for the initial stage, short term and long term are 1.49 billion yuan, 2.11 billion yuan and 3.09 billion yuan respectively. According to the operation cost elements, they can be divided into wages and welfare, materials, repairs, fuel, electricity and other costs②.

James：如果运营期出现资金短缺，请问贵方有何对策？

余工程师：运营期如出现资金短缺，需要借短期贷款，如果运营期补贴采用无息③贷款方案，则由中国出口信用保险公司提供。

James: What's your solution for capital shortage in the operation period?

Mr Yu: Short-term loans are required in case of capital shortage during the operation period. If subsidies for the operation period are supplied in interest free③ loans, they can be provided by SINOSURE.

James：请问本线运价定为多少？

James: What's the rate of this line?

余工程师：我方在定价时参考了贵国既有铁路客货运价，以成本为导向，体现出铁路运输的价格优势，并充分考虑本项目建成后运输服务质量的提高。本次暂推荐本项目货运综合运价率 0.425 元 /（t•km），客运综合运价率 0.25 元 /（人•km）。

James：本项目投资巨大，低运价会造成严重亏损，我方建议在此基础上将运价提高一些。

余工程师：过高的运价会导致运量大幅下降，运输收入将大幅降低，这样做是不经济的。

James：本次计算中还采用了哪些参数？

余工程师：本线的流动资金取 30 元 / 万换算吨公里，自筹率按 30% 考虑。铺底流动资金按 8 万元 / 正线公里。长期贷款按使用期 30 年，宽限期 6 年。年利率争取优惠利率，暂采用中国现行<u>长期（5 年及以上）贷款</u>[④]利率 6.55% 计算，按季结息。营业税按客运运输收入的 8% 提取。企业所得税税率暂按运营前 3 年全免，其后 21 年减半（15%），最后 36 年按现行税法 30% 征收。利息税按暂免考虑。

Mr Yu: During pricing, we refer to the passenger and freight rates of your existing railway, take the cost as the orientation, demonstrate the price advantage of rail transport, and take into account the quality improvement of transport services after the project is completed. The recommended comprehensive freight rate is 0.425 yuan/(t•km) and comprehensive passenger rate is 0.25 yuan/(person•km).

James: Since the project investment is huge, low rates will cause serious losses. We would advise you to raise the rates by a little bit on that basis.

Mr Yu: High rates will result in a sharp decrease in traffic volume, and transportation revenues will decline dramatically, so this measure is uneconomical.

James: What are the other parameters used in the estimation?

Mr Yu: Circulating funds of the line are considered as 30 yuan/10^4 converted ton-kilometer, and self investment ratio is considered as 30%. Initial working capital is planned as 80,000 yuan / km (main line). The period of utilization is 30 years and the grace period is 6 years for long-term loans. We will strive for preferential annual interest rates. Tentatively the current interest rate 6.55% of <u>long-term (five years or more) loans</u>[④] in China is

James: 根据贵方的计算，本项目的盈利能力如何？

余工程师： 本项目全部投资财务内部收益率税前为5.94%，税后为5.68%；自有资金财务内部收益率为2.76%。全部投资收益水平较高，自有资金收益水平较低，没有达到预设的基准收益率3%。全部投资回收期税前税后均为23.42年，自有资金投资回收期为52.96年。全部投资回收期较短，自有资金投资回收期较长。综合来看，本项目全部投资盈利能力较好，自有资金<u>盈利能力</u>[⑤]较差。

James: 本项目的借款偿还期为多久？

adopted for estimation, which is calculated quarterly for interest settlement. Business tax is considered as 8% of the passenger transportation revenue. Corporate income tax rate is free for the first three years of operation, halved (15%) in the subsequent 21 years and levied 30% in the last 36 years based on current tax laws. Interest tax is provisionally considered as free.

James: According to your estimation, how profitable do you expect the project to be?

Mr Yu: The financial internal rate of return is 5.94% before tax and 5.68% after tax for the total project investment, and it is 2.76% for self-hold capital. While the income level is high for total investment, it is low for self-hold capital, which does not reach the presupposed benchmark rate of return of 3%. The payback period is 23.42 years for total investment before and after tax and 52.96 years for self-hold capital investment. Therefore, it is short for total investment but long for self-hold capital investment. On the whole, the <u>profitability</u>[⑤] is good for the total project investment, but it is poor for self-hold capital.

James: How long is the loan repayment period of the project?

余工程师： 长期贷款偿还按固定期限等额本金偿还，贷款使用期为30年，宽限期6年；短期贷款50年还清，其中包含6年建设期。

James： 贵方将采取哪些措施确保按时还款？

余工程师： 为保证按计划还本付息，项目合资公司需要在运营期筹集其他资金来源。可用于本项目还本付息的资金来源有利润、折旧、摊销等。

James： 本项目的财务生存能力如何？

余工程师： 本项目运营初期财务生存能力较弱，为解决运营期资金缺口，项目合资公司需在运营期筹集总额不少于809.4亿元的资金。

James： 对本项目各指标影响最大的因素是什么？

余工程师： 针对本项目，最敏感的因素是运价，其次是运量，再次为投资和运营成本。当单因素向不利方向变动20%，本项目全部投资内部收益率均高

Mr Yu: Long-term loans will be repaid in equal installments of the principal repayment over a fixed period, with a loan utilization period of thirty years and grace period of six years. Short-term loans will be paid off in fifty years, including the six years of construction period.

James: What measures will you take to ensure repayment timely?

Mr Yu: The joint-venture company of the project has to raise funds from other sources to ensure the debt service on schedule. The available sources of funding for the project debt service include profit, depreciation, amortisation, etc.

James: How is the financial viability of the project?

Mr Yu: The financial viability of the project is weak during the initial operation period. In order to address the funding gap, the joint-venture company needs to raise funds with total amounts of no less than 80.94 billion yuan in the operation period.

James: What is the factor that has the greatest influence on the project indicators?

Mr Yu: For this project, the most sensitive factor is rate, followed by traffic volume, investment and operating cost. When one single factor changes 20%

于基准收益率3%,说明本项目抗风险能力较强。

James: 本项目何时可以达到盈亏平衡?

余工程师: 在运输密度一定的前提下,本线的客运在运营期第40年后才能达到盈亏平衡,货运在运营第17年达到盈亏平衡。

adversely, the internal rate of return of total project investment is still higher than the benchmark yield of 3%, which indicates a strong anti-risk capacity of the project.

James: When will the project break even?

Mr Yu: Under the premise of certain traffic density, the passenger transport of the line will break even in forty years of operation and the freight transport will break even in seventeen years of operation.

替换单词 Alternative terms

① 工程造价增长预留费 　reserve fund for project cost growth
　机车车辆购置费 　　　rolling stock acquisition cost
　铺底流动资金 　　　　initial working capital
　动态投资 　　　　　　dynamic investment
② 间接管理费 　　　　　indirect management fees
　资产保管费 　　　　　assets storage charges
　动车组运用费 　　　　EMU operation costs
　车站及附属费用 　　　station and ancillary costs
③ 低息 　　　　　　　　low-interest
　贴息 　　　　　　　　interest subsidy
　优惠 　　　　　　　　discount
④ 短期贷款 　　　　　　short-term loans
　流动资金贷款 　　　　working capital loans
⑤ 偿债能力 　　　　　　solvency
　财务生存能力 　　　　financial viability
　财务可持续能力 　　　financial sustainability

第一部分　交通工程情景会话

第三章　测量
Chapter 3　Survey

业务情景： 中方王工程师到埃塞俄比亚国家测绘局收集所需资料，Tom 接待。

Scene: Chinese engineer Mr Wang is going to the Ethiopia State Surveying and Mapping Bureau to collect the required information. Tom is receiving him.

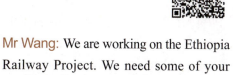

典型对话 Conversation

王工程师：我们正在进行埃塞俄比亚铁路的勘察工作，需要收集一些贵国的测绘资料，包括国家各等级三角点、水准点和各种基本比例尺地形图。

Tom：请稍等。相关材料都在这里。

王工程师：请问这些三角点采用的是<u>国家坐标系统</u>[①]吗？

Tom：是的。

王工程师：坐标系统有无参考椭球参数？

Tom：有的，坐标系采用 WGS-84 椭球，参数为长半轴 =6378137m；短半轴 =6356752.3142m；扁率 α=1/298.257223563。

Mr Wang: We are working on the Ethiopia Railway Project. We need some of your surveying and mapping data, such as triangulation points, benchmarks and all kinds of basic scale topographic maps.

Tom: Just a moment, please. Here you are.

Mr Wang: Are these triangulation points based on your <u>national coordinate system</u>[①]?

Tom: Yes, they are.

Mr Wang: Are there any reference ellipsoid parameters for the coordinate system?

Tom: Yes. For the coordinate system, the WGS-84 ellipsoid is used, the Semi-major axis is equal to 6378137m; Semi-minor axis is equal to 6356752.3142m; Flattening α is equal to 1/298.257223563.

23

王工程师：采用的是 UTM 投影[②]吗？

Tom：是的。

王工程师：可否提供你们国家坐标系统和 WGS-84 坐标系统之间的转换参数吗？

Tom：可以提供给你们。

王工程师：我们还需要水准点的高程系统以及水准点的等级分类。

Tom：水准点采用我国统一的高程系统，分为一、二、三、四等，你们需要收集哪一等级的水准点？

王工程师：地形图的坐标系统和三角点一致吗？

Tom：是一致的。我们有地形图拼接示意图，可以提供给你们。

王工程师：你们还有航空摄影的航片吗？

Tom：我查看一下，有的。

王工程师：请问摄影比例尺是多大？摄影时间是什么时候？

Tom：摄影比例尺是 1:20000，摄影时间是 2012 年 6 月。

Mr Wang: Is it UTM projection[②]?

Tom: Yes, it is.

Mr Wang: Would you please give us transformation parameters between coordinate system of your country and WGS-84 coordinate system?

Tom: Yes, we can.

Mr Wang: Would you please give us the elevation system and level of classification of benchmarks?

Tom: Benchmarks are based on a unified elevation system in our country and divided into Grade Ⅰ, Ⅱ, Ⅲ and Ⅳ, etc. Which grade do you need?

Mr Wang: Is the coordinate system of topographic maps consistent with the triangulation points?

Tom: Yes, it is. We have the splicing schematic of topographic maps and can give it to you.

Mr Wang: Do you have any aerial photos?

Tom: Let me see. Yes, we do.

Mr Wang: How about the photographic scale? What was the photography time?

Tom: It was taken in scale of 1:20 000, in June, 2012.

第一部分 交通工程情景会话

替换单词 Alternative terms

① WGS-84 坐标系　　　　　　① WGS-84 coordinate system
　54 坐标　　　　　　　　　　　54 coordinate
　80 坐标　　　　　　　　　　　80 coordinate
　工程独立坐标系统　　　　　　engineering independent coordinate system
② 横轴墨卡托投影　　　　　　② transverse Mercator projection
　高斯—克吕格投影　　　　　　Gauss-Kruger Projection

业务情景：中方王工程师参加勘测大纲评审会议，回答 Tom 的提问。
Scene: Mr Wang is participating in the review meeting of the survey outline and replying to the questions from Tom.

典型对话 Conversation

Tom：铁路勘测分哪几个阶段？

王工程师：铁路勘测分为初测、定测和补定测三个阶段。

Tom：这次初测工作主要包括哪些工作？

王工程师：这次初测工作包括航空摄影、1:2000 数字地形图测绘、控制网测量①等。

Tom：定测工作主要包括哪些工作？

王工程师：这次定测工作包括中线测量、断面测量、工点地形图测量②等。

Tom: Could you tell me how many phases there are in the railway survey?

Mr Wang: There are three, which are in the preliminary survey, the location survey and the supplemental location survey.

Tom: What will you do in the preliminary survey?

Mr Wang: We shall do the aerial photography, draw 1:2000 digital topographic maps, and make control network survey①, etc.

Tom: What will you do in the location survey?

Mr Wang: We shall do the midline survey, cross section survey, survey of topographic maps on worksite②, etc.

Tom: 什么是补定测工作？

王工程师: 补定测主要是由于方案调整进行的补充测量工作。

Tom: 请问高速铁路进行精密控制测量的主要目的是什么？

王工程师: 高速铁路进行精密控制测量的主要目的是保证旅客列车的安全性和舒适性，以及高速铁路轨道高平顺性。

Tom: 此次数字地形图的成图采用哪种方式？

王工程师: 本项目数字地形图成图方式采用航空摄影测量方法成图[3]。

Tom: 本项目为何不采用 UTM 投影而采用高斯投影？

王工程师: 采用高斯投影，通过选择适当的中央子午线和投影面高程，可把线路轨道面的长度变形控制在 10mm/km 以内，而 UTM 投影达不到此要求。

Tom: 请简要介绍高速铁路精密控制测量的原则。

王工程师: 精密控制测量，按分级布网、逐级控制的原则，建立高速铁路平面和高程控制网。

Tom: What is the supplemental location survey?

Mr Wang: The supplementary location survey is mainly taken when the scheme is adjusted.

Tom: What is the main purpose of the precise control survey for the high-speed railway?

Mr Wang: The purpose is to ensure the safety and comfort of the passenger train and the smoothness of the tracks.

Tom: Which mode will you adopt to draw the digital topographic map this time?

Mr Wang: We shall use aerial photogrammetry[3].

Tom: Why did you use the Gauss projection for this project and not UTM projection?

Mr Wang: Because by Gauss projection, we can control the length deformation of the track surface within 10mm/km by selecting the appropriate central meridian and the height of the projection surface, but the UTM projection cannot meet this requirement.

Tom: Please briefly introduce the principle of the precise control survey for the high-speed railway.

Mr Wang: The principle of precise control survey is to set the level-to-level network, control step-by-step and establish the high-speed rail plane and elevation control network.

第一部分　交通工程情景会话

Tom：本项目平面控制网如何布设？

王工程师：在平面控制网（CP0）基础上分三级布设，第一级为基础平面控制网（CPI），第二级为线路平面控制网（CPⅡ），第三级为轨道控制网（CPⅢ）。

Tom：本项目高程控制网如何布设？

王工程师：高程控制网测量分两级布设，第一级为线路水准基点控制网，第二级为轨道控制网（CPⅢ）。

Tom: How do you set the plane control network for this project?

Mr Wang: We shall adopt a three-level layout based on the plane control network (CP0). The first level is the basic plane control network (CPI). The second level is the route plane control network (CPⅡ). The third level is the track control network (CPⅢ).

Tom: How do you set the elevation control network for this project?

Mr Wang: We set two levels. The first level is the bench mark control network of the route, and the second level is the track control network (CPⅢ).

替换单词 Alternative terms

① 控制工点测量　　　　　① control worksite survey
　 控制断面测量　　　　　　 control section survey
　 气象水文资料收集　　　　 weather and hydrological data collection
② 形图修测　　　　　　　② charts revision
　 专业调查测量　　　　　　 professional investigation survey
　 专业勘测　　　　　　　　 professional survey
　 水文测量　　　　　　　　 hydrographic survey
③ 机载激光雷达（lidar）方法成图　③ digital mapping by airborne lidar
　 全站仪数字化测图　　　　 by total station
　 GPS RTK 数字化测图　　　 and by GPS RTK

业务情景：王工程师和 Tom 跟随测量队伍在野外测量中。
Scene: Mr Wang and Tom are following the survey team in the field.

典型对话 Conversation

Tom：平面控制网主要有哪些建立方法？

王工程师：平面控制网的建立，可采用卫星定位测量①。

Tom：GPS 控制网沿线路如何布设？

王工程师：GPS 控制网应由一个或若干个独立观测环构成，各等级控制网同步图形之间的连接采用边联式或网联式。

Tom：GPS 控制点点位图有何要求？

王工程师：GPS 控制点均采用混凝土固桩，均应在现场填写点位说明，绘制点位示意图，做好点标记。

Tom：本次导线测量的布网方式是哪种？

王工程师：导线控制网布设为附合导线②。

Tom：具体的测站观测采用什么顺序进行？

Tom: How do you establish the plane control network?

Mr Wang: We can utilise the satellite positioning survey①.

Tom: How do you set the GPS control network along the route?

Mr Wang: GPS control network consists of one, or several independent observation rings. The connection between synchronising graphics of each level control network is to be achieved by using edge coupling or net coupling.

Tom: Are there any requirements for the diagram of GPS control points?

Mr Wang: GPS control points are all made of solid concrete stakes. The point description shall be done at the site, and the schematic diagram of point must be drawn.

Tom: What is the layout mode of this traverse survey?

Mr Wang: The traverse control network is set as the connecting traverse②.

Tom: What is the observation sequence at a specific station?

王工程师：测站观测顺序按"后视—前视—前视—后视"的观测模式进行。

Tom：这些仪器是否在检校期内？

王工程师：在这次出工前，我们已确认仪器都在检校期内，并进行了出工前仪器检查测试。

Tom：现场调绘的地名、河流名称等采用哪种语言注记？

王工程师：现场所有地形图名称注记均采用英文注记。

（询问当地人）王工程师：这个村子北边是不是有个水准点？你知道它具体在什么位置吗？

当地人：这个村子北边是有个点，但是不知道是否是你们说的水准点，我带你们去，就在那个山顶上。

王工程师：请问这条河最大洪水位在哪一年？

当地人：资料显示，最大洪水位发生在1921年。

王工程师：请问你们这个火车站的股道图在哪里能找到？

当地人：你到那边火车站办公室问问吧。

Mr Wang: The station observation sequence is done by the observation model of "rear sight-fore sight-fore sight-rear sight".

Tom: Are the instruments in the calibration period?

Mr Wang: We have confirmed the instruments are in the calibration period and we have carefully inspected and tested the equipment before work.

Tom: Which language is used to note the names of places and rivers?

Mr Wang: All annotations of topographic maps shall be written in English.

(Asking a local person)Mr Wang: Excuse me, is there a benchmark in the north of the village? Do you know its specific position?

Local person: Yes, it is on the top of the mountain, but I don't know exactly whether it is what you are looking for. I will lead you there.

Mr Wang: Excuse me, which year did the maximum flood level take place in this river?

Local person: The data shows that it took place in 1921.

Mr Wang: Do you know where we can find the track diagram of this station?

Local person: You can ask someone in station office there.

替换单词 Alternative terms

① 导线测量
　三角网测量

② 闭合导线
　导线网

① traverse survey
　triangulation network survey

② closed traverse
　traverse network

业务情景：勘察成果完成，正在进行成果汇报。
Scene: Having completed the survey, Mr Wang is reporting the results to Tom.

典型对话 Conversation

Tom：请简要介绍一下本项目采用的主要测量设备。

王工程师：本项目使用的主要测量设备有全站仪和电子水准仪①。

Tom：本项目引用的技术标准有哪些？

王工程师：采用的技术标准主要有《铁路工程测量规范》（TB 10101—2009）②。

Tom：本项目采用的平面和高程控制网基准是什么？

王工程师：平面基准为 WGS-84 椭球，高程采用当地高程系统。

Tom: Please briefly introduce the main equipment used in this project.

Mr Wang: In this project we mainly use total stations and electronic level①.

Tom: Which technical standards do you adopt in the project?

Mr Wang: The main technical standard is *Code for Railway Engineering Survey* (TB 10101—2009)②.

Tom: What is the datum for plane and elevation control network in this project?

Mr Wang: The plane control network is based on the WGS-84 ellipsoid, and for the elevation we use is the local elevation system.

第一部分　交通工程情景会话

Tom：请详细介绍本项目使用的坐标和高程系统。

王工程师：本项目使用的坐标系统是工程<u>独立坐标系统</u>③，中央子午线是117°，投影面高程500m，采用的高程系统是当地高程系统。

Tom：请介绍本项目各阶段采用的地形图比例尺及成图方法。

王工程师：预可研阶段采用了1:50000和1:10000比例尺地形图，用矢量化方法成图；可研阶段采用1:2000<u>航空摄影数字图</u>④；定测阶段采用1:500航空摄影数字地形图。

Tom：本项目生产过程中如何保证资料质量？

王工程师：本项目的生产内外业均采用"两级检查、一级验收"的方法，保证测绘资料的质量。

Tom: Please introduce, in detail, the coordinate system and elevation system used in this project.

Mr Wang: In this project we use the engineering <u>independent coordinate system</u>③. The central meridian is 117 degrees and the height of the projection surface is 500 metres, and we use the local elevation system.

Tom: Please briefly tell us the scales of the topographic maps used in different phases and the mapping methods.

Mr Wang: In the phase of preliminary feasibility study, we used topographic maps with the scales of 1:50000 and 1:10000 and drew the maps by vectorising method; in the feasibility study phase we adopted <u>aerial photography digital map</u>④ with the scale of 1:2000; in the location survey phase we used digital topographic map of aviation photography with the scale of 1:500.

Tom: How did you ensure the quality of data during the survey in this project?

Mr Wang: Working in the field and office, we adhere to the "Two-level inspection and one-level acceptance" method to guarantee the quality of the surveying and mapping data.

替换单词 Alternative terms

① GPS 测量仪器
数字摄影工作站
航摄像片扫描仪

② 《工程测量规范》（GB 50026—2007）

《城市轨道交通工程测量规范》（GB 50308—2008）

《全球定位系统（GPS）测量规范》（GB/T 18314—2009）

③ 2000 坐标系
54 坐标
80 坐标

④ 机载激光雷达方法成图
全站仪数字化测图
GPS RTK 数字化测图

① GPS measuring instrument
digital photogrammetric workstation
aerial photograph scanners

② *Code for engineering surveying* (GB 50026—2007)

Code for urban rail transit engineering survey (GB 50308—2008)

Specification for global positioning system (GPS) surveys (GB/T 18314—2009)

③ 2000 coordinate system
54 coordinate system
80 coordinate system

④ drawing by airborne lidar
digital mapping by total station
digital mapping by GPS RTK

第一部分　交通工程情景会话

第四章　地质
Chapter 4　Geology

业务情景：中方张工程师到国土资源部门收集所需资料，Martin 博士接待。

Scene: Chinese engineer Mr Zhang is collecting data at the Ministry of Land and Resources and Dr. Martin is receiving him.

典型对话 Conversation

张工程师：我们需要收集贵国基础地质研究资料，如沿线 1:20 万的区域地质报告及图件、沿线抗震设防区划①、矿产分布图等相关资料。

Mr Zhang: We need to collect the basic data of geological researches of your country, such as regional geological maps with the scale of 1:200000 and reports, related data on the seismic fortification zoning ① and the distribution of mineral resources along the route.

Martin：没问题。

Martin: No problem.

张工程师：我们需要你们引荐几位地质专家向其咨询一些地质勘察方面的问题。

Mr Zhang: Could you be kind enough to introduce us a few geologists so that we can consult with them about some questions of geological investigation?

Martin：可以！你可在我国的岩土工程勘察协会网站上查到很多你所关注的信息。我熟悉几位岩土工程勘察协会注册的地质专家，可以在你方便的时候介绍你们相互认识。

Martin: Certainly! You can visit our website of Geotechnical Engineering Investigation Association and get the relevant information. I'm familiar with some geologists registered in the association, and I'd like to introduce them to you at your convenience.

33

张工程师：十分感谢。
Martin：我会尽快向他们介绍你的情况，约好时间地点后通知你。

张工程师：谢谢。

Mr Zhang: Thanks a lot.
Martin: I'll let them know you as soon as possible, and I'll inform you when the appointment is fixed.
Mr Zhang: Thanks.

替换单词 Alternative terms

① 地震动参数　　　　　　　　① seismic ground motion parameters
　地震区划图　　　　　　　　　　map of seismic zoning
　地质灾害分布图　　　　　　　　distribution map of geological disasters
　地震报告　　　　　　　　　　　earthquake reports

业务情景：中方李工程师汇报地质勘察大纲，外方工程师 Allen 对审查内容提问。
Scene: Chinese engineer Mr Li is giving an account of the outline of geological survey, and Allen (an engineer representing the owner) is questioning on the statement.

典型对话 Conversation

大纲分为9部分，
第1部分为工程地质勘察概况，包括编制依据、工程概况、重大工程的分布及以往勘察情况等；

The outline is composed of nine parts.
Part 1. General description on engineering geological investigation, including the basis of compilation, overview of the project, and the distribution of important works and the past investigation results;

第2部分为地质概况，包括沿线地形地貌特征、主要岩性及地质特征、工程地

Part 2. Geological overview, including the landform and geomorphic characteristics,

质及水文地质概况、沿线不良地质及特殊岩土的分布状况等；

第 3 部分为技术要求及勘察工作原则，包括执行的标准、规范，主要技术要求，勘察工作的主要内容和原则，重大工程、重点不良地质及特殊岩土的勘察原则；

第 4 部分为勘探方法的选用、勘探点的布置原则及主要工作量；

第 5 部分为勘察工作的质量目标和质量管理；

第 6 部分为勘察组织机构、人员及设备配置，安全保障措施；

第 7 部分为计划进度安排及保证措施；

第 8 部分为资料编制的原则，应交成果资料种类和数量等；

第 9 部分为其他需要说明的问题。

main lithology and geological characteristics, general description on engineering geology and hydrogeology, distributions of unfavorable geology and the special rock and soil along the route;

Part 3. Technical requirements and principles of investigation, including the standards, codes and main technical requirements, major content and principles involved in the investigation, and principles for the investigation on important works, key unfavorable geology and special rock and soil;

Part 4. Selection and employment of exploration methods, principles of layout of exploration points and the main workload;

Part 5. Quality target and management of the investigation;

Part 6. Organizations, staff and equipment, as well as safety protection measures;

Part 7. Planning schedule and guarantee measures;

Part 8. Principles of documents compilation, variety and quantity of achievement documents which shall be delivered;

Part 9. Other issues to be explained.

业务情景： 汇报结束后，汇报人回答审查人提问。
Scene: The reporter is answering the examiner's questions after he finishes his statement.

典型对话 Conversation

Allen: 请简要介绍一下本次勘察设计的主要工作内容，布置原则及计划工作量。

Allen: Please give us a brief introduction to the major contents, principles of arrangement and anticipated workloads for this investigation and design.

李工程师： 我们计划采用综合勘察方法[①]，查明沿线的地形地貌、地层岩性、地质构造、水文地质特征等工程地质条件；查明各类不良地质和特殊岩土的成因、类型、性质、分布、发展规律以及对线路的危害程度等。我们会根据场地地质条件，合理布置勘探、测试工作。按照工程设置特点，我们勘察工程类型分为路基工程、桥涵工程、隧道工程、站场和房屋建筑工程、供水工程、天然建筑材料场地六类。

Mr Li: We intend to use comprehensive investigation methods[①] to ascertain the geological conditions along the route, including landform, lithology, geological structure and hydro-geological features etc., as well as the cause of formation, types, properties, distribution and development law of various unfavorable geologies and special rock and soil, and their extent of harm to the route. Investigation and tests will be arranged rationally in accordance with the geological conditions of worksites. Based on the engineering characteristics, there are six engineering types: subgrade, bridges and culverts, tunnels, stations and yards and housing structures, water supply and quarries for natural building materials.

Allen: 根据沿线膨胀岩土发育的特点，我建议将路堑细分为不高于5m的路堑和高于5m的路堑边坡工程。

李工程师: 你的建议很好，我们会按要求修改。对于大纲，还有其他意见吗？

Allen: 在大纲中应加入质量保证体系，包含技术管理和质量监控管理，其中技术管理应包含工作步骤流程图和投入人员设备情况表等信息。

李工程师: 我们会将这部分补充进去的。

Allen: 上述意见将会在本次会议的会议纪要中反映，请编制方在两星期内，也就是下个月5号前，根据意见完成工程咨询大纲修改、完善工作，提交正式文件。

李工程师: 我们将根据审查意见尽快完成修改工作。

Allen: According to the development characteristics of expansive rock and soil along the route, I suggest cuttings should be divided into two types, one is below 5m high, and the other is above 5m high.

Mr Li: That's a very good advice. We will modify our design as required. Do you have any other opinions on the outline?

Allen: A quality assurance system shall be added into the outline, including technical management and quality control management. Information like the flow chart of working procedures and deployment of manpower and equipment shall be included in the technical management.

Mr Li: We'll add this part to the outline.

Allen: The above opinions shall be recorded in the meeting minutes. I'd be obliged if you would fulfill the modification of this consultation outline accordingly within a fortnight or before 5th of next month, and submit the official document.

Mr Li: We'll finish the modification according to the reviews as soon as possible.

替换单词 Alternative terms

① 地质测绘	① geological survey
钻探	drilling
物探	geophysical prospecting
原位测试	in-situ test
室内试验	laboratory test
资料分析	data analysis

业务情景： 中方杨工程师请求铁路公司项目经理 Perry 协助进行钻探进场野外作业，并就钻探中的技术问题进行探讨。

Scene: Chinese engineer Mr Yang is asking Perry, the project manager of Railway Company to assist him in carrying through the drilling in the field and discussing techniques of drilling.

典型对话 Conversation

Perry: 你们最近工作进展怎么样？

杨工程师: 还比较顺利。但在某些地段，我们的钻探工作遇到一些麻烦，需要请求你们的帮助。

Perry: 是什么样的问题？

杨工程师: 是这样，我们须在某某公司的地界内进行局部钻孔，希望贵方能出面协调。

Perry: 没问题。

Perry: How are you getting along with your recent work?

Mr Yang: Not bad, but we have run into trouble in drilling at a worksite, we need your help.

Perry: What trouble have you met?

Mr Yang: We have to perform some partial drillings within the boundary of a company. Could you negotiate with that company for us?

Perry: No problem.

第一部分　交通工程情景会话

杨工程师： 我们还有一段线路正好经过市中心 D-A 大道，这条大道交通非常繁忙，我们钻机准备进场施钻，但是交通警察阻止了我们，说是要造成交通堵塞。

Perry： 为什么必须在这个路段开钻？

杨工程师： 只有通过钻探才能了解下部地基土的详细情况，才能确保这段路基的设计准确无误。

Perry： 我们将以函件的形式尽快通知相关公司和城市交管局，同时也将给你们派发一份关于支持铁路建设的函件。

杨工程师： 那真是太好了！谢谢您对我们工作的支持。

Perry： 这是我们应该做到的，项目的顺利推进对双方都有好处。

杨工程师： 这是我们现场的特大桥的钻探工作。这个特大桥目前我们总共安排有 3 台钻机正在施钻，钻孔工作预计 5 天左右全部结束。

Perry： 这个桥总共多少个墩台？你们布置钻孔的原则是什么？

Mr Yang: It also happened that a section of our line precisely passes through the congested D-A Avenue in downtown. There is a heavy traffic on this avenue, we were held back by traffic policemen when we got there to drill for the likelihood of causing traffic jam.

Perry: Why must this part of road be drilled?

Mr Yang: Only by drilling can we reveal the detailed underground condition, and consequently we can ensure the correct design for the subgrade of this section.

Perry: We'll send correspondence to inform the company concerned and the City Traffic Authorities, and at the same time, we'll prepare a letter for you on supporting railway construction.

Mr Yang: That's really great! Thank you for your support.

Perry: We've done no more than our duty. We both benefit when things go smoothly.

Mr Yang: This is the drilling worksite for a super major bridge. Three drilling machines are working, and all of the drilling tasks are estimated to be completed within 5 days.

Perry: How many piers and abutments will be built for this bridge? What are your principles for drilling arrangement?

杨工程师： 这个桥总共33个墩，本阶段我们原则上是隔墩布孔，根据地质调绘掌握的地质情况，若基岩出露、地质条件相对简单的墩台我们就会隔2~3墩进行布孔。另外本座桥除了钻探工作外，我们还布置有物探工作，以物探、钻探两种勘察手段相互验证，以求查清桥基情况。

Perry： 对中国地质钻探的技术特点和工艺，我希望能有更多的了解。

杨工程师： 我们本次地质勘探的采用的是中国运来的XY-1T150型钻机，该型钻机最大钻探深度为150m，采用机械回旋钻进，钻头直径110-75mm，依据岩土层特点可选用合金或金刚石钻头。在钻探过程中可进行SPT原位测试、原状土取样。

Perry： 我国一般采用的钻头直径为BX-NX，口径为45~55mm，你们采用更大的钻头直径对岩芯鉴定、取样更为有利。

Mr Yang: 33 piers are designed for the bridge. As a rule, boreholes will be arranged for every other pier in this phase. In accordance with the results of geological mapping, boreholes will also be arranged for every other 2-3 piers when the piers are situated on outcropped bed rock or on bases with simple geological conditions. Apart from drilling, moreover, geophysical prospecting is employed to get a mutual authentication in an attempt to make a thorough investigation of the pier bases.

Perry: I'd like to enrich my knowledge of your the technical features and workmanship in geological drilling.

Mr Yang: We use XY-1T150 drilling rigs manufactured in China for this geological exploration. With a drill bit that is 110-75mm in diameter and driven by circling mechanical force, this model has a maximum drilling depth of 150m. An alloy or diamond drill bit is optional depending on the characteristics of the rock and soil. SPT in-situ test and undisturbed soil sampling are available in the process of drilling.

Perry: Drill bit in BX-NX diameter and 45-55mm in caliber is commonly used in our country, but a larger drill bit in your drilling would be better for identification of rock core and sampling.

杨工程师：我完全同意您的观点。

Perry：SPT 测试①和取样有什么具体要求？

杨工程师：对于在黏性土、砂层内钻探，我们要求每米必须进行一次 SPT 试验，记录击数。当 SPT 击数连续两次大于 50 击时才能停止实验。取样方面，同一土层每 2m 取一组土样，岩层中分层采取一组样品。

Perry：请注意，我国规范要求在岩石全风化层内也应进行 SPT 试验，直到击数大于 80 击方可停止。

杨工程师：谢谢你的提醒。

Perry：此外，在取样方面我有一点建议：土层每米取一个样品，我国规范要求根据土样颗粒粒径、含水率、液塑限、风化程度、抗压强度等结果进行分类，相邻深度样品如判定为同一类岩土方可合并为一层，因此，取样密度直接决定岩土层划分的准确性及抗压强度。

Mr Yang: I quite agree with you.

Perry: Do you have any specific requirements on SPT test① and sampling?

Mr Yang: One SPT test with recorded strike number is required in each meter when drilling is performing in cohesive soil or sand. The test should not be stopped until the number of SPT strike surpasses fifty for two times in succession. As to sampling, one group of soil sample is taken in each 2 meters within the same soil layer and one group of samples is taken in each rock stratum.

Perry: Please note, that in accordance with the specifications enacted by our country, SPT test is required for the completely weathered rock strata and the test should not be stopped until the strike number surpasses eighty.

Mr Yang: Thank you for reminding me of that.

Perry: I also have some suggestions for taking samples. In accordance with the specifications in our country, one sample taken at each meter in soil shall be classified based on its grain size, water content, liquid and plastic limit, rate of weathering and compressive strength, etc.; samples taken at the adjacent depth may be regarded as taken from the same layer provided the identical rock is defined.

杨工程师：我们会按照贵国规范要求进行取样的。

Perry：现场钻探、原位测试及取样等如何保证质量？

杨工程师：首先，我们的钻探工人都是经过专业培训的，能够熟练地进行钻探、原位测试、取样等工作。其次，我们的地质工程师会经常对钻探工作进行检查。再次，每一个钻孔的完成，都必须得到现场地质工程师的确认方能终孔，以确保现场钻探、原位测试及取样工作的质量。

Perry：还有一点提醒，野外工作请注意人员设备安全，最好能配备保安人员。

杨工程师：您说得对，我们也正在联系保安公司。

Therefore, the sampling density directly determines the exact classification of rock and soil layers and their compressive strength.

Mr Yang: We'll take samples according to the requirements in your specifications.

Perry: How will you guarantee the quality of in-site drilling, in-situ test and sampling?

Mr Yang: First, all our drill operators have gone through professional training and are skillful at drilling, in-situ testing and sampling. Second, drilling operations are under the close observation of our geological engineers. And at last, each drilling would not be regarded as accomplishment until the approval from our on-site geological engineers. This gives qualified field drilling, in-situ test and sampling.

Perry: One thing needs special attention: every precaution has to be taken to ensure the safety of personnel and equipment in the wild. It would be best to hire some security guards.

Mr Yang: Quite right, we are now in touch with a company that can supply us with security guards.

替换单词 Alternative terms

① 标准贯入
　动力触探
　静力触探

① standard penetration test
　dynamic penetration test
　static cone penetration test

第一部分　交通工程情景会话

业务情景：张工程师向铁路公司经理 Dobor 等汇报中方的勘察成果，张工程师汇报结束后，Dobor 先生与张工程师就相关问题进行了讨论。
Scene: Chinese engineer Mr Zhang is reporting the survey results to Dobor, the manager the of Railway Company, and other officials, and discussing issues of surveying.

典型对话 Conversation

Dobor: 本线勘察过程中，采用了哪些综合勘察手段[①]？

张工程师: 在本线勘察中，主要采用了遥感解译、地质测绘、钻探、物探、静力触探、动力触探、室内试验、资料分析等综合勘察手段。

Dobor: 请介绍一下此次勘察的布孔原则。

张工程师: 由于项目工期要求，我们在研究了贵方提出的勘察技术要求后，结合沿线地形平坦、地质条件相对简单的特点来考虑勘探孔布置原则及勘探工作量。确定了普通路基地段按200m左右布置1个钻孔，桥梁工程隔一墩或多墩布置1个钻孔的原则，并按此实施了全线地质钻探。

Dobor: What comprehensive investigation methods[①] did you use in the investigation of this route?

Mr Zhang: We undertook comprehensive investigation methods for this route, including remote sensing interpretation, geological mapping, drilling, geophysical prospecting, static cone penetration tests, dynamic penetration test, laboratory tests and data analysis, etc.

Dobor: Please introduce the principles of the boreholes arrangements for this investigation.

Mr Zhang: To meet the deadline and your technical requirements in the investigation, we worked out our principles of boreholes arrangements and investigation workload, with consideration of the flat terrain and simple geological conditions of the route. We concluded the principles that one borehole was drilled at the points roughly

43

Dobor: 请介绍一下沿线主要的不良地质[②]和特殊岩土[③]。

张工程师: 沿线主要不良地质有活动性断裂等。主要特殊岩土有膨胀土、软土。

Dobor: 请介绍一下本线所经过地区的主要地质构造。

张工程师: 线路大部分位于东非大裂谷中，Beseke 湖附近的地裂对线路工程影响较大，建议以路基通过。

Dobor: 全线勘察效果如何？

张工程师: 目前已施工段落，未因地质情况不符而引起变更，证明我们可以在控制钻探量的情况下保证勘探精度，同时可以控制工程造价、保证工程按期完成。

every 200m on normal subgrade section and one borehole was drilled for every other or more piers for the bridge project, and the geological drilling along the route is implemented accordingly.

Dobor: Please give us a description of the unfavorable geology[②] and special rock and soil[③] along the route.

Mr Zhang: The unfavorable geology essentially consists of active faults; special rock and soil largely consists of expansive soil and soft soil.

Dobor: Please give us a description of the basic geological structure in the area where the route is laid.

Mr Zhang: The line is largely laid in the Great Rift Valley of East Africa and the fractures near Beseke Lake would heavily affect the line, so we propose this part of line be built with subgrade.

Dobor: How do you value the investigation results of the route?

Mr Zhang: So far, we have never altered our design in construction because of inconformity of geological conditions. It has proved we are able to guarantee the investigation accuracy with controlled amount of drillings, and at the same time, keep the cost within the required limit and accomplish the project on time.

Dobor: 你的汇报中,沿线膨胀岩土较多,在这样的地质条件下施工,你们有何建议?

张工程师: 我们明确提出沿线的膨胀岩土不能用作路基填料。对于膨胀土地段的路堑边坡,我们根据路堑段内膨胀岩土强弱程度建议边坡率为1∶1.75~1∶2。

Dobor: 那么作为填料,是对膨胀岩土进行改良,还是在别处寻找合格填料呢?

张工程师: 我们考虑到铁路沿线多为膨胀岩土的工程地质特性,针对黏土岩、页岩作了改良试验,主要增加水泥,其试验结论是对于高塑性黏土岩、页岩,要达到规范规定的95%的压实度及无侧限抗压强度,需要添加7%~9%的水泥;对于低塑性的黏土、粉土需要添加3%~5%的水泥。如果采用水泥进行土质改良,将需要很大的水泥量,而且费用会增加很多。综合比较,我们建议在别处寻找合格的卵砾石土填料相对经济。

Dobor: We've learned from your report that expansive rock and soil is found abundantly along the line. Do you have any suggestions on construction under these geological conditions?

Mr Zhang: We need to point out here that expansive rock and soil must not be used as filling for subgrade. As for the cutting slope with expansive rock and soil, we suggest the slope gradient should be 1∶1.75-1∶2 according to the intensity of expansive rock and soil in the cutting section.

Dobor: Then, as for filling, do you prefer to make some improvement to expansive rock and soil, or look for a suitable substitute in other places?

Mr Zhang: As expansive rock and soil is largely spread along the railway route, we carried out tests for improving the clay-stone and shale by adding cement. The conclusion indicated that an additional 7%-9% cement is suitable for high plastic limit clay-stone and shale to meet the 95% compactness and unconfined compressive strength specified by the Specification, and an additional 3%-5% cement is needed for low plastic limit clay and silt soil. If we use the above methods to improve the soil, a great quantity of cement is needed and the cost

Dobor: 地下水的侵蚀性对工程影响如何？

张工程师: 我们专门进行了地表水下渗、土壤淋滤引起的侵蚀性问题研究。钻孔揭示浅部地层没有地下水，加之黏土岩、页岩属于相对隔水层，降雨或地表水难以在地层中形成浅部地下水，也不容易在土壤中产生淋滤作用，进而形成侵蚀性地下水对桩基及各类工程基础产生侵蚀性。所以经综合分析，我们认为沿线不存在地下水、土壤侵蚀的问题，为本段铁路工程节约了不少工程投资。

will be very high. By comprehensive comparison, we suggest looking for proper gravel-cobble soil as filling in some other places. That will be more economical.

Dobor: How does the erosion caused by underground water affect the project?

Mr Zhang: We carried out special researches of the erosive effect on the project caused by infiltration of surface water and leaching of soil. Since the drilling revealed that there is no underground water in shallow strata, and additionally, clay-stone and shale belongs to the relatively water-resisting layers, it is hard for rainwater or surface water to infiltrate through strata and form shallow underground water. Therefore, eluviation will hardly be developed in soil to form erosive underground water and erode pile foundation and other bases. By the above analysis, we conclude that the route is free from erosion caused by underground water and soil and this would bring the cost down to this railway project.

替换单词 Alternative terms

① 地质测绘　　　　① geological mapping
　 钻探　　　　　　　 drilling
　 物探　　　　　　　 geophysical prospecting
　 原位测试　　　　　 in-situ test

室内试验	laboratory test
资料分析	data analysis
② 崩塌	② collapse
泥石流	debris flow
地裂	ground fracturing
③ 膨胀土	③ expansive soil
软土	soft soil

第五章 线路
Chapter 5　Route

业务情景：中方总体（线路负责人）张工程师向业主项目经理 Yonas 搜集资料。

Scene: Mr Zhang, chief engineer in charge of the route from the Chinese side, is collecting materials from Yonas, the project manager of the employer.

典型对话 Conversation

张工程师：我方需要贵方提供线路沿线的城市规划①资料，包括公路、铁路、地下管线②以及军事区等资料。

Mr Zhang: We expect that you can provide us with urban planning① materials along the line, including road, railway, underground pipelines②, military zone, etc.

Yonas：城市规划资料我方可立即提供给你方，但涉及市政、路政、水利等部门的其他资料，提供时间可能会有所延迟。

Yonas: We could give you urban planning materials right now. However, the materials from municipal administration, road administration, water conservation department and others may be delayed.

张工程师：工期紧迫，请你方尽快办理。在收集到上述资料后，我方将对方案作优化调整，使设计更加经济合理。

Mr Zhang: As the construction time is limited, could you please handle it soon? After the successful collection of the above-mentioned materials, we can optimise the scheme so as to make the design more economical and reasonable.

第一部分　交通工程情景会话

Yonas：好的,我们立即与相关单位联系,敦促他们收集相关资料。不过军事区的相关资料属于军事机密,我们爱莫能助。

Yonas: No problem, we will contact relevant agencies as soon as possible, and urge them to collect the relevant materials. unfortunately the materials about the military zone are classified, we cannot not help you.

张工程师：军事区资料和其他资料一样重要,以便我们在方案设计中尽量避绕这些敏感点,以免造成今后勘察、设计、施工中不必要的麻烦。

Mr Zhang: The materials about military zone are as important as the others, they would help us avoid sensitive points in our design scheme so as to prevent unnecessary troubles in the following jobs of survey, design and construction.

Yonas：我们会尽力而为。

Yonas: We will try our best.

张工程师：一旦完成上述资料的收集,请立即通知我们。

Mr Zhang: Please inform us immediately after all the materials mentioned above have been collected.

替换单词 Alternative terms

① 城市生态与环境保护
　城市交通
　城市市政工程规划
　区域规划

② 输油管道
　输电管道
　给排水管道
　供暖管道

① urban ecological and environmental protection
　urban transport
　urban municipal engineering planning
　regional planning

② oil pipelines
　power transmission lines
　water supply and drainage pipelines
　heating pipelines

49

业务情景：中方线路专业刘工程师与外方工程师 Mandela 就技术问题进行沟通。

Scene: Mr Liu, engineer of the route from the Chinese side, is exchanging ideas with Mandela, the engineer from the foreign side, about technical issues.

典型对话 Conversation

刘工程师：我方已收到你方提供的本市规划道路①的平面图资料。请告知该平面图所使用的平面坐标系统，包括投影高、中央子午线经度。

Mandela：我方使用的是 WGS-84 坐标系，TM 投影，投影高 $H=950m$，中央子午线经度 $L=41°30′$。

刘工程师：我方还需要该规划道路的纵断面图以及该纵断面图使用的高程系统。

Mandela：我会通过电子邮件将纵断面图发给你，该图虽使用与你方不一致的高程系统，但与你方高程系统误差很小，可以忽略不计。

Mr Liu: We have received the plans of planned roads① for the city. Please tell us the plane coordinate system used in the plans, including projection height and the longitude of central meridian.

Mandela: We use WGS-84 coordinate system and TM projection. The projection height H is 950m, and longitude of central meridian L is 41°30′(41.5 degrees).

Mr Liu: We also need profiles of the planned roads and the height systems used by the profiles.

Mandela: I will send the profiles to you via e-mail. Although the elevation systems in the profiles are different from yours, the deviation is small and can be ignored.

替换单词 Alternative terms

① 港口	① port
车站	railway station
货场	freight yard
油库	oil depot
军事区	military zone

第一部分　交通工程情景会话

业务情景： 项目前期中方总体王工程师与业主项目总工 Peter 商讨技术标准。

Scene: At the initial stage, Mr Wang, the team director from the Chinese side, is discussing technical standards with Peter, the chief project engineer of the employer.

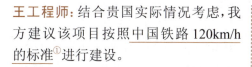

王工程师： 结合贵国实际情况考虑，我方建议该项目按照<u>中国铁路 120km/h 的标准</u>①进行建设。

Peter： 这个标准是不是稍微低了点？目前已经步入高铁时代，尤其是中国近些年大力发展高铁，速度目标值 120km/h 的是否已经过时？标准就不能再高点？

王工程师： 提高标准在技术上没有问题，我们也理解贵国政府发展铁路交通的决心，不过我们对不同时速方案进行过比较，认为速度目标值 120km/h 的方案最符合贵国国情也最经济。

Peter： 何以见得？

王工程师： 经过和 160km/h 方案投资额进行比较，本方案更加经济实惠。根据本线功能需求而言，以货为主、兼顾客运，因此本线采用速度目标值为 100km/h

Mr Wang: Given the actual conditions of your country, we suggest building the project according to <u>China Railway 120km/h Standard</u>①.

Peter: Is the standard a little low? It's the high-speed railway era now, and China takes great efforts to develop high-speed railways in recent years. Is the target speed, 120km/h, out of date? Could you set the standard higher?

Mr Wang: There is no technical problem in increasing the standard, and we appreciate your decision in developing railway transport. However, after comparing schemes of different speeds per hour, we think 120km/h is the best choice as well as the most economical one.

Peter: Why?

Mr Wang: Compared with the investment amount of 160km/h scheme, the scheme is more economical. According to the function of the line which handles freight

51

已经足够，同时考虑到贵国经济强劲的发展势头，我方经过仔细的研究和比较，决定推荐你方采用 120km/h 标准进行建设，为今后预留足够的发展和升级空间。

Peter: 同我们双方签订的上一个合同相比，该项目地形地质条件更好，桥、隧比重更小，因而工程投资应该更省，在不增加投入的情况下，应该具备将技术标准提高的客观条件。

王工程师: 考虑到上一项目也是按照速度目标值 120km/h 的标准进行建设，从便于维修、养护、运营以及站后机电设备的兼容等方面着想，我们强烈建议使用同一标准。

Peter: 鉴于你们提议的技术标准和我方预期有一定差距，我觉得有必要将你方意见向交通部长进行汇报，然后我们再作进一步商洽。

and passenger transport but the former is the key function, 100km/h is enough. Meanwhile, with the strong economic development momentum of your country taken into account, we suggest you adopt 120km/h standard after careful study and comparison, but reserve enough development and upgrade space for the future.

Peter: Compared with the previous contract signed between our two parties, this project enjoys better geological and landform conditions as well as smaller bridge and tunnel proportions, so the project investment should be lower. Without increasing investment, there should be objective conditions for higher technical standards.

Mr Wang: The previous project was also constructed as per 120km/h standard. From the aspects of maintenance, repair, operation and integration of M/E electromechanical equipment, we strongly recommend the same standard as the previous project.

Peter: As your recommended standard is different from our expectation, I think it is necessary for me to report your opinions to the transport minister. And then we will discuss it further.

第一部分　交通工程情景会话

替换单词 Alternative terms

① UIC 标准速度目标值 120km/h　　① UIC Standard Target Speed 120km/h

业务情景：中方总体赵工程师向业主项目经理 Nicolas 寻求支持。
Scene: Mr Zhao, team director from Chinese side, is asking Nicolas, project manager of the employer, for support.

典型对话 Conversation

赵工程师： 我们下月就要开始全线的初测①工作了，为保证我方设计人员②的作业安全，请你方以业主的身份为我方给线路沿线的军、政、警察机关拟一份支持函。

Mr Zhao: We will start our preliminary survey① of the whole line in the next month. In order to ensure the safety of our designers②, we hope you could give us a support letter to military, political and police agencies along the line in the name of the Employer.

Nicolas： 不必担心，我们已经通知了沿线的军、政、警察部门，你们将在接下来的几个月在他们的辖区进行外业工作。

Nicolas: Don't worry. We have informed military, political and police agencies along the line that you will carry out field work within their jurisdictions in the following months.

赵工程师： 为了避免不必要的冲突而耽误外业工作时间或影响员工安全，我方坚持你方提供书面的支持函件，以便我方员工在接受军警盘查时或受当地居民阻挠时出示。

Mr Zhao: In order to avoid delaying of field work and to protect the designer's safety from unnecessary conflicts, we insist that we have a written letter of support from you, so that we can use it when soldiers and policemen question us or local residents hinder our work.

Nicolas: 好的,会后我们立即着手这项工作。

赵工程师: 我们需要英语和当地母语两个语言版本的支持函,且需要你们在上面签章。

Nicolas: 没有问题。

赵工程师: 还请你方提供沿线主要军警部门负责人的联系方式,在沿线某些路段,我们可能会聘用当地军警人员来执行我方员工的外业安保工作。

Nicolas: 好的,我方会先电告相关的军警负责人你们的需求,并提供相关责任人的联系方式。

Nicolas: Ok, we will prepare the letter immediately.

Mr Zhao: We hope the support letter can be written in both English and the local language; it also needs your stamp.

Nicolas: No problem.

Mr Zhao: Could you please give us the contact information for the directors of major military and police agencies along the line. In some sections, we may employ local military and police personnel to do field security work for our staff.

Nicolas: Ok, we will inform the relevant military and police directors of your requirements, and give you the contact details of relevant persons.

替换单词 Alternative terms

① 现场调查　　　　　① on-site investigation
　现场踏勘　　　　　　 on-site survey
　定测　　　　　　　　 location survey
　补定测　　　　　　　 supplementary location survey
② 测量员工　　　　　② survey staff
　地勘员工　　　　　　 geological survey staff
　当地员工　　　　　　 local staff

第一部分　交通工程情景会话

业务情景: 中方线路专业李工程师与外方工程师 Sisay 探讨线路方案。
Scene: Mr Li, the route engineer from the Chinese side, is discussing route schemes with Sisay, the engineer from the foreign side.

典型对话 Conversation

关于线路断链（中国铁路和公路线路设计中所使用的断链是某些国外咨询公司没有的，在尼日利亚和埃塞俄比亚都曾出现业主和咨询机构询问关于断链的问题和要求取消断链的业务情景）

About broken chain of the line (the broken chain used in Chinese railway and road alignment design is not used by foreign consulting companies, and in Nigeria and Ethiopia, there are cases that the employer and advisor ask questions about broken chain and require to cancel broken chain.)

李工程师：该方案线路全长 310km。

Mr Li: In the scheme, the line is 310km.

Sisay：为什么线路平面图上显示终点里程是 322km，而线路全长才 310km。

Sisay: The total length is 310km, so why is the terminal mileage on the plan 322km?

李工程师：因为线路存在长链和短链。

Mr Li: Because there are lengthened chain and short chain.

Sisay：什么是长链[1]和短链？

Sisay: What are lengthened chain[1] and short chain?

李工程师：长链和短链是在设计或测量过程中产生的里程断链，使线路里程不连续。

Mr Li: Lengthened chain and short chain are broken chains that occur during design or survey process, which makes the line discontinuous.

Sisay：请举例说明。

Sisay: Please give an example.

55

李工程师：比如有一段100km长的线路，中间第20~60km处有40km长的线路需改线优化，改线优化后的线位可能比原来的40km长或短。若是41km长，则在原60km处产生1km的长链；若是39km长，则在原60km处产生1km的短链。原60km处的里程因此而不连续，断链由此产生。

Sisay：能不能把线路方案中的断链取消，使里程连续？

李工程师：若取消断链，会改变断链后原有的线路里程。外业勘察和方案确定是一个互动过程，由于随着工作的深入，为了在线路方案改线后继续使用断链后原有的测量、地勘和各专业的设计资料，减少各专业设计人员的内业修改工作量并保持各阶段设计资料的一致性，我方强烈建议保留断链。

Mr Li: Take a 100km line for example. At the 20-60km, there is a 40km line that needs to be rerouted and optimized. After that, the line length may be shorter or longer than the original length of 40km. If it is 41km in length, there will be a 1km lengthened chain at the original stake of 60km; if it is 39km in length, there will be a 1km short chain reduced at the original stake of 60km. As a result, the mileage at the original stake of 60km is discontinuous, which results in a broken chain.

Sisay: Could you cancel the broken chain in the alignment scheme and make the line continuous?

Mr Li: Canceling broken chain will change the original mileages. Field survey and scheme determination are interactive to each other. As the work gets further, we strongly suggest you keep broken chain, so that the design materials from original survey, geological exploration and other disciplines can be used after the alignment scheme is rerouted, the modification workloads of designers from different disciplines can be reduced, and the design materials of all stages can be consistent.

第一部分 交通工程情景会话

替换单词 Alternative terms

① 长链
  短链
  断链

① lengthened chain
  short chain
  mileage broken chain

业务情景： 中方总体（线路负责人）周工程师与外方工程师 Nash 讨论线路方案。
Scene: Mr Zhou, the team director (also the engineer in charge of the route) from Chinese the side, is discussing route scheme with Nash, the engineer from the foreign side.

典型对话 Conversation

Nash： 为什么在 DK18+350~DK45+500 里程段，线路位于半山腰，而不在山脚下的平地？

周工程师： 半山腰的地质条件优于山脚下平坦地段，路基施工不用采取诸如填料改良或换填等措施。线路位于半山腰，不会受到雨季水位影响。

Nash： DK35+500~DK35+800 处线路既没有跨越任何既有公路也没有跨越任何河流，为何设置桥梁？

Nash: Why did you set the DK18+350-DK45+500 section on hillside instead of the flat place at the foot of the mountain?

Mr Zhou: Because the geological conditions at the hillside are better than those at the foot of mountain, and measures like improvements or replacement of filling materials could be avoided for subgrade construction. The line located on the hillside will not be influenced by the water level in the rainy season.

Nash: Why have you set a bridge at DK35+500-DK35+800 which does not cross over any existing road or river?

57

周工程师：该处设置桥梁并非为了跨越河流或既有建筑物，而是为了克服地形缺陷而设置的桥梁。
Nash：为何不采用路基填方直接通过？
周工程师：填方过高，经过比选反而不如设桥经济，且填方过高也不安全。

Nash：DK45+500~DK85+500 段线路位于地势平坦地带，为何不直线通过而要舍近求远，添加几个曲线后从南侧通过？

周工程师：原因有三点，一是根据最新收集的城市规划资料，若以直线通过，会穿越城市<u>工业园规划区</u>①，并与几条主干道发生交叉。为了便于城市今后的发展，线路应尽量绕避这些规划的设施，以免造成过多的相互干扰。二是若以直线通过，会造成线路附近几处重要的<u>居民楼</u>②的拆迁，为了避免这些重要建筑物的拆迁，线路绕至这些建筑物的东侧通过。三是我们外业踏勘时发现该处设有一军用雷达站，若线路直线通过，则距离雷达站太近，铁路的通信信号系统可能会和军用雷达产生电磁干扰。为了保证足够的安全距离，我们将线路从雷达站旁移开。

Mr Zhou: We set a bridge here because of landform defects instead of crossing over any river or existing buildings.
Nash: Why don't you use an embankment?
Mr Zhou: Because the required embankment would be too high, making it less economical than building a bridge. Besides, high embankment is not safe.
Nash: As for the DK45+500-DK85+500 which is located in a flat area, why do you add several curves and make it go to the southern side instead of going straight?
Mr Zhou: There are three reasons: firstly, according to the urban planning materials collected by us, if the line goes in a straight line, it will go through the <u>planning zone of industrial park</u>①, and will also intersect with some trunk roads. For the future development of city, the line should be clear of these planned facilities to avoid mutual interference. Secondly, if it goes in a straight line, some important <u>residential buildings</u>② nearby will have to be demolished and relocated. In order to avoid it, the line passes round the buildings at their eastern side. Thirdly, we found a radar station for military purposes while we were doing field work. If the line is straight, the distance between it and the radar station is too short, which may result in electromagnetic

Nash：从 DK90+200 至 DK92+100，线路经过的地区已被开发商买下，经我方协调，开发商不愿做出置换土地的让步，请你们考虑别的线路方案绕避开该区域。

周工程师：我们马上回去进行方案研究，从现有情况来看，方案修改后不会明显地增大工程数量或工程难度，改线方案基本可行，但要待比较方案完善后再给你方正式答复。

Nash：什么时候能提供比较方案？

周工程师：三天之后吧。
Nash：好，请尽快开展工作。为何这个客运站③不设置在该处，设站于该处可有效减少站场土建工程数量。

周工程师：我方已考虑过该处设站的方案，但若在该处设站，会造成出站端土方量过大（或出现长桥）。经方案比选后，我方确定了现在的站位。

interference between the communication signals of railway and the radar station. To ensure enough safe distance, we have kept the line away from the radar.

Nash: The land that DK90+200-DK92+100 section passes through has been bought by a developer. Although we negotiated with him, he was not willing to make a concession of land replacement, so please consider other alignment scheme to avoid going through the area.

Mr Zhou: We will study it soon. From the current condition, the modified scheme will not obviously increase the quantity or difficulty for the project. The rerouting scheme works, but we need to complete the comparison scheme and then give you a formal feedback.

Nash: When will you give us the comparison scheme?

Mr Zhou: Three days later.
Nash: Ok, please do it as soon as possible. Why don't you set the passenger station③ at this place? If so, the civil engineering quantity for the station yard could be effectively reduced.

Mr Zhou: We also considered setting the station here, but if so, it will result in excessive earthwork quantity at the train departure side of the station (or a major bridge). After comparison of the schemes, we decide to choose the current station location.

Nash: DK126+200处，铁路线路与既有高速路交叉，该既有高速路是连接该地区和外界的主干道，车流量大，公路局要求我方转达他们在此处设置铁路跨线桥与公路立交的意见。

周工程师: 我方同意公路局在此处设置立交的观点，但是不同意铁路上跨公路的意见。我方已做了铁路桥上跨公路和公路桥上跨铁路两个比较方案。结论是公路上跨铁路更为经济，故推荐采用改移公路抬高公路路面高程，设置公路桥上跨铁路的方案。

Nash: At DK126+200, the railway will intersect with an existing highway which is a trunk road linking this region with other places. It has high traffic flow. The Road Bureau requires us to consider their suggestion of building a railway bridge to overfly the road.

Mr Zhou: We agree with Road Bureau about setting a flyover here but we disagree about setting the railway bridge crossing over the highway. We have made two comparison schemes, firstly a railway bridge crossing over the highway and secondly a highway bridge that crosses over the railway. The result is that the latter one is more economical. Therefore, we suggest diverting the highway and elevating the road. We prefer the scheme of the highway bridge crossing over railway.

替换单词 Alternative terms

① 居住区　　　　　　　　　① residential area
② 工厂厂房　　　　　　　　② factory building
　 教堂　　　　　　　　　　　 church
　 电站　　　　　　　　　　　 power plant
　 泵房　　　　　　　　　　　 pumping station
　 温室大棚　　　　　　　　　 green house
③ 货运站　　　　　　　　　③ freight station
　 中间站　　　　　　　　　　 intermediate station
　 越行站　　　　　　　　　　 crossing station
　 会让站　　　　　　　　　　 passing station

第一部分　交通工程情景会话

业务情景：中方总体（线路负责人）蒋工程师与外方咨询师 Smith 进行沟通。

Scene: Mr Jiang, the team director (also the engineer in charge of the route) from the Chinese side, is exchanging ideas with Smith, the consultant from the foreign side.

典型对话 Conversation

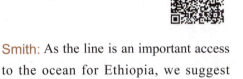

Smith：由于本线为埃塞俄比亚的重要出海通道，建议 ADAMA-DEWELLE 段按双线设计。

蒋工程师：根据业主提供的经济运量报告，ADAMA-DEWELLE 段采用单线通过增开车站的方式即可满足远期运量的需求，为节省投资，ADAMA-DEWELLE 段按单线设计实施。

Smith：线路选线要充分减少施工成本[1]。

蒋工程师：线路方案已经得到业主批复，为减小工程投资，在设计过程已经充分考虑减少施工成本。

Smith：在会让站，需要在车站两端设置安全侧线，以保证对向行车安全。

Smith: As the line is an important access to the ocean for Ethiopia, we suggest that the Adama-Dewelle section could be designed as double track.

Mr Jiang: According to the economy and traffic volume report from the employer, single track for Adama-Dewelle section can meet the requirements of long-term traffic volume by adding new stations. To save investment, Adama-Dewelle section is designed as single track.

Smith: The route selection should fully reduce construction cost[1].

Mr Jiang: The alignment scheme has been approved by the employer. In order to reduce the engineering investment, the reduction of the construction cost has been fully considered during the design process.

Smith: Catch sidings should be set at both sides of the passing station to ensure the safety of trains travelling in opposite directions.

蒋工程师：进站方向的纵坡是大于6‰的下坡，列车才有刹车失控的风险，此时才有必要设置安全线。

Mr Jiang: While the longitudinal slope of the arriving direction is the minus grade with gradient over 6‰(6 permil), there would be the risk of an out-of-control brake. In this circumstance, it's necessary to set a catch siding.

Smith：需要补充绕行 AWASH 公园线路方案。

Smith: We require you to supplement the alignment scheme of detouring around Awash Park.

蒋工程师：对 AWASH 公园南北[2]侧绕行方案已作研究，经比较横穿方案线路最短、工程最省，同时设计方案已报请业主和公园管理方，并征得双方的书面同意，线路方案靠近既有公路与之并行，尽量减少征地，并按照公园管理方提出的环保要求为野生动物设置了动物通道。

Mr Jiang: We have studied the scheme of the north–south[2] detouring around Awash Park. After comparison, the crossing-through scheme features the shortest length and is the most efficient. Meanwhile, the design scheme has been submitted to the employer and park administration agency, and they have approved it. The alignment scheme is adjacent to the existing road and parallel to it, which could reduce land acquisition. We also set a passageway for wild animals to achieve environment protection required by the park administration agency.

替换单词 Alternative terms

① 土方　　　　　① earthwork
　 工期　　　　　　construction time
　 人力投入　　　　manpower input
② 东西　　　　　② east-west

第一部分　交通工程情景会话

业务情景：中方龙工程师做方案汇报，外方工程师 Robert 提问。
Scene: Chinese engineer Mr Long is delivering the scheme report, and the foreign engineer Robert is asking questions.

🔊 典型对话 Conversation

Robert：请问你们的设计依据？

龙工程师：我们的设计依据有两个：一是埃塞俄比亚铁路公司于2010年8月15日下发的《关于尽快开展埃塞俄比亚至吉布提铁路项目 SEBETA-MIESO 段初步设计/施工图设计的函》。二是埃塞俄比亚铁路公司/咨询公司2011年3月15日《关于尽快开展埃塞俄比亚至吉布提铁路项目 SEBETA-MIESO 段可行性研究的报告的审查意见》。

Robert：请问你们的研究范围？

龙工程师：SEBETA-MIESO 段正线及相关联络线工程。正线工程的线路总长329.065km，从 SEBETA 至 ADAMA 为双线①。相关工程有 LABU 客车联络线②，全长3.50km。研究年度为初期2020年③。

Robert: Could you introduce your design basis?

Mr Long: We have two design basis: firstly, *Letter about Starting Preliminary Design/ Construction Drawing Design of SEBETA-MIESO Section of Ethiopia-Djibouti Railway as Soon as Possible* issued by the Ethiopian Railway Corporation on August 15, 2010. Secondly, *Review Comments about Starting Feasibility Study of SEBETA-MIESO Section of Ethiopia-Djibouti Railway as Soon as Possible* issued by Ethiopian Railway Corporation/consulting company on March 15, 2011.

Robert: Could you please introduce your study scope?

Mr Long: Main line of SEBETA-MIESO section and the relevant connecting line works. The total length of the main line is 329.065km, and SEBETA-ADAMA is a double track① section. Relevant works include LABU passenger train connecting line②, 3.50km in length. The studied stage is 2020 as beginning stage③.

63

Robert: 请介绍一下主要技术标准。

龙工程师: 我们设计的正线数目：SEBETA 至 ADAMA 段为双线，ADAMA 至 MIESO 为单线；速度目标值为 120km/h；最小曲线半径：一般 1200m，极限 800m；最大坡度：限制坡度 9‰，加力坡度 18.5‰；牵引种类为电力；机车类型是 HXD 系列；4000t 牵引质量；到发线有效长 850m，双机牵引 880m；4m 线间距；自动闭塞④。主要工程数量包括全线桥梁/隧道总长 12.505km，占线路长度 3.8%。全线设置 10 个车站，其中 8 个中间站，两个会让站⑤。全线铺轨 451.021km。路基填方量⑥ 1850 万 m³。新建房屋 5.31 万 m²。建设工期为 4 年，项目总投资约 18.141 万美元。

Robert: Could you please introduce the major technical standards?

Mr Long: The number of main lines designed by us: SEBETA-ADAMA section is double track, and ADAMA-MIESO section is single track; the target speed is 120km/h; minimum radius of curve: 1200m in general condition, and 800m in extreme condition; largest gradient: 9‰ for limiting gradient, and 18.5‰ for pusher gradient; traction type is electric traction; locomotive type is HXD series; 4000 tons tractive tonnage; the effective length of arrival–departure line is 850m, double locomotive traction 880m; the distance between centres of tracks is 4m; automotive blocking④. The major quantity of works includes bridge/tunnel in a total length of 12.505km, about 3.8% of the line. There are ten stations, namely eight intermediate stations and two passing stations⑤. The track laying length of the whole line is 451.021km. The embankment amount⑥ of subgrade is 18500000m³. The newly-built buildings are 53100m². The construction period is 4 years, and the total investment is 181410 USD.

第一部分　交通工程情景会话

替换单词 Alternative terms

① 单线
② 货车联络线
③ 近期 2025 年
   远期 2035 年
④ 半自动闭塞
   电器路签闭塞类型
⑤ 越行站
⑥ 挖方
   坉工量

① single track
② freight train connecting line
③ short-term stage is 2025
   long-term stage is 2035
④ semi-automotive blocking
   electric train staff blocking type
⑤ crossing station
⑥ excavation
   masonry amount

业务情景： 中方总体吴工程师和业主代表 Brown 探讨设计工作工期的问题。
Scene: Mr Wu, the team director of the Chinese side, is talking about the design period with Brown, the employer representative.

典型对话 Conversation

Brown：我们仔细阅读了本次初步设计的全部文件，里面没有反映如通信①专业所需设备的具体型号。

吴工程师：初步设计阶段还无法确定这些专业所需设备的具体型号，要待完成设备招标后才能确定设备的具体型号。

Brown：那什么时候才能完成设备招标呢？

吴工程师：一般在施工图设计之前。

Brown: We have read all the documents for preliminary design, but they do not cover the specific type of communication① equipment.

Mr Wu: The specific equipment type for this discipline cannot be determined in the preliminary design stage until the completion of equipment bidding.

Brown: When could you complete the bidding for equipment?

Mr Wu: Usually before the construction drawing design.

65

Brown: 那你们什么时候能开展施工图设计？

吴工程师：根据合同，我们将在两周后也就是2月28日收到你们业主方对我方初步设计的正式书面评估意见。之后我们将按照评估意见开展我们的施工图设计工作。

Brown: 能适当调整一下工期么？我们认为时间太长了，咨询公司正等着审查你们前述设备的相关资料呢。

吴工程师：本着对你们业主负责的原则，我们希望你方为我方留足时间，以便我们把施工设计图做得尽可能详细，以免未来出现过多的变更。

Brown: 好的，我们会尽快给你们书面的初步设计评估意见，也请你方尽快按计划开展工作。

Brown: When could you start the construction drawing design?

Mr Wu: According to the contract, we will receive a formal written assessment about our preliminary design from the employer on February 28, namely two weeks later. After that, we will begin the construction drawing design as per the assessment comments.

Brown: Could you adjust the design period? We think it's too long, and the consulting company is waiting to review the relevant materials of the above-mentioned equipment.

Mr Wu: With the principle of being responsible for the employer, we hope you can give us enough time so that we can make the construction design drawing more detailed and avoid modifications as much as possible.

Brown: Ok, I will give you the written assessment comments about the preliminary design as soon as possible, please carry out your work soon.

替换单词 Alternative terms

① 信号
电气化

① signal
electrification

第一部分　交通工程情景会话

业务情景：中方线路专业杨工程师和业主方工程师Lorry探讨变更设计的问题。
Scene: Mr Yang, the route engineer of the Chinese side, is talking about design modification with Lorry, the engineer of the employer.

典型对话 Conversation

杨工程师：我方是按照所签订的道路改移协议进行该处的道路改移，且道路改移方案通过了咨询单位的审查，为何现在要求变更？

Mr Yang: The road relocation is carried out according to the road relocation agreement signed by both parties, and the consulting company has reviewed the road relocation scheme, why do you want to modify it?

Lorry：其实要求变更的是当地政府官员。他们在铁路左侧①300m处新建了一所学校，希望你们在此处改移的这条道路连接到学校门口。

Lorry: The modification is required by local officials. They built a new school about 300m on the left① of the railway, and they hope that you can relocate the road to link it to the school gate.

杨工程师：就技术上而言，这没有问题。不过该变更非我方设计失误引起，变更责任方应是当地政府部门，故变更设计费和因此而增加的工程投资费应另计，不包含在合同的总价里。

Mr Yang: There is no problem from a technical perspective, but the modification is not caused by our design failure, and the responsible party should be the local government. Therefore, the modification cost and the increased engineering investment cost due to the modification should not be included in the total contract amount.

Lorry：这次变更增加的投资费用应该不大，而且我们不可能再支付合同总价之外的费用。这个问题希望贵方有所通融。

Lorry: There may only be a little extra investment caused by the modification, and it's impossible for us to pay extra fees other than the total contract amount. We would appreciate your understanding.

67

杨工程师：按照惯例，我方没有义务把道路连接到新建学校。如果你方不能负担变更费用，那就请变更责任方负担变更费用。

Lorry：那我们还得和当地政府谈谈，不过你们能否先提供一个连接学校的道路改移方案并附相应的工程量及造价？以便我们和当地政府协商。

杨工程师：我们可以先提供一个草图，在明确变更费用的问题之后我们才能做正式的变更设计图。

Lorry：草图也行，什么时候提供给我们？

杨工程师：3天后。

Lorry：好的，去这个工点踏勘时，希望你们能和我们一起和当地政府协商此事。

Mr Yang: In normal conditions, it's not our obligation to link the road to the new school. If you do not pay for the modification fees, the party responsible for the modification should pay it.

Lorry: We need to talk with the local government about it. Can you please give us a road location scheme that links it to the school, together with the quantity of works and the construction cost? Then we could negotiate with the local government.

Mr Yang: We can give you draft drawings, but the formal modification design drawings can not be provided until the issue of modification fees is solved.

Lorry: Draft drawings are ok. When could you give them to us?

Mr Yang: In three days time.

Lorry: Ok, when we carry out the on-site survey, we hope to negotiate with the local government with you present.

替换单词 Alternative terms

① 右侧　　　　　　　　　　① right side

第一部分　交通工程情景会话

第六章　路基
Chapter 6　Subgrade

业务情景：中方王工程师与外方工程师 Alex 讨论线路方案。
Scene: Mr Wang, the engineer from the Chinese side, is discussing the route scheme with Alex, the engineer from the foreign side.

典型对话 Conversation

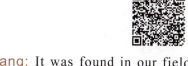

王工程师：经我们外业踏勘发现，原方案会穿过一片很大的湿地①区域；为了当地的环境保护及可持续发展，我们建议绕开这片湿地。

Mr Wang: It was found in our field reconnaissance that the line in the original scheme passes through a large area of wetland①. It is preferable to bypass this area for the purposes of environmental protection and the sustainable development of this area.

Alex：这样会增加工程量么？

Alex: Will this increase the quantities?

王工程师：会增加近 2km 的线路。

Mr Wang: It will increase the length of the alignment by 2km.

Alex：我们建议按照原方案通过。

Alex: We suggest adopting the original scheme.

王工程师：绕避方案虽然线路增加了 2km，但避开了湿地范围内的不良地质情况，减少了软基处理的费用；因此工程造价相差不大。

Mr Wang: Although the bypass scheme increases the alignment length by 2km, it avoids unfavorable geological conditions in the wetland, and reduces soft foundation treatment cost. So there won't be a big difference in project cost.

Alex：请你提供两个方案的详细对比，这边便于我们向上级汇报情况。

Alex: Please provide us a detailed comparison between the two schemes so that we can brief our superiors.

王工程师：目前我们还没有相关资料，三天后我们可以提供主要工程数量的可研精度比较。

Alex：好的，谢谢。

Mr Wang: We do not have the relevant materials yet, but we can provide a comparison of the quantities of works in a feasibility study in three days.

Alex: Ok, thanks.

替换单词 Alternative terms

① 原始森林　　　　　　① virgin forest
　耕地　　　　　　　　　arable land
　经济作物　　　　　　　economic crop

业务情景：中方王工程师与外方工程师 Alex 讨论路基工点措施。
Scene: Mr Wang is discussing measures of subgrade construction site with Alex.

典型对话 Conversation

Alex：你方的设计文件，总体上看不错，我们很满意，谢谢。但就个别地方我们还想与你们再详细探讨一下。

王工程师：好的。请讲。

Alex：设计图中 K120+500~K120+700 段的地基处理采用了 CFG 桩①，投资较高，是否可以采用其他的替代方案？

王工程师：对于此段，我们进行了必要的计算，建议维持原设计方案。

Alex: Your design documents are of sound quality overall. We are satisfied. But I would like to discuss some details with you.

Mr Wang: Ok. Let's talk about it.

Alex: CFG pile① is adopted for the foundation treatment at K120+500~K120+700 section in your drawing. But as CFG pile requires a high investment, is there any alternative?

Mr Wang: We have conducted the necessary calculations on this section. It is recommended to keep the original design.

第一部分　交通工程情景会话

替换单词 Alternative terms

① 塑料排水板　　　　　① plastic drainage board
　 碎石桩　　　　　　　　 gravel pile
　 水泥搅拌桩　　　　　　 cement mixing pile
　 旋喷桩　　　　　　　　 jet grouting pile
　 注浆　　　　　　　　　 slip casting

业务情景：中方王工程师向外方工程师 Alex 进行路基工点汇报。
Scene: Mr Wang is reporting subgrade construction site to Alex.

典型对话 Conversation

王工程师：该工点位于CK11+990~CK12+790右侧，长800m。

Alex：请问周边环境怎样？

王工程师：本工点位于本国首都西南方向，属高原台地及浅丘区地貌，地形平坦开阔，植被不发育，测区地面高程2108~2298m，相对高差2~15m，自然坡度2°-10°，最大挖方高度约26m，交通条件较好。

Alex：请你介绍一下这个工点的地质情况。

Mr Wang: This construction site is on the right side of CK11+990−CK12+790 with a length of 800m.

Alex: How about the surrounding environment?

Mr Wang: This site is on the southwest of the capital. The landform is high plateau and low hills, with flat terrain and undeveloped vegetation. The ground elevation is 2108−2298m, relative height difference is 2−15m, natural slope is 2°−10°, and the maximum excavation height is 26m. The traffic condition is relatively good.

Alex: Please brief us on the geological condition of this site.

71

王工程师：该段地表上覆第四系破残积（Qs）黑棉土、粉质黏土，下伏基岩为三叠系（Ti3）凝灰岩，三叠系（Tt2）玄武岩。

Alex：设计的地震参数如何考虑？

王工程师：本段地震动峰值加速度小于0.1g，地震动反应谱特征周期为0.35s。

Alex：请提供本工点详细的地质参数。

王工程师：黑棉土<3-1>：$\gamma=19kN/m^3$、$c=30kPa$，$\varphi=10°$、$\sigma_0=150kPa$；属于中~强膨胀土粉质黏土<3-2>：$\gamma=19kN/m^3$、$c=35kPa$，$\varphi=12°$、$\sigma_0=160kPa$；玄武岩<5-3>W4：$\gamma=20kN/m^3$，$c=25kPa$，$\varphi=18°$，$\sigma_0=200kPa$。

Alex：请说明这个工点主要工程措施。

王工程师：我们考虑了两个工程措施方案：方案一，路堑坡脚设锚固桩[①]加固；路堑坡脚设重力式路堑挡土墙[②]；除墙顶平台外，各级护坡顶平台设截水沟排水。方案二，路堑坡脚设重力式路堑挡土墙，墙顶以上第一、二边坡，采用人字

Mr Wang: The surface is covered by Quatenary (Qs) regur and silty clay, and the underlying rock is Triassic (Ti3) tuff and Triassic (Tt2) basalt.

Alex: What are your considerations of the seismic parameters?

Mr Wang: Ground motion peak acceleration of this section is less than 0.1g, and characteristic cycle of the ground motion response spectrum is 0.35s.

Alex: Please provide a detailed geological parameter of this site.

Mr Wang: Regur<3-1>: severe γ is $19kN/m^3$, cohesion c is 30kPa, internal friction angle φ is 10°, basic bearing capacity σ_0 is 150kPa; medium~strong expansive soil. Silty clay<3-2>: severe γ is $19kN/m^3$, cohesion c is 35kPa, internal friction angle φ is 12°, and basic bearing capacity σ_0 is 160kPa; Basalt<5-3>W4: severe γ is $20kN/m^3$, cohesion c is 25kPa, internal friction angle is 18°, and basic bearing capacity σ_0 is 200kPa.

Alex: Please describe the major engineering measures of this construction site.

Mr Wang: We considered two engineering schemes: In Scheme Ⅰ, anchored pile[①] is set at the cutting toe for reinforcement; a gravity type retaining wall for cutting[②] is set at cutting toe; an intercepting ditch is set at every bench of slope for drainage

截水骨架护坡③。除墙顶平台外，各级护坡顶平台设截水沟排水。

Alex：两个方案的主要区别在哪里？

王工程师：方案一圬工量较大，但可以减少本工点用地数量；方案二可以节约大量圬工，但土石方开挖及工点用地数量均会有所增加。

except for a bench at the wall top. In Scheme Ⅱ, a gravity type retaining wall for the cutting is set at the cutting toe, and a herringbone intercepting slope protection③ is adopted for the first and second layer of the side slope over the wall top. An intercepting ditch is set at every bench of the slope for drainage except for the bench at wall top.

Alex: What is the main difference between the two schemes?

Mr Wang: The quantity of masonry for scheme Ⅰ is larger but it reduces land occupation while Scheme Ⅱ saves a lot of masonry work, but increases earthwork excavation and land occupation.

替换单词 Alternative terms

① 锚索桩
   预加固桩
   抗滑桩
② 土钉墙
   短卸荷板式挡土墙
   锚杆挡土墙
   锚定板挡土墙
   空窗式护墙
③ 拱形截水骨架内绿化护坡

   方格截水骨架内绿化护坡

① anchor cable pile
   pre-consolidation pile
   anti-slide pile
② soil-nailed wall
   short unloading plate retaining wall
   anchored retaining wall
   anchored plate retaining wall
   empty window curtain wall
③ greening slope protection in the arched intercepting framework
   greening slope protection in the grid intercepting framework

锚杆框架梁内植生袋护坡	slope protection of seed-nutriment-soil sacks in anchored frame beam
喷混植生护坡	slope protection of spraying seeds mixing base material
喷锚网护坡	slope protection of shotcrete rockbolt mesh

业务情景: 中方王工程师向外方工程师 Alex 进行路基工点汇报。
Scene: Mr Wang is reporting on the subgrade construction site to Alex.

典型对话 Conversation

Alex: 请介绍一下这个工点的情况。

Alex: Please explain the situation at this site.

王工程师: 这是位于CK155+832~CK155+950左侧的一个陡坡路基工点。

Mr Wang: This is a steep slope embankment site on the left side of CK155+832-CK155+950 section.

Alex: 这个工点工程环境概况怎样？

Alex: How is the engineering environment of this site?

王工程师: 本段线路地面高程1200~1446m，相对高差2~20m，自然坡度2°~10°，线路主要以填方通过，中心最大填方高度约14m，桥址附近有城镇公路相通，交通条件较好。

Mr Wang: The elevation of this section is 1200~1446m, and the relative height difference is 2~20m, with a natural slope of 2°~10°. The alignment passes the section mainly in the form of filling, and the maximum filling height at the centre is about 14m. There are roads to towns near the bridge, and the traffic situation is relatively good.

Alex: 地质情况能否说明一下？

Alex: Can you explain the geological conditions?

王工程师: 本段地表覆盖粉质黏土:黄褐色,硬塑状,含砂质较重;基岩为玄武岩,灰色、浅灰色,中~粗粒结构,块状构造,含黑曜石矿物,岩体破碎,强风化层较厚。

Alex: 请问你们在这个工点是否考虑了地震的影响因素?

王工程师: 本段地震动峰值加速度小于0.1g,地震动反应谱特征周期为0.35s。

Alex: 本工点各个土层的物理力学指标是否已通过试验得出?

王工程师: <3-2>粉质黏土:γ=19kN/m³,c=30kPa,φ=10°,σ_0=160kPa。<5-3>W3玄武岩:γ=23kN/m³,c=45kPa,φ=0,σ_0=350kPa。

Alex: 请说明这个工点主要的工程措施。

王工程师: 工点左侧设置桩基托梁衡重式路肩挡土墙[①];墙顶设置角钢立柱栏杆;路肩墙墙背衡重台处平铺双向土工格栅。

Mr Wang: The surface of this section is covered by silty clay: tawny, hard plastic, and highly sandy; the bedrock is basalt, gray, light gray, medium-coarse grained, massive structure, containing obsidian minerals, rock mass crushed, and heavily weathered layer is relatively thick.

Alex: Did you consider seismic factors for this construction site?

Mr Wang: Ground motion peak acceleration of this section is less than 0.1g, and characteristic cycle of ground motion response spectrum is 0.35s.

Alex: Did you have the physico-mechanical index of various layers of this site from experiment?

Mr Wang: <3-2> silty clay: severe γ is 19kN/m³, cohesion c is 30kPa, internal friction angle φ is 10°, and basic bearing capacity σ_0 is 160kPa. <5-3>W3 basalt: severe γ is 23kN/m³, cohesion c is 45kPa, internal friction angle φ is 0, and basic bearing capacity σ_0 is 350kPa.

Alex: Please explain the major engineering measures for this site.

Mr Wang: The balance weight retaining wall with capped pile foundation[①] is set at the left shoulder of the construction site; and an angle steel baluster railing is set at wall top; a bidirectional geogrid is laid at the backside of the wall.

Alex：请问这个点的墙后填土有没有具体要求。

王工程师：对于填土，基床底层采用 A、B 组② 填筑，基床以下采用挖方填筑。填筑前必须进行路堤填筑试验，以获得适合的施工参数。

Alex: Are there any specific requirements on the filling?

Mr Wang: Group A and B ② are adopted as fillings at the bottom of bedding and excavation is adopted as fillings underneath the bedding. Embankment filling tests must be conducted before filling to acquire the appropriate construction parameters.

替换单词 Alternative terms

① 重力式路堤挡土墙
　路肩桩板墙
　悬臂式挡土墙
　扶壁式挡土墙
　加筋土挡土墙
② 改良土

① gravity embankment retaining wall
　sheet-pile wall of shoulder
　cantilever retaining wall
　buttress retaining wall
　reinforced earth retaining wall
② improved soil

业务情景：外方工程师 Alex 向中方王工程师确认提供资料工期。
Scene: Alex is confirming with Mr Wang about the delivery time of materials.

典型对话 Conversation

Alex：我们已收到贵公司给我们提供的 1 标段路基施工图纸，非常详细，谢谢。但请给我们提供一份相应的设计计算说明书好吗？

Alex: We have received your subgrade construction drawing for Lot 1. We are grateful that it is very detailed. But can you provide us a design and calculation description?

王工程师：好的，但我们需要一点时间整理一下，下星期一给你们行吗？

Alex: 好的。请问什么时候能确定下一阶段路基图纸的交付日期。

王工程师：下一阶段图纸的交付日期是本阶段正式批复后90个工作日后。但是现在我们没有本阶段的正式批复文件。

Alex：那是因为我们还没有收到本次审查意见的答复。

王工程师：相关答复我们已经在上个周五以书面文件发到您的公司。

Alex: 我回去会查收，那样的话我们批复文件会尽快下发的。

王工程师：谢谢。

Alex: 我们希望尽快得到这段路基图纸，涵洞和桥梁图纸可以晚些交付。

王工程师：路基图纸需要涵洞及桥梁专业[①]提供相应设计范围，然后才能确认出图。

Alex: 好吧，我们还是按90个工作日交图吧。

Mr Wang: Ok, but it will take some time. Can I give it to you next Monday?

Alex: Ok, when can we determine the delivery date of next stage's subgrade drawing?

Mr Wang: The delivery date of the next stage's subgrade drawing is 90 working days after official approval of this stage's drawing. But we haven't received the approval yet.

Alex: That's because we haven't received the reply on this review.

Mr Wang: We sent our written reply to your company last Friday.

Alex: I will check it. In that case, we will issue our approval as soon as possible.

Mr Wang: Thank you.

Alex: We hope we can get the subgrade drawing as soon as possible, and the culvert and bridge drawings can be delivered a little later.

Mr Wang: Subgrade drawing requires the relevant design scopes provided by the culvert and bridge designers[①], and then the drawing can be worked out.

Alex: Ok, please deliver the drawing in 90 working days.

替换单词 Alternative terms

① 站后专业　　　　　　　　　① electrical & mechanical discipline
　 站场专业　　　　　　　　　　 station & yard discipline

业务情景：咨询方和设计方共同参与工程咨询大纲审查。
Scene: The consulting party and the designing party are participating in the review of the engineering and consulting outline.

典型对话 Conversation

咨询方：请问你们的设计文件为什么采用中国规范标准，而不采用英国标准？

设计方：因为合同中明确了此项目设计规范采用中国规范。

咨询方：但是在合同的第 ## 部分也明确说了如果标准低于英国标准时，则采用英国标准。

设计方：是的，但我们认为我们的规范标准是高于英国标准的。

Alex：我们今天需要明确一些基本的计算方法，这样方便大家咨询工程中计算资料的沟通与审查。
王工程师：比如挡墙土压力的计算方法？

Consulting party: Why did you adopt the Chinese standard rather than the British standard in your design document?

Designing party: Because the contract specifies that the Chinese standard is adopted for this project .

Consulting party: But it is also specified in the ## section of the contract that if the Chinese standard requires a lower standard than the British one, the British standard should be adopted.

Designing party: Yes, but we believe that our standard requirements are higher than the British one.

Alex: We should explicit some basic calculation methods to facilitate our communication and review.
Mr Wang: Such as the calculation method of pressure on the retaining wall?

第一部分　交通工程情景会话

Alex：你是说作用在墙背的主动土压力么？

王工程师：是的。

Alex：我们一般采用<u>库仑土压力</u>①理论进行计算。

王工程师：看来这点上我们是一致的。

Alex：你们目前对于路堤和地基的整体稳定性计算采用的是何种方法？

王工程师：我们通常采用<u>圆弧滑动法</u>②进行计算。

Alex：好的，我们知道了。

王工程师：顺便我们也想明确一下我们交付文件的格式规定。

Alex：请讲。

王工程师：按照合同，我们提交咨询时文件应为不可编辑的 PDF 格式。

Alex：我们认为 CAD 格式的文件更方便我们的咨询工作。

王工程师：抱歉，按照目前的合同规定，我们不能满足你的要求。

Alex：会后我会向业主提交相关要求的。

Alex: Do you mean the active earth pressure on the wall back?

Mr Wang: Yes.

Alex: We usually adopt <u>Coulomb's earth pressure theory</u>① for calculation.

Mr Wang: We use the same method.

Alex: What method do you use for stability calculation of subgrade and foundation?

Mr Wang: We usually adopt the <u>arch glide method</u>② for calculation.

Alex: Ok, I get it.

Mr Wang: And I would also like to explain the format of our documents.

Alex: Ok.

Mr Wang: According to the contract, the consulting document we submit should be in non-editable PDF format.

Alex: We believe CAD format is conducive to our consulting work.

Mr Wang: I'm sorry that we can't meet your requirements based on the current contract.

Alex: We will submit these requirements to the employer after the meeting.

替换单词 Alternative terms

① 朗肯土压力理论
② 折线滑面法
　　不平衡推力法

① Rankine's earth pressure theory
② sliding surface method
　　imbalance thrust force method

第七章 桥梁
Chapter 7　Bridge

业务情景：中方王工程师与外方政府官员 Jones 讨论桥梁设计所需收集相关水文资料事宜。
Scene: Mr Wang, the engineer from the Chinese side, is discussing hydrological data collection for bridge design with Jones, the government officer from the foreign side.

典型对话 Conversation

王工程师：我方正在开展磨丁至万象新建铁路的初步设计工作，需要收集一些桥梁设计所需的气象、水文资料。

Jones：请问需要哪些资料。

王工程师：首先我们需要收集铁路沿线所经过的省份的气象资料，主要包括<u>年平均气温</u>①、年平均降雨量、历史最高和最低气温值等。

Jones：我们将尽快联系当地气象部门，他们会将资料提供给你。

王工程师：其次，我们需要收集琅勃拉邦和万象地区湄公河的水文资料，包括历年最大水位及流量值。

Mr Wang: We are conducting the preliminary design of the Boten-Vientiane railway project, and we need to collect some meteorological and hydrological data for bridge design.

Jones: What do you need?

Mr Wang: Firstly, we need to collect meteorological data of the provinces the railway passes by, including the <u>annual average temperature</u>①, annual average rainfall, and the highest and lowest recorded temperatures.

Jones: We will contact the local meteorological department to get that information for you.

Mr Wang: Secondly, we also need hydrological data of the Mekong River in the Luang Prabang and Vientiane region, including recorded the maximum water level and discharge.

Jones: 我们会尽快联系当地水文部门,请问你们所设计的铁路防洪等级是多少年一遇呢?

王工程师: 设计洪水频率按100年一遇进行设计。

Jones: 很好,需要提醒你们的是,像湄公河这样的河流,我们规划了很多水库,请在铁路桥梁设计时考虑当地的规划要求。

王工程师: 好的,规划水库的资料能否一并提供给我们呢?

Jones: 没有问题,我们也会尽快通知水利部门。

Jones: We will contact the local hydrological department. What is the flood control level in your railway design?

Mr Wang: The designed flood frequency is once in 100 years.

Jones: Very well. I have to remind you that we have planned numerous reservoirs for rivers like Mekong River, please consider the restrictions, by local planning, in railway bridge design.

Mr Wang: Ok. Can you provide us with the materials for reservoir planning?

Jones: No problem. We will inform the water conservancy department as soon as possible.

替换单词 Alternative terms

① 年雷暴天数　　　　　　　　① annual thunderstorm days

业务情景: 中方王工程师与外方政府官员 Jones 讨论铁路桥梁设计方案。
Scene: Mr Wang is discussing with Jones on railway bridge design scheme.

典型对话 Conversation

王工程师: 我方正在开展磨丁至万象新建铁路的初步设计工作,关于跨越湄公河的桥梁方案需要同贵方进行探讨。

Mr Wang: We are conducting a preliminary design on Boten-Vientiane railway project, and we need to discuss for the scheme of bridge crossing the Mekong River.

Jones: 请问你们跨越湄公河的桥梁，主跨度将采用多少米？

王工程师: 因为现在湄公河的通航等级为Ⅳ级，跨越湄公河的主航道的桥梁将采用104m的跨度。

Jones: 已经满足通航需要了，现在设计的桥梁与河道的交角是多少度呢？

王工程师: 琅勃拉邦湄公河特大桥方案受地形、水文及琅勃拉邦车站站位的控制，现方案桥梁与河道的交角是85°。

Jones: 非常好，需要提醒的是，请在设计文件中考虑下施工期间的通航①调度组织问题。

王工程师: 我们已经开始着手这方面的工作了，施工期间通航安全是我们设计时需考虑的重要因素。

Jones: How long is the main span of that bridge?

Mr Wang: The navigation level of the Mekong River is Level Ⅳ, so a span of 104m is adopted for the bridge crossing the main channel of the river.

Jones: It meets the requirement of navigation. How many degrees is the crossing angle of the river?

Mr Wang: The Luang Prabang Mekong River Super Major Bridge is restricted by topography, hydrology and the position of Luang Prabang Station. It intersects the river at an angle of 85°.

Jones: Very well. I have to mention that the organization of navigation① should be considered during the construction phase.

Mr Wang: We are working on this. The security of navigation during construction is an important factor considered in our design.

替换单词 Alternative terms

① 防汛　　　　　　　　　　　① Flood control

第一部分　交通工程情景会话

业务情景: 中方王工程师与外方政府官员 Jones 讨论道路立交净空问题。
Scene: Mr Wang is discussing with Jones on the clearance for grade separation.

典型对话 Conversation

王工程师: 我方正在开展磨丁至万象新建铁路的初步设计工作关于铁路与地方道路的立交净空问题,我们需要征求贵方的意见。

Jones: 这条铁路是否采用铁路上跨道路的形式进行设计?

王工程师: 原则上是的,特殊情况会采用公路桥的形式在地方道路上跨铁路。城市道路的立交净空按 4.5m 进行设计。

Jones: 这已满足城市道路的需要了,请问跨越乡村道路的净空是多少?

王工程师: 仅为人力车及人行而设的铁路桥涵按净高 2.5m 考虑,若是机耕及畜力车通道,我们将按 3m 净高进行设计,同时桥涵出入口两侧都会设置限高架。

Jones: 需要提醒的是,我们现正规划有几条<u>高速公路</u>[①],立交净空请按 5m 进行设计。

Mr Wang: We are conducting a preliminary design for the Boten-Vientiane railway, and we need to discuss with you the clearance for grade separation of railways and local roads.

Jones: Is this railway designed to overpass the road?

Mr Wang: In principle, it is. The railway also underpasses road in the form of highway bridges under special circumstances. The grade separation clearance is designed as 4.5m.

Jones: It meets the requirements of the municipal road. How much is the clearance of crossing country road?

Mr Wang: The clearance for railway bridges with only man-powered vehicles and pedestrians is considered as 2.5m, and that for tractors and animal-powered vehicles is designed as 3m. Height restrictions will be set on both sides of the bridges and culverts.

Jones: We are planning several <u>highways</u>[①], please design the grade separation with a clearance of 5m.

83

王工程师：好的，请提供给我们规划高速公路的资料，以便我们进行下一阶段的设计工作。

Jones：没问题，我们会通知交通规划单位与你方接洽。

Mr Wang: Ok. Please provide us with the relevant materials to facilitate our design in the next stage.

Jones: No problem, we will inform the planning authority to contact with you.

替换单词 Alternative terms

① 轻轨　　　　　　　　　　① light rail

业务情景：中方王工程师与外方施工单位工程师 Gavin 讨论桥梁施工问题。

Scene: Mr Wang is discussing with Gavin, the engineer from the foreign construction company on bridge construction.

典型对话 Conversation

Gavin：我是施工单位的 Gavin。湄公河大桥施工设计中关于梁部结构的施工图设计完成了么？

王工程师：梁部的设计，我们已经按期完成了，并于昨天将图纸寄了出去。请你们及时查收。

Gavin：还有个问题要和你们沟通一下，我们在施工桥墩及桩基础时，发现桥位处地质情况与目前的设计图上有差异，可能会影响到结构设计。

Gavin: I am Gavin from the construction company. Have you finished the construction drawings of beams for the construction of the Mekong River Major Bridge?

Mr Wang: We have finished the beam design on time and sent it to you yesterday. Please check it without delay.

Gavin: I have another issue to discuss with you. In the construction of the pier and pile foundations, we found that the geological condition was different from that shown in the current design drawing, which might affect the structural design.

第一部分　交通工程情景会话

王工程师：请您把最新的地质情况以报告的形式发给我们。

Gavin：好的，随后我会发给你。还有个问题是，关于图纸中墩身①钢筋的数量有遗漏，我将一并通过电子邮件发给你，麻烦你们重新核查一下图纸。

王工程师：非常感谢。我会及时对你提出的问题进行回复。

Mr Wang: Please send us a report on the latest geological information collected.

Gavin: Ok. I will send it to you later. Another problem is that some quantity of the steel reinforcement for pier① is omitted. I will send you the e-mail together with it, please recheck the drawing.

Mr Wang: Thank you very much. I will respond to you in time.

替换单词 Alternative terms

① 承台　　　　　　　　　　　　　① Bearing platform

业务情景：设计院代表王工程师向业主代表 Gavin 及施工单位代表工程师 Tom 做工程设计技术交底。
Scene: Mr Wang is carrying out a technical disclosure with Gavin, the employer's representative and Tom, the representative engineer from the constructor.

典型对话 Conversation

Gavin：下面请设计代表汇报湄公河大桥的设计情况及施工注意事项。

王工程师：湄公河大桥的设计情况如下：该桥中心里程为DK881+980，桥梁全长880m，主桥为（40+64+40）m三跨预应力混凝土连续梁结构，引桥采用32m

Gavin: Now let's invite the designer to brief us about attention points on the design and construction of the Mekong River Major Bridge.

Mr Wang: The design of the Mekong Major Bridge is as follows: the total length of the bridge is 880m, with a centre mileage of DK881+980. (40+64+40)m three-span

简支箱梁[①]。全桥最高墩高为40m，最低墩高为21m，墩身采用矩形截面，桥梁墩、台基础均采用桩基础。该桥设计施工工期为24个月。

prestressed concrete continuous beams are adopted for the main bridge, and 32m simple box girder is used for the bridge approach[①]. The highest pier is 40m, and the lowest one is 21m. Rectangular cross-section is adopted for the pier, and pile foundations are adopted for bridge piers and abutments. The construction period of the bridge is designed as 24 months.

Gavin: 对湄公河大桥的设计情况，施工单位有没有什么问题？

Gavin: Are there any questions from the construction company about the design of the Mekong River Major Bridge?

Tom: 从目前交付的施工图图纸来看，没有明确交代合龙段施工时的注意事项。希望设计方说明一下这个问题。

Tom: From the current construction drawing, there are no specific notes on the construction of the closure section. Please explain this issue.

王工程师: 对于这个问题，我们在第二册梁部施工图总说明中有详细说明。一般来说，为保证合龙段混凝土的质量，要求合龙段在一天的最低气温下施工。

Mr Wang: We have detailed instructions about this issue in Volume Ⅱ Beam Construction Drawing. In general, construction is required under the lowest temperature to insure the concrete quality of the closure section.

Tom: 我们会认真阅读施工说明并按设计要求进行施工。

Tom: We will read the instructions carefully and construct accordingly.

替换单词 Alternative terms

① 简支T形梁

① simply supported T beam

第一部分　交通工程情景会话

第八章　隧道
Chapter 8　Tunnel

业务情景：中方罗工程师与外方工程师Jones讨论设计方案。
Scene: Mr Luo, the engineer from the Chinese side and Jones, the engineer from the foreign side, are talking about the design scheme.

典型对话 Conversation

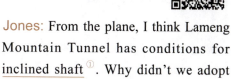

Jones： 从平面图看，拉孟山隧道有设置斜井①的条件，为什么不采用斜井方案呢？

罗工程师： 首先该隧道洞身穿越可溶岩强烈发育地层，施工中遭遇突水突泥的工程风险较大，为实现顺坡排水，我们选择设置平行导坑的方案。

Jones： 该方案是否满足工期要求？

罗工程师： 平行导坑方案的工期比控制工期少3个月，满足工期要求。

Jones： 但是该隧道设置辅助坑道总长1234m，工程量较大，能否进行优化？

Jones: From the plane, I think Lameng Mountain Tunnel has conditions for inclined shaft①. Why didn't we adopt inclined shaft?

Mr Luo: The tunnel body crosses highly developed Karst strata, so the risk of water inrush and mud bursting is high in construction. We chose the parallel drift method to realize downslope drainage.

Jones: Can this option meet the requirements of the construction period?

Mr Luo: Construction with the parallel drift method is 3 months less than the critical path time, so it can meet the requirements of the construction period.

Jones: But the total length of the service gallery is 1234m in length, which generates large quantities of works. Can it be optimized?

87

罗工程师：平行导坑的方案是各方案中造价较少而且工程风险较低的方案，所以我们推荐该方案。

Mr Luo: The parallel drift method is a low-cost one with lower risk among all the options. Therefore, we recommend this option.

Jones：希望你们能提供比较方案的材料给我们。

Jones: We hope you can provide us with materials for option comparison.

罗工程师：我们已经准备好了，资料在这里，请您过目。

Mr Luo: We've already prepared them, here you are.

替换单词 Alternative terms

① 横洞；竖井　　　　　　　　　① horizontal adit; vertical shaft

业务情景：中方罗工程师与外方工程师 Jones 讨论出口渣场位置。
Scene: Mr Luo is discussing with Jones about muck disposal.

典型对话 Conversation

罗工程师：万荣隧道临近万荣市的风景旅游区，隧道出口位置设计渣场是否会影响到该风景旅游区？

Mr Luo: Wanrong Tunnel is near the tourist site of Wanrong City. If the muck disposal is located by the entrance, will it influence the tourist site?

Jones：我认为这里弃渣会影响到风景区的景观，不适合修建弃渣场。

Jones: I think the tourist site would be influensed if we set it here. It is not a good place for muck disposal.

罗工程师：好的，希望贵方能提供风景区范围的平面位置图，以方便我们进行设计。

Mr Luo: Ok. Please provide us with the plane of the tourist site to facilitate our design.

Jones：进口右侧1000m的位置不行吗？

Jones: Is 1000m away to the right of the tunnel entrance a good place?

罗工程师：该处存在滑坡①，不宜弃渣。

Jones：我们会尽快给您提供相关资料。

罗工程师：谢谢，希望您下周一前将资料以邮件的形式发给我们。

Jones：没问题。

Mr Luo: The place has potential for landslides①, it is not suitable for muck disposal.

Jones: We will provide you with the materials as soon as possible.

Mr Luo: Thank you! Please send it to us by email before next Monday.

Jones: No problem.

替换单词 Alternative terms

① 泥石流　　　　　　　　① mud flow
　岩堆　　　　　　　　　　rock heap
　落水洞　　　　　　　　　sinkhole

业务情景：中方罗工程师汇报设计方案，外方工程师 Jones 参加。
Scene: Mr Luo is briefing the design scheme to Jones, the foreign engineer.

典型对话 Conversation

罗工程师：我是隧道专业设计负责人。我汇报的主题是万荣隧道方案研究。汇报内容主要有以下三个部分：1. 隧道概况介绍，2. 分别从经济性、施工风险和施工工期等方面对三种不同的施工组织方案进行比较，3. 重点介绍推荐方案及具体的工程措施。（详细汇报略）

Mr Luo: I'm in charge of tunnel design. My briefing is mainly on the study of Wanrong Tunnel Design, which is composed of three parts: 1. Overview of the tunnel; 2. Comparison of three different construction plans from three aspects, namely economy, construction risk and construction duration; 3. Detailed introduction of recommended option and specific engineering measures. (Detailed report is omitted.)

Jones: 感谢隧道专业设计负责人的汇报，我们非常认可贵方的推荐方案，该方案既经济，又大大降低了施工风险。但是我们注意到该隧道DK123+456~DK123+789里程穿越含瓦斯地层，对该段的施工安全方面，贵方有没有具体的一些工程措施呢？

罗工程师： 推荐方案采用进口平导+出口横洞①的施工组织形式，进口平导在通过瓦斯地段时可以与正洞一起实现巷道式通风，大大降低隧道中的瓦斯浓度，同时在通过瓦斯地段时应加强超前探测、设置瓦斯自动监测系统等措施。

Jones: 运营通风方面，贵方是如何考虑的呢？

罗工程师： 经计算分析，隧道内不考虑运营机械通风。

Jones: 隧道衬砌有没有进行特殊设计呢？

罗工程师： 对通过瓦斯地段的隧道衬砌采用全封闭衬砌，并且安装水气分离装置防止瓦斯渗漏入隧道，确保隧道运营安全。

Jones: Thanks for your excellent report. We accept your recommended option, which is economical and has a lower construction risk. However, we noticed that DK123+456- DK123+789 of the tunnel crosses gas strata. Do you have any specific engineering measures for construction safety?

Mr Luo: The construction organization of parallel drift for the entrance and horizontal adit for the exit① is adopted in the recommended option. Ventilation by ducts can be adopted for the parallel drift for the entrance with the main tunnel when it crosses the gas strata, which can greatly lower the gas density in the tunnel. In addition, such measures as advanced detection, automatic gas monitoring system should be taken when crossing gas strata.

Jones: What are your considerations on operation ventilation?

Mr Luo: After analysis and calculation, mechanical ventilation is not necessary for the tunnel.

Jones: Is there any special design for the tunnel lining?

Mr Luo: For the part of the tunnel that crosses the gas strata, we will use a fully enclosed lining, and install a gas-water separation device to prevent gas from leaking into the tunnel and guarantee operational safety.

替换单词 Alternative terms

① 进口横洞 + 出口平导　　① horizontal adit for entrance and parallel drift for exit

　　进口平导　　　　　　　　parallel drift for entrance

业务情景：外方工程师 Jones 与中方罗工程师讨论设计工作安排。
Scene: Jones and Mr Luo are discussing the arrangements for the design work.

典型对话 Conversation

Jones: 拉孟山隧道发现大型溶洞①，贵方在 10 月 30 日前能否按时交付施工图呢？

罗工程师: 请您放心，我们一定能在规定时间内保质保量完成。

Jones: 具体工作是怎么安排的呢？

罗工程师: 目前，该隧道的设计方案已经通过集团公司级会审确定下来，我们已经安排精兵强将进行该方案的绘制。具体安排是这样的：10 月 1 日提交施工咨询图，咨询意见返回后，5 日内完成修改并逐级审查，预计 10 月 25 日左右能提交施工图。

Jones: A large karst cave① is found in Lameng Mountain Tunnel, so can you deliver the construction drawings on time before October 30?

Mr Luo: Don't worry! We will deliver them within the required time with both quality and quantity guaranteed.

Jones: Can I be informed of your specific arrangement?

Mr Luo: Currently, the design of the tunnel has been already confirmed by the final review of CREEC. We appointed excellent designers to make the designs. The specific schedule is as follows: We will deliver construction drawings for consulting on Oct. 1, and complete modifications and all levels of reviewing within 5 days after we receive consulting

Jones: 请你们务必按计划完成。
罗工程师: 没问题。

opinions. We are supposed to deliver final construction drawings on Oct. 25.
Jones: Please follow your schedule.
Mr Luo: No problem.

替换单词 Alternative terms

① 突水突泥
   软岩大变形
   岩爆

① water inrush and mud bursting
   large deformation of soft rock
   rock burst

业务情景: 外方工程师 Jones 与中方罗工程师讨论交图。
Scene: Jones is discussing with Mr Luo about drawings delivery.

典型对话 Conversation

Jones: 万荣隧道设计图纸是否已经完成了呢？
罗工程师: 由于地质资料还未全部返回，设计未全部完成。

Jones: 能否将进出口图纸先交付给施工方，便于施工？

罗工程师: 可以考虑以阶段性施工图的形式出图，但需按双方签署合同中有关交图的进度方案的条款办理。

Jones: Have you finished the drawings of Wanrong Tunnel?
Mr Luo: Because the geological data is not fully returned, the design is not completely finished.

Jones: Can you deliver the drawings of inlet and outlet to the constructor first, so that they can start the construction?
Mr Luo: We can consider delivering construction drawings in stages, but it has to be carried out according to the terms of the drawings delivery schedule in the signed contract.

第一部分　交通工程情景会话

Jones: 好的。辅助坑道洞口图①希望也一起出了。

罗工程师: 我们会按合同条款内容交付图纸。

Jones: Ok. We hope that the drawings of service gallery portal① can be delivered together.

Mr Luo: We will deliver the drawings according to the contract terms.

替换单词 Alternative terms

① 渣场设计图　　　　　　　　① drawings of muck disposal design
　 进口排水设计图　　　　　　　 drawings of entrance drainage design
　 施工组织设计图　　　　　　　 drawings of construction organization design
　 辅助坑道洞身设计图　　　　　 drawings of service gallery body design
　 衬砌参考图　　　　　　　　　 drawings of lining reference

业务情景: 外方工程师Jones与中方罗工程师讨论变更设计。
Scene: Jones is discussing with Mr Luo about design alteration.

典型对话 Conversation

Jones: 据现场反映，南坡隧道在DK123+456里程发现一充填溶洞①，已严重影响施工进度，贵方是否根据收到的变更指令完成了设计？（黄皮书）或者是否与总包单位进行了协调，完成了变更设计（银皮书）？

Jones: According to feedback from the construction site, an infilled karst cave① is found on DK123+456 in Nanpo tunnel, which has severely hampered construction progress. Have you finished the design according to the alteration instruction you received? (Yellow Book) Or have you finished alteration design based on coordination with the Main Contractor (Silver Book)?

罗工程师：现场隧道专业负责人和总工已经在现场进行了踏勘，了解了现场具体情况，通过研究，提出了具体方案，目前正在进行图纸绘制。

Jones：该隧道现在的施工进度已经滞后于工期要求，贵方考虑如何处理？

罗工程师：我们将在发现充填溶洞处设计迂回导坑②，确保隧道能继续施工，保证工期要求。

Jones：希望贵方能与施工单位协同配合，确保工期。

罗工程师：我们在现场有施工配合人员，能及时跟施工单位沟通协调。

Jones：现场配合人员有几个人？

罗工程师：现在该工点有两名设计人员。

Jones：两名设计人员够么？

罗工程师：没问题，现场设计人员都是经验非常丰富的，从事设计已经有十年时间。

Mr Luo: The engineer in charge of tunnel design on site and the chief engineer have already performed site reconnaissance to assess the situation there. After study, a specific scheme will be proposed and the drawings will be made.

Jones: Since the construction progress of the tunnel is behind schedule, what will you do about it?

Mr Luo: We will set a detour drift② at the location of the infilled karst cave and continue tunnel construction to ensure the timely completion of the tunnel.

Jones: Please coordinate with the Constructor to make sure the tunnel will be completed on time.

Mr Luo: We have site coordinators to facilitate timely communication with the Constructor.

Jones: How many coordinators are there on site?

Mr Luo: We appointed two coordinators for the site now.

Jones: Is that enough?

Mr Luo: No problem. The designers we appointed on site are very experienced. They have been working in this trade for 10 years.

第一部分　交通工程情景会话

替换单词 Alternative terms

① 富水溶腔　　　　　　① water-rich karst cave
　岩溶暗河　　　　　　　karst underground river
　富水断层　　　　　　　water-rich fault
② 桩基托梁跨越结构　　② pile foundation underpinning structure
　泄水洞　　　　　　　　drain cavern
　帷幕注浆　　　　　　　curtain grouting

业务情景：外方工程师 Jones 与中方罗工程师讨论技术标准。
Scene: Jones is discussing with Mr Luo about technical standards.

典型对话 Conversation

Jones：本线对混凝土耐腐蚀性有考虑么？

罗工程师：是的，已纳入设计。
Jones：衬砌①设计使用年限是多久？

罗工程师：按 100 年考虑。
Jones：本线有没有考虑运营通风？

罗工程师：本线隧道长度均小于 10km，均不考虑运营机械通风。

Jones：依据是什么呢？

罗工程师：依据规范及计算分析得出的结论。

Jones: Do you have any considerations of corrosion resistance of concrete for this line?
Mr Luo: Yes, it is included in the design.
Jones: How long is the design service life of the lining①?
Mr Luo: 100 years.
Jones: Have you considered the operation ventilation?
Mr Luo: Each tunnel on the line is shorter than 10km, so mechanic ventilation is not considered.
Jones: What is the basis of that conclusion?
Mr Luo: We concluded it according to codes and analysis.

替换单词 Alternative terms

① 洞门　　　　　　　① portal
　沟槽　　　　　　　　 trench
　永久防护　　　　　　 permanent protection
　辅助坑道　　　　　　 service gallery
　预加固桩　　　　　　 pre-consolidation pile

业务情景：外方工程师 Jones 与中方罗工程师讨论车站影响。
Scene: Jones is discussing with Mr Luo about the effect of the stations.

典型对话 Conversation

Jones：本线共有几座隧道受车站影响？

罗工程师：共 7 个车站进入隧道，影响 11 座隧道。

Jones：受影响段与其他段落的主要区别是什么？

罗工程师：主要区别是受影响段为双线隧道，开挖断面较单线隧道大。

Jones：设计上是如何确保大断面开挖安全的？

罗工程师：对大断面开挖段采用台阶法加临时仰拱法①等特殊工法，并加强支护措施，确保安全。

Jones: How many tunnels on this railway line are effected by stations?

Mr Luo: There are seven stations entering tunnels, influensing eleven tunnels.

Jones: What are the main differences between the effected sections and other sections?

Mr Luo: The primary difference is that the effected section is double-track tunnel, which has a larger excavated section than that of single-track tunnel.

Jones: How do you ensure the safety of large-section excavations in design?

Mr Luo: As for large-section excavation, we adopt special construction methods, such as the bench method and the temporary inverted arch method①, and we have strengthened support to ensure safety.

第一部分　交通工程情景会话

Jones：衬砌结构与单线隧道保持一致？

罗工程师：不是的，首先断面不一致，双线隧道断面较大；其次衬砌厚度和配筋量有所增加，以满足结构计算要求；再次排水等措施根据相关要求进行调整。

Jones：这样造价会提高不少了？

罗工程师：是的，车站隧道造价约是单线隧道的两倍。

Jones: Is the lining structure consistent with that of a single-track tunnel?

Mr Luo: No. Firstly, the cross sections are different. Double-track tunnels have a larger cross section. Secondly, the lining thickness and amount of steel bars are increased to satisfy the structural requirement. Thirdly, some other measures such as drainage will be adjusted according to relevant requirements.

Jones: Will this substantially increase the construction cost?

Mr Luo: Yes. The cost of a station tunnel is twice of that of single-track tunnel.

替换单词 Alternative terms

① 双侧壁导坑法　　　　　　　　① twin-side heading method
　 三台阶七步作业法　　　　　　　 three-bench seven-step method
　 交叉中隔壁法　　　　　　　　　 cross diaphragm method

业务情景：外方工程师 Jones 与中方罗工程师讨论工期。
Scene: Jones is discussing the duration of construction with Mr Luo.

典型对话 Conversation

Jones：空朗村隧道的建设工期是多少年呢？

罗工程师：总工期是 45 个月。

Jones: How long is the construction period of Konglang Village Tunnel?

Mr Luo: A total of forty five months.

Jones: 是否已考虑施工场地整平及进场时间。

罗工程师: 已按3个月时间考虑。

Jones: 进度指标是怎么确定的呢？

罗工程师: 参照规范确定的。

Jones: 具体指标情况是怎样的？

罗工程师: 正洞施工进度为Ⅱ级围岩140m/月，Ⅲ级围岩100m/月，Ⅳ级围岩55m每月，Ⅴ级围岩35m/月。

Jones: Ⅴ级围岩段落是否太慢？

罗工程师: 上述指标是综合考虑沿线地形、地质①等因素，经工程类比得到的，是比较合理的。

Jones: Does it include the time for site leveling and equipment mobilization?

Mr Luo: Yes. We counted it as three months.

Jones: How did you determine the progress target?

Mr Luo: We determined it based on the related codes.

Jones: What about the detailed schedules?

Mr Luo: The construction progress targets for the main tunnel are 140m per month for Grade Ⅱ surrounding rock, 100m per month for Grade Ⅲ surrounding rock, 55m per month for Grade Ⅳ surrounding rock, and 35m per month for Grade Ⅴ surrounding rock.

Jones: Is it too slow for Grade Ⅴ surrounding rock?

Mr Luo: The above progress targets are reasonable because they are obtained from engineering comparisons of such factors as topography, geology①.

替换单词 Alternative terms

① 气候	① climate
交通	transportation
工人素质	staff quality
材料供应	material supply

第一部分　交通工程情景会话

业务情景：外方工程师 Jones 与中方罗工程师讨论地质问题。
Scene: Jones is discussing geological issues with Mr Luo.

📢 典型对话 Conversation

Jones：本线主要工程地质问题有哪些？

罗工程师：主要有<u>高地应力、滑坡、岩堆及岩溶</u>[①]等。

Jones：本线瓦斯问题是否突出？

罗工程师：本线含瓦斯等有害气体隧道共 19 座，均为低瓦斯隧道。

Jones：存在软岩大变形风险的是哪座隧道？

罗工程师：森村隧道存在软岩大变形风险。该隧道岩性为砂岩、泥岩，埋深 400~730m，经分析可能发生轻微大变形。

Jones：贵方是如何考虑设计的？

罗工程师：施工中加强超前地质预报及监控量测，根据检测结果采取合理的支护措施及衬砌结构。

Jones: What are the major engineering geological issues of this line?

Mr Luo: Mainly <u>high ground stress, landslide, talus and karst</u>[①], etc.

Jones: Is the issue of gas distinct in this line?

Mr Luo: There are nineteen tunnels with gas or other hazard gas. All of them are low gas tunnels.

Jones: Which tunnel has the risk of large deformation in soft rock?

Mr Luo: It is Sencun Tunnel. The lithology of it is sandrock and mudrock, with a depth of 400~730m. After analysis, we think minor large deformation may occur in this tunnel.

Jones: How has this been taken into consideration in your designs?

Mr Luo: Advance geology forecasts and monitoring measurements should be strengthened in construction. Reasonable supports and lining structures should be adopted.

替换单词 Alternative terms

① 高地温　　　　　　　　　　① high ground temperature
　黄土　　　　　　　　　　　　 loess
　多年冻土　　　　　　　　　　 permafrost
　膨胀性围岩　　　　　　　　　 swelling wall rock
　大变形　　　　　　　　　　　 large deformation

第九章　站场
Chapter 9　Station and Yard

业务情景：中方王工程师到埃塞俄比亚阿达玛市政府收集所需资料，Tom 接待。

Scene: Mr Wang, the Chinese engineer, is going to the municipal government of Adama in Ethiopia for data collection. Tom is receiving him.

典型对话 Conversation

王工程师：我们正在进行埃塞铁路的设计工作，该铁路在阿达玛市设置车站，需要收集相关规划资料，并就车站的位置征求贵方的意见。

Tom：好的，你们需要收集哪些资料？

王工程师：我们需要阿达玛市城市总体规划图[1]，最好能够提供电子版。

Tom：请稍等，我们马上把相关资料拷给你。

王工程师：另外，我们把车站的初步选址给你介绍一下，并希望能得到市政府对于该选址的正式意见。目前的方案是将阿达玛车站设置在城市边缘 Wuse 村附近，国家 1 号公路外侧，车站距离市中心约 3km。车站长 1.6km，站坪最

Mr Wang: We are designing an Ethiopian railway, and there is a station set in Adama city, so we would like to collect some related data and ask for your opinions about the location of the station.

Tom: Fine, what kind of data do you need?

Mr Wang: We need the master plan[1] of Adama city, and a soft copy would be better.

Tom: A moment, please, we will give it to you right now.

Mr Wang: Furthermore, we want to introduce the initial location of the station to you, and wish to receive your official comments. In the current proposal, Adama station is designed around Wuse village on the edge of the city, outside the

宽处约200m,总占地约18hm², 地块现状情况下为旱地, 有少量民房, 车站东侧为工厂区, 有几家制鞋工厂。

Tom: 车站拆迁房屋的量有多大, 房屋的类型是什么?

王工程师: 车站方案避开了工厂区, 需要拆迁的是少量民房, 约1000m², 为砖墙瓦房②。

Tom: 车站与城市道路的交通连接是如何考虑的?

王工程师: 拟修建一条道路连接车站与阿达玛A大道, 道路宽14m, 双向4车道, 采用混凝土路面③。

Tom: 好的, 我们稍后会将车站的选址向市长进行汇报, 之后给你们进行书面回复。

national No.1 highway and about 3km from the city centre. The station is 1.6km long, with a maximum width of about 200m, covering a total area of about 18hm². The land area is dry with a few houses. There is an industrial district to the east of the station where several shoe-making factories.

Tom: What is the amount of house demolition required for the construction of station? What kind of houses are they?

Mr Wang: Since the station is kept away from the factory district, only about 1000m² of private houses with tile roofs and brick walls② will need to be demolished.

Tom: What do you think about the traffic connection between the station and the urban roads?

Mr Wang: It is planned to construct a road, 14m in width, connecting the station and Adama Avenue A, which is four bidirectional lanes with a concrete pavement③.

Tom: Ok, we will report to the mayor about the siting of the station and then give you a written reply.

第一部分　交通工程情景会话

替换单词 Alternative terms

① 城市交通规划图　　　　　① urban traffic plan
　市政管线位置图　　　　　　 map of municipal pipeline location
　工业区规划图　　　　　　　 industrial park plan
　物流园规划图　　　　　　　 logistics park plan
② 土墙瓦房　　　　　　　　② tile-roofed house with cob wall
　石墙瓦房　　　　　　　　　 tile-roofed house with stone wall
　砖混房屋　　　　　　　　　 brick-and-concrete house
③ 泥结碎石路面　　　　　　③ clay-bound macadam pavement
　沥青路面　　　　　　　　　 asphalt pavement

业务情景：中方王工程师与咨询工程师 Tom 讨论阿达玛站站场布置方案。
Scene: Chinese engineer Mr Wang is discussing the layout plan of Adama station with consulting engineer Tom.

典型对话 Conversation

Tom: 请王工介绍一下阿达玛站的平面布置方案。
王工程师: 好的。阿达玛站为中间站①，车站采用横列式布置②，设到发线 6 条。车站设客运站台两座，设货场 1 处。

Tom: 客运站台的尺寸是多少，基本站台和中间站台之间是否设置跨线设施？

Tom: Could you please present the layout plan of Adama station?
Mr Wang: All right. Adama station is an intermediate station① with six receiving-departure tracks, which adopts a lateral-type layout②. There are two passenger platforms and one freight yard.
Tom: What is the size of the passenger platform? Is there any over-line facility between the main platform and intermediate platform?

103

王工程师：客运站台长 300m，宽 8m，轨面到站台面的高度差是 0.5m。车站站台之间设置<u>人行天桥</u>③。

Tom：车站货场的规模有多大，每年的装卸能力是多少？

王工程师：货场设尽头式货物线两条，货物线长 300m，另设有货物站台和仓库。货场设施能满足每年装、卸货物 15 万 t 的要求。

Tom：每年 15 万 t 的装卸能力是否偏小？

王工程师：根据我们的调查和测算，货场规模能满足近期的货运需求；在远期，随着经济发展，货场能力不足时，可以考虑对货场进行扩建。

Tom：车站是否设有铁路维修设施？

王工程师：车站设有工务工区、信号工区、接触网工区。

Tom：车站东侧为工厂区，根据地方政府的规划，远期要建设铁路物流园，车站的设计是否考虑了这个问题。

Mr Wang: The passenger platform is 300m long and 8m wide, and the height difference between the rail level and the platform surface is 0.5m. <u>Pedestrian overcrossing</u>③ is set between platforms.

Tom: What is the scale of the freight yard? How about the annual load and unload capacity?

Mr Wang: Two dead-end freight lines are designed in the yard, each of which is 300m in length. Besides, freight platforms and storages are also designed. The facilities in the yard could meet the requirement of annual load and unload capacity of 150000 ton.

Tom: Is the capacity a little bit small?

Mr Wang: According to our investigation and calculation, the yard scale could satisfy the near-term demand of freight transportation; for the long term, when the capacity is not enough with the economic development, the yard could be expanded.

Tom: Is the station equipped with railway maintenance facilities?

Mr Wang: There are permanent way maintenance sections, signal sections and OCS sections in the station.

Tom: It is a factory district on the east side of the station, and in accordance with the planning of local government, a railway

第一部分　交通工程情景会话

王工程师：我们考虑了这一因素，对车站左侧咽喉的道岔布置进行了调整，预留了铁路专用线的引入条件。铁路物流园建设时，能顺利地进行接轨，不会产生废弃工程。

Mr Wang: Of course we did. We adjusted the layout of the switch in the throat on the left of the station and reserved conditions for leading in special railway lines. Therefore, when the logistics park is constructed, the track connection can be carried out smoothly, and no works will be discarded.

替换单词 Alternative terms

① 会让站　　　　① passing station
　越行站　　　　　overtaking station
　区段站　　　　　district station
　编组站　　　　　marshaling station
② 纵列式布置　　② longitudinal-type layout
③ 人行地道　　　③ pedestrian underpass
　行包地道　　　　luggage tunnel

业务情景：中方工程师与业主关于 INDODE 站的讨论。
Scene: The Chinese engineer is discussing Indode station with the owner.

典型对话 Conversation

Tom: 王先生，INDODE 车站很大，请问这个站的性质是什么？

Tom: Mr Wang, Indode station is very big, so what is the character of the station?

105

王工程师：INDODE 站是这全线的技术作业中心，是区段站①。

Tom：请问 INDODE 站由哪几个部分组成？

王工程师：本站设有到发场、调车场、货场、机务车辆段、综合维修中心几个部分。

Tom：能介绍一下到发场和调车场的作用吗？

王工程师：好的，到发场主要负责列车的到达、始发和通过。调车场主要负责从吉布提过来的货物列车的解体和编组，以及发往吉布提方向货物列车车辆的集结。

Tom：请问机务车辆段是干什么用的？

王工程师：本站机务车辆段主要负责从亚的斯亚贝巴—吉布提铁路全线机务、车辆的维修、保养和检查作业，同时负责 LABU 客运站和 INDODE 站客货运机车、调车机车及客车车辆的整备作业。

Mr Wang: Indode station is a district station①, and is a centre for technical operation on the whole line.

Tom: What is Indode station composed of?

Mr Wang: It is composed of a receiving-departure yard, shunting yard, freight yard, locomotive and rolling stock depot and a comprehensive maintenance centre.

Tom: Could you tell me the function of the receiving-departure yard and shunting yard?

Mr Wang: Fine, the receiving-departure yard is mainly responsible for the arrival, departure and passing of the trains. The switching yard is responsible for the decoupling and marshaling of the freight train coming from Djibouti, as well as the coupling of the freight cars to Djibouti.

Tom: What is the function of locomotive and rolling stock depot?

Mr Wang: It is mainly responsible for repair, maintenance and inspection of the locomotives and rolling stock for the whole of the Addis Ababa—Djibouti line. Meanwhile, it is also responsible for the servicing works for passenger and freight locomotives, shunting locomotives and passenger cars in Labu passenger station and Indode station.

第一部分　交通工程情景会话

Tom: 那综合维修中心的作用是什么，我总是不能把综合维修中心和机务车辆段区分开。

王工程师: 综合维修中心负责对铁路轨道、路基、桥涵、电力、通信、信号、给排水及房屋建筑等铁路设施设备做维修和养护；而机务车辆段则是对机车、车辆进行维修养护的部门。

Tom: 我看到本站有一组交叉渡线，其他站都没有，请问这个道岔有什么作用？

王工程师: 交叉渡线主要是为了缩短车站咽喉布置，减少用地和机车车辆走行距离而设计的，因为本站规模很大，为了布置紧凑才使用了交叉渡线。而其他中间站规模相对较小，因此不用设置交叉渡线。

Tom: So, what is the comprehensive maintenance centre used for? I can't distinguish between the comprehensive maintenance centre and the locomotive and rolling stock depot.

Mr Wang: The comprehensive maintenance centre is responsible for the repair and maintenance of railway facilities, like track, subgrade, bridge & culvert, electric power, communication, signal, water supply and drainage and building. The locomotive and rolling stock depot is responsible for locomotive and rolling stock only.

Tom: There is a scissors crossing only in this station, but no in other stations, so I want to know what it is used for.

Mr Wang: The scissors crossing is designed primarily to shorten the throat layout of the station and decrease the land use and the running distance for locomotive and rolling stock. Since the station is big, we use it for a compact layout. But for other intermediate stations, their scales are comparatively small, so it is unnecessary to use it.

替换单词 Alternative terms

① 会让站　　　　　① passing station
　越行站　　　　　　overtaking station
　区段站　　　　　　district station
　编组站　　　　　　marshaling station

业务情景：中方王工程师与咨询工程师 Tom 在阿达玛车站工地讨论施工技术问题。

Scene: The Chinese engineer Mr Wang is discussing the technical problems of construction with consulting engineer Tom on the site of Adama station.

典型对话 Conversation

Tom: 请问车站线路的路基和区间正线路基一样吗？为什么？

王工程师：车站正线路基和区间正线路基是一样的。到发线和其他站线如果和正线有排水槽等隔开设备隔开，则到发线和其他站线路基表层和底层填料厚度不一样，如果没有隔开，则和区间正线一致。这主要是因为到发线和其他站线没有列车直接通过，运行速度较低，因此技术要求没有区间正线那么高。

Tom: 我看到车站到发线的线间距有的间距是 5.3m，有些股道线间距是 5.0m，为什么会有差异？

王工程师：到发线 II 道和 4 道间距为 5.3m，主要是为了满足 II 道和 4 道同时接发超限货物列车的需要，根据建筑限界和机车车辆限界要求，需要 5.3m 才

Tom: Is the subgrade under the station's tracks the same as that under the main line? If so, why?

Mr Wang: The subgrade under the station's main track is the same as that under the main line. If the receiving-departure tracks and other station tracks are separated by some facilities, like a drainage chute, their filling thickness for the surface and bottom layers of the subgrade is different, but if there is no separation, it is the same as that of the main line. It is mainly because the train running on the receiving-departure track and other station tracks normally has a low speed, the technical requirement is not as high as that of the main line.

Tom: I found that some distances between centres of receiving-departure lines are 5.3m, while some are 5.0m, why?

Mr Wang: For the receiving-departure tracks No. II and No.4, their distances between centres of lines are 5.3m, in order to meet the requirement of receiving

能满足要求，如果不是同时接发超限货物列车，则采取 5.0m 线间距就可以了。

Tom: 车站单身宿舍的场坪比车站其他房屋的场坪高，说说为什么这么做。

王工程师：我们车站站房和场坪设计有很多种形式，本站采用线上式①。这些布置都是根据不同的地形和用地投资综合考虑。本站是为了减少用地和减少大量的开挖，依据地形进行设计，站房采用线平式，单身宿舍采取线上式，减少大量挖方，减少对环境的破坏，让建筑适应自然。

and departing of out-of-gauge freight trains simultaneously, if not, 5.0m would be fine. According to the requirement of structure gauge and locomotive and rolling stock gauge, only 5.3m could satisfy receiving and departing of out-of-gauge freight train simultaneously.

Tom: Why is the site for the bachelor quarters higher than that for other buildings in the station?

Mr Wang: We have different types when designing the station buildings and yards. Higher-than-the-line style① is used for this station. All these layouts are comprehensively considered according to the different landforms and land investment. The design of the station is in harmony with the landform to decrease the land use and avoid mass excavation. Same-level-with-the-line style is adopted for the station building while higher-than-the-line style is for bachelor quarters, so that a great deal of excavation is reduced and damage to the environment is lessened, and in that way, the buildings are friendly with nature.

替换单词 Alternative terms

① 线平式
　 线下式

① same-level-with-the-line
　 lower-than-the-line

第十章　轨道
Chapter 10　Track

业务情景：中方林工程师与业主代表 Roger 讨论轨道专业设计方案。
Scene: Mr Lin, the engineer from the Chinese side, is discussing the design of track with Roger, the representative of the employer.

典型对话 Conversation

Roger: 请问本线设计速度和年通过总质量是多少？

林工程师：正线[1]设计速度为120km/h，年通过总质量达到25Mt。

Roger: 正线是采用60kg/m 钢轨吗？

林工程师：是的。

Roger: 如果采用50kg/m 钢轨，采购成本应该更低，可以节约投资。

林工程师：是的，若选用50kg/m 钢轨，可以减少约18%的初期投资。

Roger: 那么，为什么不采用50kg/m 钢轨？

林工程师：钢轨类型的选择应保证轨道具有良好的动力响应特性和更大的稳定性，在长期运营中保持良好的平顺性，

Roger: What are the design speed and annual carrying capacity of the railway line?

Mr Lin: The design speed of the main line[1] is 120km/h, and the annual carrying capacity is 25Mt.

Roger: Is 60kg/m rail used for the main line?

Mr Lin: Yes.

Roger: If we use 50kg/m rail, the procurement cost will be lower, so the investment can be reduced.

Mr Lin: Yes, if we use 50kg/m rail in the initial stage, the cost can be reduced by 18%.

Roger: Then, why don't you use 50kg/m rail?

Mr Lin: When selecting rail type, we shall ensure good dynamic response and greater stability of the track, so as to

减少养护维修工作量并延长使用寿命。

Roger: 有没有具体的数据呢?

林工程师: 相对于50kg/m钢轨,60kg/m钢轨抗弯截面模量会增加37%,弯曲应力减少28%,枕上压力减少30%~40%,安全疲劳寿命延长75%以上,养护维修工作量减少40%,乘坐舒适性和减振降噪的性能也明显提高。

Roger: 原来是这样,在经济允许的情况下,我们采纳你们的建议,选用60kg/m钢轨。本线有没有采用双层道砟的地段?

林工程师: 有的。

Roger: 哪些地段铺设了双层道砟?

林工程师: 非渗水土质路基地段应采用双层道砟,其中上层为面砟,下层为底砟。

Roger: 其余地段是否全部采用单层道砟?

林工程师: 是的。

Roger: 为什么全线不统一采用单层道砟,以节约投资?

maintain the smoothness of track during railway operations, reduce maintenance works and extend the service life of tracks.

Roger: Can you give me any specific numbers?

Mr Lin: Compared to 50kg/m rail, bending section modulus can be increased by 37% in using 60kg/m rail, bending stress is decreased by 28%, pressure on sleepers is decreased by 30%-40%, safe fatigue life is extended by 75%, maintenance works are reduced by 40%. The riding comfort and mitigation on vibration and noise is also improved.

Roger: Oh, I've got it. We accept your suggestion to use 60kg/m if it is affordable in the project. Are there any sections with double-layer ballast on the line?

Mr Lin: Yes.

Roger: Where are they?

Mr Lin: The section with non-permeable subgrade should use double-layer ballast. The upper layer is called top ballast, and the lower layer is called bottom ballast.

Roger: And all other sections use single-layer ballast?

Mr Lin: Yes.

Roger: Why don't you use single-layer ballast for the whole line to save investment?

林工程师：为了防止路基及道床病害的发生，非渗水土质路基地段得采用双层道砟。

Roger：底砟层的主要功能是隔离面砟层和路基基床表层？

林工程师：是的，底砟层可以防止上层碎石和下层路基土颗粒之间的相互掺混，对从碎石到基床表层之间的渗水性能起过渡作用，防止基床表层在暴雨时被冲刷，防止地下水通过毛细管作用向上渗透，对基床表层起保温防冻作用。

Roger：有砟轨道经过一百多年的发展，技术是否已经成熟？

林工程师：是啊！它结构简单，弹性好，减振降噪效果好，造价较低，但道床本身容易变形，养护维修工作量较大。

Roger：无砟轨道呢？

林工程师：无砟轨道稳定性好，轨道几何形位易于保持，但造价高，对线下基础的工后沉降要求高，在中国国内多用在养修条件较差的长大隧道或者高速

Mr Lin: Double-layer ballast must be used for non-permeable subgrade sections to prevent defects in the subgrade and ballast bed.

Roger: Is the main function of bottom ballast to separate the top ballast and the subgrade bed surface?

Mr Lin: Yes, the bottom ballast can prevent the top ballast from mixing with the soil grains in the subgrade, play a role as a permeable medium between the gravel and the subgrade bed service, protect the bedding from scouring during storms, prevent the upward infiltration of groundwater by capillary action. The bottom ballast can also protect the bedding surface from freezing.

Roger: Is the technology of ballasted track mature enough after more than 100 years' development?

Mr Lin: Yes! It has many advantages, such as simple structure, good elasticity, good effect of vibration and noise mitigation, low cost. However, the ballast bed can be deformed easily, causing a heavy maintenance workload.

Roger: How about ballastless track?

Mr Lin: Ballastless track has good stability, and track geometry is easy to maintain. But the cost is higher and the requirements on post construction

铁路上。

Roger: 有砟轨道与无砟轨道哪一种更适合我们这条线呢？

林工程师：本线全是地面线，设计速度120km/h，天窗时间也是足够的，有砟轨道应是正确的选择。

settlement after construction are stricter. Ballastless tracks are mostly used on long tunnels with poor maintenance conditions or high speed railways.

Roger: Which type is more suitable for this railway line, ballast or ballastless?

Mr Lin: Considering that the whole line is on the ground, the design speed is 120km/h, and the skylight time is long enough, ballast track should be a better option.

替换单词 Alternative terms

① 辅助线　　　　　　　　① auxiliary line
　 专用线　　　　　　　　　 special line
　 联络线　　　　　　　　　 link line
　 疏解线　　　　　　　　　 relief line

业务情景：中方林工程师向业主代表 Roger 讨论汇报轨道设计方案。
Scene: Mr Lin is briefing the design of track to Roger.

典型对话 Conversation

Roger: 请简要汇报一下轨道的设计方案。

林工程师：好的，我汇报的内容主要包括正线轨道设计类型、无缝线路以及主要工程数量。

Roger: Please briefly introduce the design of tracks.

Mr Lin: Ok. My introduction mainly includes the design type of main line track, continuously welded rail track and main quantity of works.

Roger: 先说一下主要工程数量吧！

林工程师: 正线铺轨 26km，其中铺设有砟轨道 12km，无砟轨道 14km。全线正线共铺设Ⅰ级面砟 36000m³，底砟 9600m³。

Roger: 正线不是全部采用的无砟轨道么？

林工程师: 正线采用<u>重型</u>①轨道类型，一次铺设跨<u>区间无缝线路</u>②，长度大于等于 6km 的隧道内铺设无砟轨道，其余地段铺设有砟轨道。

Roger: 好的，采用的是什么扣件？

林工程师: 扣件采用<u>弹条Ⅱ型扣件</u>③。

Roger: 无砟轨道是什么类型？

林工程师: <u>弹性支承块式无砟轨道</u>④。

Roger: 好的，还有什么要补充的没？

林工程师: 正线铺设<u>Ⅲ型混凝土轨枕</u>⑤，按 1667 根/km 铺设。钢轨焊接采用的<u>闪光焊</u>⑥。

Roger: Please start from the quantity of works.

Mr Lin: The tracks laid for the main line is 26km, including 12km ballast tracks and 14km ballastless tracks. 36000m³ (36000 cubic meters) Grade I top ballast and 9600m³ bottom ballast are laid for the entire main line.

Roger: Isn't ballastless track used for the whole main line?

Mr Lin: <u>Heavy</u>① track is adopted for the main line, laid continuously as <u>trans section CWR</u>②. For tunnels no shorter than 6km, ballastless track is adopted, while ballast track is adopted for other parts.

Roger: Ok, what type of fastening is adopted?

Mr Lin: We use <u>type Ⅱ tension clamps</u>③.

Roger: What is the type of ballastless track?

Mr Lin: Ballastless track with <u>elastic bearing block</u>④.

Roger: Ok. Do you have anything more to report?

Mr Lin: <u>Type Ⅲ concrete sleepers</u>⑤ are laid for the main line, on the basis of 1667 pieces per kilometer. <u>Flash welding</u>⑥ is adopted for the welding of rails.

第一部分　交通工程情景会话

替换单词 Alternative terms

① 次重型
　轻型
② 区间无缝线路
　有缝线路
③ 弹条Ⅰ型扣件
　弹条Ⅲ型扣件
④ 双块式无砟轨道
　板式无砟轨道
⑤ Ⅱ型混凝土轨枕
　新Ⅱ型混凝土轨枕
⑥ 铝热焊
　移动式接触焊

① secondary heavy
　light
② section CWR
　rail with joints
③ type I tension fastening
　type III tension fastening
④ double-block ballastless track
　slab ballastless track
⑤ Type II concrete sleepers
　new Type II concrete sleepers
⑥ thermit welding
　mobile contact welding

业务情景： 中方林工程师和业主方代表 Roger 讨论隧道无砟轨道施工的问题。
Scene: The Chinese engineer Mr Lin is discussing issues concerning the laying of ballastless track in the tunnel, with Roger.

典型对话 Conversation

Roger：设计图上无砟轨道结构高度为 0.6m，具体是指的哪一部分的高度？

林工程师：指的是轨道内轨顶至隧道回填层上表面的最小高度。

Roger：经过我们核对，东山隧道无砟轨

Roger: The ballastless track structure on the design drawing is 0.6m high. What does it represent?

Mr Lin: It is the minimum height from the top of the inner rail to the top of the backfilling layer in the tunnel.

Roger: After reviewing the drawings,

道设计图上曲线地段的线间距与线路专业的不一致,如何处理?

林工程师:曲线地段①的线间距②按线路及隧道设计图中的线间距进行施工。

Roger:好的。对于无砟轨道混凝土的现场施工,有什么特别需要注意的呢?

林工程师:混凝土入模后,立即插入振动棒振捣。对轨枕底部位置混凝土要加强振捣,确保混凝土的密实性,避免出现离析、麻面现象。

Roger:施工过程中,希望你们加强现场配合指导工作,明确无砟轨道施工现场配合人员,确保准确按设计图纸施工。

林工程师:没问题,我们一定会按照合同规定,做好配合施工的工作。

we found the distance between tracks in the curved section in Dongshan Tunnel ballastless track design drawing is different from that given by alignment discipline. Can you explain that?

Mr Lin: During construction, the distance between tracks① in the curved section② is adopted according to that in the route and tunnel design drawings.

Roger: Ok. For the site construction of ballastless track concrete, what are the cautions?

Mr Lin: The vibrator should be inserted immediately after the concrete is casted into the mould. The concrete on the bottom of sleepers should be vibrated intensely to ensure the compactibility of concrete and avoid segregation and a pitted surface.

Roger: During construction, we hope you can strengthen on-site coordination and specify coordinators for ballastless track construction to ensure that the construction exactly follows drawings.

Mr Lin: No problem! I'm sure that we will follow the contract and perform the construction coordination well.

替换单词 Alternative terms

① 直线地段
② 轨道中心距

① straight section
② distance between centres of tracks

第一部分　交通工程情景会话

业务情景：轨道咨询方孙工程师和业主方代表 Simon 在咨询会上的对话。

Scene: Mr Sun, the engineer of the track consultant, is having a conversation with Simon, the representative of the employer, in a consulting conference.

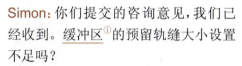

Simon：你们提交的咨询意见，我们已经收到。缓冲区①的预留轨缝大小设置不足吗？

孙工程师：是的，预留轨缝应保证在最高轨温时两轨端不顶紧，在最低轨温时轨缝不应超过构造轨缝，以使螺栓不受弯剪作用。经过我们的计算，预留轨缝还需要增加 2mm。

Simon：还好你们及时发现了这个问题，若施工了就麻烦了。

孙工程师：这是我们应该做的。

Simon：另外还有一册"线路信号标志"设计图，请你们在一周内完成咨询工作，现在我们着急用这份图纸。

孙工程师：好的，没有问题，我们一定按时提交咨询成果。

Simon: We've already received your consulting advice. Is the reserved rail gap in buffer section① sufficient?

Mr Sun: No, the reserved rail gap should ensure that the two rail ends are not too tight under the highest temperature, and that there is not an excess structural gap under the lowest temperature to prevent bolts from bending or shearing. According to our calculation, the reserved rail joint gap should be increased by 2mm.

Simon: Thanks for pointing out this problem, which may cause big trouble in construction.

Mr Sun: You're welcome.

Simon: A copy of the "railway signal" design drawing hasn't been delivered. Please complete the consultation within a week, because we need the drawings urgently.

Mr Sun: Ok. No problem. We will submit all deliverables of consultation on time.

替换单词 Alternative terms

① 伸缩区　　　　　　　　　　① breathing zone
　 固定区　　　　　　　　　　　 non-breathing zone

业务情景：中方林工程师向业主代表 Roger 讨论汇报咨询意见。
Scene: Mr Lin is discussing and reporting the consulting results to Roger.

典型对话 Conversation

Roger: 对于轨底坡①，你有什么样的咨询意见呢？

林工程师: 轨底坡的规定，建议改为"应根据轮轨匹配的要求合理设置轨底坡，一般可为 1/40、1/30、1/20"。

Roger: 其余还有什么意见？

林工程师: 城市铁路的减振降噪是轨道设计的重点内容之一，建议作适当的补充规定，如振动及噪声的设防等级划分及对应的设防标准等。

Roger: 这条意见提的太棒了！

Roger: What are your advisory opinions for rail cant①?

Mr Lin: The specification of rail cant should be modified as "rail cant shall be reasonably set based on the requirement of wheel-track match. It is often set as 1/40 (one fortieth), 1/30 (one thirtieth) or 1/20 (one twentieth)".

Roger: Any other suggestions?

Mr Lin: The mitigation on vibration and noise is one of the keys in the track design for urban railways. We recommend that some provisions on this aspect should be added, such as grading of vibration and noise mitigation and corresponding mitigation standards.

Roger: That's a great suggestion!

林工程师：总的来说，工程设计基本执行了强制性规程规范及历次审查意见，安全性、经济性较好，图件较完善、齐全，数量准确，根据咨询意见修改后，可满足设计深度要求。

Roger：好的。

Mr Lin: Generally speaking, the mandatory regulations and codes and previous review opinions are basically executed in the engineering design. Safety and economic efficiency are good. The drawings are complete. The quantity of drawings is right. After modifications according to consulting opinions, the design can meet the requirement at design stage.

Roger: Ok.

替换单词 Alternative terms

① 轨顶坡　　　　　　　　　　　　① rail top slope

第十一章 机务车辆
Chapter 11　Locomotive & Rolling Stock

业务情景: 中方周工程师同业主方代表 Tony 讨论工程方案。
Scene: Mr Zhou, the engineer from the Chinese side, is discussing the project programme with Tony, the employer's representative.

典型对话 Conversation

Tony: 本次 EPC 项目,你方为我方设计的杰贝尔机辆段,请问规模是如何考虑的?

周工程师: 机务方面设机车整备线 6 条①,设机车外皮清洗②、自动上砂、冷却水制备等相应运转整备设备,车辆方面设车辆存车线 5 条;检修库机车、车辆合设,设机车中修两台位,小修 6 台位,设置转向架、轮对、电机、车上部件检修设备;设车辆中修两台位。

Tony: 机车、车辆合设后,检修设备能否共用?

Tony: Please specify your design on the scale of the Jebel locomotive & rolling stock depot in this EPC project.

Mr Zhou: For locomotives, six locomotive service tracks① will be set, equipped with locomotive surface cleaning②, automatic sanding, cooling water preparation and other relevant service equipment; for rolling stock, five rolling stock storage sidings will be set. Locomotive maintenance depots and rolling stock maintenance depots are constructed jointly, with two locomotive intermediate overhaul stands and six minor overhaul stands; install bogie, wheel-set, electric machinery, onboard component maintenance equipment; and two rolling stock intermediate overhaul stands.

Tony: After the maintenance depots for the locomotive and rolling stock are jointly

第一部分　交通工程情景会话

周工程师：我们在设计时已充分考虑，按照机车、车辆检修修程，部分设备③在设计时考虑共用。

Tony：整备及检修规模是如何确定的？

周工程师：根据本线及相邻线引入枢纽列车开行对数、机车配属情况确定。整备线按照1条/20对车考虑，当出入段机车每日大于60台次时，设出入段线两条。定位修机车检修台位数量根据所承担机车检修工作量、定检公里和占用检修台位时间、进车不平衡系数计算确定。

Tony：总图方面，整备与检修按横列式布置，请问能否改为纵列式布置，以便于今后的使用？

周工程师：根据段址地形，段址在宽度方向工程地质条件较好，若按纵列式布置，长度方向有河道需要迁改，我们在详细对比两方案后再向你方汇报。

constructed, can the maintenance equipment be shared?

Mr Zhou: We have fully considered this issue in the design; therefore, some equipment③ could be shared according to the maintenance process of locomotive and rolling stock.

Tony: How do you determine the scale of service and maintenance?

Mr Zhou: It depends on pairs of trains led into this line and adjacent lines, as well as locomotives allocation. Assume service track as 1 track / 20 pairs of trains, set two entrance and exit lines if locomotives that enter or exit from the depot are more than sixty vehicle times. Amount of fixed locomotive overhaul stand shall be calculated according to overhaul workload, running kilometers between predetermined repairs, overhaul stand occupying time and train access unbalanced coefficient.

Tony: Service and maintenance has a transverse layout in general drawing. Is that possible to change it to longitudinal type for convenient utilization in the future?

Mr Zhou: According to the terrain of depot site, the engineering geological condition along the width direction is favorable for depot's arrangement. If longitudinal

Tony：好的。若按纵列式布置，河道迁改需要办理哪些手续？

周工程师：根据我方经验，待总图方案确定后，设计方给出河道迁改走向初步方案，报当地水务主管部门审批，期间需进行行洪论证。

Tony：整备场工艺设计如何考虑？

周工程师：为提高作业效率，改善作业环境，整备场设计有三层作业平台；为保证作业安全，整备台位在作业时按接触网无电考虑，机车进出整备场采用引车入库方式。

Tony：接触网无电区是否有警示设施？

周工程师：接触网在整备台位设有接触网分段绝缘器、带接地的隔离开关，并设有隔离开关标志灯系统。

arrangement is made, watercourse would be diverted along the length direction. We will report to you after we make a detailed scheme comparison.

Tony: Ok, what procedures are required for relocating watercourse if longitudinal arrangement is selected?

Mr Zhou: According to our experience, after general drawing is confirmed, the designer will propose preliminary watercourse relocating scheme and report it to the local department in charge of water affairs for approval. During this period, flood discharge assessment shall be done.

Tony: What is your consideration for technological design of service yard?

Mr Zhou: In order to improve working efficiency and working environment, three-storey working platform will be designed for the service yard. To ensure working safety, OCS is designed to be not energized when work is proceeding at service stand, and locomotives are led into service yard.

Tony: Is there any warning facility in OCS non-energized area?

Mr Zhou: Section insulator, grounded disconnection switch as well as disconnection switch identification lamp system for OCS are set at service stand.

Tony: 检修库线间距能否加大,能否由 7.5m 加大为 9m?

周工程师: 贵方在标书中明确检修库房线间距按照 7.5m 考虑,我方在技术文件中已做澄清,7.5m 线间距略显不足,我方建议线间距按照 8m 设计,加大检修工具车、人员通行通道。

Tony: 设备检修是否考虑流水线?

周工程师: 本次设计特点为部件拆解、清洗系统集中布置。转向架、轮对、电机等大线检修设置流水线,其余附件检修按照定位修考虑。

Tony: 清洗设备是否考虑中水回用?

周工程师: 已考虑,部分设备自带水循环处理功能,部分设备用水采用经污水处理场处理后的中水,另外中水系统还将用于段内绿化。

Tony: Is it possible to increase distance between centres of tracks in maintenance workshop from 7.5m to 9m?

Mr Zhou: You have specified in the tender document that distance between centres of tracks in the maintenance workshop is 7.5m, but we have clarified in our technical document that 7.5m is slightly insufficient, so we suggest that this distance shall be designed as 8m, which can widen passageway for maintenance tool vehicle and staff.

Tony: Is assembly line considered for equipment maintenance?

Mr Zhou: This design features disassembling parts and centralized cleaning system. Assembly line will be set for the maintenance of bogie, wheel-pair, electrical machine, etc. while fixed maintenance for other accessories.

Tony: Have you thought about reusing reclaimed water for equipment cleaning?

Mr Zhou: Yes, we have. Some equipment has water circulation function themselves; some equipment use reclaimed water processed from sewage farm. Besides, reclaimed water system is used for greening works within the depot.

替换单词 Alternative terms

① 预留两条
② 机车外皮清洗
　自动上砂
　冷却水制备
③ 机车外皮清洗
　转向架
　轮对检修设备

① reserved 2 lines
② locomotive external surface cleaning
　automatic sanding
　cooling water preparation
③ locomotive external surface cleaning
　bogies
　wheel-pair service equipment

业务情景：中方赵工程师代表设计方向业主代表 Wade 汇报设计方案。
Scene: Chinese engineer Mr Zhao, on behalf of the Design Company, is presenting design scheme report to the Employer's Representative, Wade.

典型对话 Conversation

Wade：首先，感谢你们设计单位能来到现场为我们设计地铁车辆段，对你们的到来表示欢迎。其次，今天想请你们介绍一下目前的设计方案，以便了解是否满足我们的需求。

赵工程师：我们能参与到贵方的地铁项目设计中也感到非常荣幸。通过前期的工作，目前已经完成车辆段的总平面布置方案，我们也想通过今天的方案汇报，进一步修改完善，以便开展下一步的设计工作。

Wade: First of all, we would like to express our appreciation and welcome to you design company for design metro depot on site. Today we would like to listen to your introduction of current design scheme, so that we could know whether it fulfills our requirements.

Mr Zhao: It is a pleasure for us to take part in the design of your metro project. Thanks for your works done at early stage, currently general plan layout of depot has been completed. We would also like to improve our design based on today's

Wade: 目前吉布提车辆段的功能定位及设计规模是怎么样的？

赵工程师： 经过对项目前期规划资料的分析，吉布提车辆段定位为定修段，主要承担本线地铁车辆的<u>定修</u>①等。

Wade: 除车辆运用检修设施外，段内的其他生产办公设施如何设置？

赵工程师： 根据车辆段的功能定位，段内还设有物资总库，承担本线生产物资的存放；设有综合维修中心，承担车辆段及线路区间的机电设备维修以及其他必要的生产生活及办公等设施的维修，这些设施包括<u>牵引降压变电所</u>②等。

Wade: 根据我们现场的了解，车辆段用地区域里还有两条沟渠和1条高压电缆，那么在总图布局中如何处理，是否需要迁改？

赵工程师： 是的，以上因素是总图布局中两个非常大的限制条件，我们在总图设计时也十分重视。根据目前的总图方案，两条沟渠需要进行迁改，沿车辆

report, so the design work of the next step can be carried out.

Wade: Now what is the functional position and design scale of Djibouti depot?

Mr Zhao: Based on analysis of initial planning data of the project, Djibouti depot is built for periodical repair, mainly undertaking <u>periodical repair</u>① for metro vehicles, etc.

Wade: Except vehicle service facilities, how to set up other production and office facilities?

Mr Zhao: As per depot's functional position, general warehouse for material supplies is set within the depot, storing goods and materials for this railroad; comprehensive maintenance centre is set for the repair of electromechanical equipment in railroad section and other essential facilities for living and office works facilities which include <u>traction and step-down substation</u>②, etc.

Wade: We found on site that there are two ditches and one high voltage cable, how shall we deal with them in general layout drawing? Do they need to be relocated?

Mr Zhao: Yes, the factors mentioned above are two great restrictions in general layout, to which we've paid much attention when we designed general

段围墙外通过。高压电缆由于电压等级较低,且位于出入段线的上空,按照有关规范要求,不必迁改。

drawing. According to current general drawing scheme, two ditches are needed to be relocated to go outside the depot's enclosure. Since high voltage cables are of low voltage grade and are high above the entrance-exit line, it is not necessary to relocate them as per relevant code.

Wade: 车辆段需要供水、供气以及污水排放,与市政设施的接口如何考虑?

Wade: Water supply, gas supply and sewage discharge are essential for depot, what is your consideration for the integration with municipal facilities?

赵工程师: 根据现场对既有市政管线的调查,在车辆段西侧的既有道路上,已经铺设有市政自来水管道、污水管道和燃气管道,目前考虑从市政管网进行接驳。

Mr Zhao: Based on investigation on existing municipal pipelines on site, municipal tap water pipes, sewage pipes and gas pipes are laid on the road at west side of depot. Now we're thinking about the connection from municipal pipe network.

Wade: 洗车机库的线路布置是什么形式?是否对出入段线有干扰?

Wade: What is the alignment layout of train washing machine workshop? Will it have any interference on entrance-exit track?

赵工程师: 通过我们对线路的优化调整,目前洗车机库采用"八"字线布置,具备出段或者入段洗车条件,对出入段线无干扰,满足作业需求。

Mr Zhao: Since we have optimized and adjusted the alignment, now the alignment in train-washing workshop is in funnel form, which enables washing the train both entering and departing and meets work requirement, without any interference with entrance-exit track.

Wade: 请介绍一下目前整个总图方案的布局形式。

Wade: Could you talk about layout scheme in current general drawing please?

第一部分　交通工程情景会话

赵工程师：车辆段采用顺向并列式布局，车辆入段后通过咽喉区，能直接进入<u>运用库</u>③，作业流程顺畅，段内走行距离短。

Wade：图上停车列检线之间的间距为4.8m，是不是过小，可否增大？

赵工程师：根据车辆限界以及作业规范的间距要求，目前4.8m的间距是可以满足要求的，如果增大线间距，可能导致用地面积增加，建议维持目前方案。

Wade：库内的车辆检修作业方式是什么样的？

赵工程师：车辆检修作业方式有现车修和换件修两种。现车修是将待修车上的零部件，经过修理消除其缺陷后，仍安装在原车上。换件修是指将待修车上分解下来的零部件，经修理后可以装到其他车上的修理方法。从提高修车效率出发，车辆检修宜采用以大部件换件修为主，部分零部件现车修为辅的检修作业方式。车辆定修及以下修程的作业工艺均采用整列入库定位作业方式。

Mr Zhao: The depot adopts forward side-by-side layout, the train passing the throat area after entering the depot, directly going into the <u>running shed</u>③. The operation process is smooth, with a short run in the depot.

Wade: The space between train inspection-parking lines is 4.8m in the drawing. Is it too small? Is it possible to be increased?

Mr Zhao: As per the spacing requirements of rolling stock clearance and work specification, spacing of 4.8m can fulfill the requirements currently. If the line spacing is increased, more land area may be needed. So it is recommended to maintain the current scheme.

Wade: What kind of rolling stock maintenance is in the workshop?

Mr Zhao: There are two kinds of maintenance: part repair and part replacement. Part repair means that the parts removed from the car are still installed in it after repair. Part replacement means that the parts removed from the car are installed in another car. In order to improve repair efficiency, it is preferable to adopt part replacement for big components as main maintenance manner, backuped by part repair for some

Wade: 总图中试车线的长度是多少米？能满足试车需要吗？

赵工程师: 本线采用的是最高速度80km/h的地铁车辆，根据计算，目前的试车线长度约有1200m，满足车辆全速试车的需要。

components. Maintenance process for periodical repair level and under it shall be done by the means of entire train entering workshop for fixing operation.

Wade: How long is the testing line in general drawing? Can it meet test requirement?

Mr Zhao: This line has metro vehicle with the maximum speed of 80km / h. It is calculated that the current testing line is about 1200m in length, which meets the needs of testing vehicle at full speed.

替换单词 Alternative terms

① 定修　　　　　　　　　　① periodical repair
　 临修　　　　　　　　　　　 temporary repair
　 周月检　　　　　　　　　　 weekly and monthly inspection
　 日常检查和停放　　　　　　 routine inspection and parking
② 牵引降压变电所　　　　　② traction and step-down substation
　 污水处理站　　　　　　　　 sewage treatment plant
　 材料棚　　　　　　　　　　 materials shed
　 洗车机库　　　　　　　　　 washing machine workshop
　 镟轮库　　　　　　　　　　 wheel lathing workshop
　 危险品库　　　　　　　　　 dangerous goods workshop
　 试车线　　　　　　　　　　 testing line
　 综合办公楼　　　　　　　　 complex office building
　 食堂浴室　　　　　　　　　 canteen bathroom
③ 检修库　　　　　　　　　③ maintenance workshop

第一部分　交通工程情景会话

业务情景：中方黄工程师同业主方代表 Parkman 讨论设计工作安排。
Scene: Mr Huang is discussing design work arrangement with the Employer's Representative, Parkman.

典型对话 Conversation

Parkman: 今天请贵方来参加会议，主要是为了落实车辆段设计进度的问题，需要对设计阶段和完成时间达成一致，并按时执行。

黄工程师: 是的，项目的设计工作已经正式启动，我们也有义务按照既定的时间节点完成设计工作，满足项目进度要求。

Parkman: 目前，车辆段设计的相关专业是否已经到位了呢？

黄工程师: 根据业主的要求，目前车辆段设计的全部专业都已经到达现场开始了工作，主要包括<u>工艺</u>①等专业的工程技术人员。

Parkman: 根据我们的工期安排，希望你们能在 6 月 30 日提交初步设计文件，不知是否能按时完成？

Parkman: Today we invite you to the meeting, mainly for confirming design schedule. We need to agree on the design phases and completion time, and execute them on schedule.

Mr Huang: Yes, the design work of the project has been officially started. We have the obligation to complete the design in accordance with the established time node and fulfill the project schedule requirement.

Parkman: Have the design engineers from disciplines related to rolling stock depot come to the site now?

Mr Huang: According to the requirement of the Employer, now design engineers of all related disciplines have arrived at the project site and started working, mainly including discipline for <u>process design</u>①.

Parkman: According to our project's schedule, I hope you will submit preliminary design document on June 30. Is it possible to complete on time?

黄工程师：根据目前的设计进度，主要是受制于测量和地勘的工作进度，如果在 6 月 30 日前能提供测量和初勘资料，那么我方能按时完成初步设计文件。

Parkman：除了测量和地勘资料外，还有其他影响设计进度的问题吗？

黄工程师：除了测量和地勘资料外，还有用地边界条件的问题。由于段址用地范围尚没有最终明确，对总图方案的稳定有较大影响，因此需要业主尽快与有关规划部门对接，尽快确定用地边界条件。

Parkman：在初步设计文件提交之后，希望能在一个月内提交施工图文件，能否按时完成？

黄工程师：由于施工图文件是一个详细设计的过程，加上车辆段设计涉及专业多、接口复杂，在一个月内提交全部施工文件较为困难，我方建议分批提供施工图文件。

Mr Huang: Current design schedule is mainly constrained by geological survey and exploration. We can complete preliminary design on time if geological survey and advanced exploration data could be provided by June 30.

Parkman: Besides geological survey and exploration data, are there other issues affecting design schedule?

Mr Huang: Boundary of land use is another issue. As depot land area is not determined, it has a great impact on the general layout plan. The employer is kindly required to discuss with relevant department as soon as possible to determine the land boundary.

Parkman: After submission of preliminary design, we hope that you can submit construction drawing within one month, can you complete it on time?

Mr Huang: Because construction drawing needs a detailed design process, many disciplines are involved in depot design, and the interface between disciplines is complicated, it is difficult to submit all the construction drawings within one month, we suggest providing construction drawings by stages.

第一部分　交通工程情景会话

替换单词 Alternative terms

① 站场　　　　　① Station & yard
　 轨道　　　　　　 track
　 路基　　　　　　 subgrade
　 桥涵　　　　　　 bridge & culvert
　 接触网　　　　　 OCS
　 房建　　　　　　 housing construction
　 给排水　　　　　 water supply and drainage
　 暖通　　　　　　 HVAC
　 电力　　　　　　 electrical power
　 施预　　　　　　 construction budget

业务情景：工程技术交底，典型对话双方为中方黄工程师和车辆、房建部门业主方代表Parkman。

Scene: During engineering technical handover, the conversation is being made between Chinese engineer Mr Huang and Parkman, the Representative of the Employer from depot and housing sector.

典型对话 Conversation

Parkman：现在开始吉布提动车运用所技术交底工作，请设计方简要介绍设计方案。

黄工程师：感谢相关主管部门参加本次技术交底会。吉布提动车运用所设动车组存车线33条（预留12条）、检查线4条（预留两条）、临修线和不落轮镟线各1条。利用出入所线兼作动车组外

Parkman: Now we start technical disclosure about Djibouti EMU running depot, we would like the Designer to make a brief introduction on design scheme.

Mr Huang: We would like to appreciate relevant authorities attending this technical disclosure. Djibouti EMU running depot has thirty-three vehicle storage tracks (twelve reserved), four inspection tracks

131

皮洗刷线和轮对踏面诊断线，并配套设有生产、办公、生活房屋及必要的检修设备。动车组 3~5 级修考虑由吉布提动车检修基地承担。

Parkman：动车组 1-5 级修如何划定？

黄工程师：动车组 1~2 级修①承担动车组日常的检查维护②。

Parkman：动车组外皮清洗请增加端面洗功能，且增设视频监控功能。

黄工程师：修改设计方案，补强以上功能后需增加设备及相关专业投资，我方一并给出增加投资部分预算。

Parkman：检查库综合管沟是否考虑排水、通风？

黄工程师：设计时已考虑，综合管沟内设有 6 台 1m³ 排水泵，检查地沟污水通过管道进入排水泵，并最终排入库外污水井；综合管沟设计未考虑通风，该综合管沟人员进入频率不高，设计可以增

(two reserved), one temporary repair track and one un-wheeling lathing track line. Depot access track is concurrently used for EMU external surface washing and wheel tread diagnostics, production, office, living houses and essential maintenance equipment are provided. EMU maintenance grade 3-5 may be undertaken by Djibouti EMU maintenance base.

Parkman: How to divide EMU maintenance grade 1-5?

Mr Huang: EMU maintenance grade 1-2① includes EMU routine inspection and maintenance②.

Parkman: End face cleaning shall be added in EMU outside cleaning, and video monitoring shall also be added.

Mr Huang: If the functions mentioned above are included in modified design, there will be additional cost for equipment and related items, we will propose additional investment budget together.

Parkman: Have you thought about water drainage and ventilation in multi-function sewerage in inspection workshop?

Mr Huang: Yes, we have considered it in the design. Six 1m³ (1 cubic meter) drainage pumps are installed in multi-function sewerage. Sewerage from inspection ditch flows into pump through

加通风设施。

Parkman: 临修库转向架更换设备能否实现轮对更换？

黄工程师: 可以实现。设计中充分调研动车组检修工艺。实际使用过程中，动车组存在大量的换轮作业。我们配备的转向架更换设备可同时实现轮对单独更换。

Parkman: 检查库内是否考虑无线网络，便于便携式设备的使用？

黄工程师: 检查库内设有有线网络，可增加无线网络功能，在库内补充无线网络接口。

Parkman: 通信、信号等检修人员是否考虑间休室？

黄工程师: 已考虑，检修人员间休室设于检查库边跨一层，房间内设有空调，保证人员办公环境。

pipe, and finally into outdoor water well. Ventilation design is not considered due to low frequency of personnel going into the multi-function sewerage. But it is possible to add ventilation facility.

Parkman: Can wheel-pair be replaced by bogie replacement equipment in temporary repair workshop?

Mr Huang: Yes, possible. During the design, make full investigation on EMU maintenance process. During actual utilization process, there is a lot of wheel changing work for EMU. The bogie replacement equipment supplied by us can simultaneously replace wheel pair separately.

Parkman: Have you thought about Wi-Fi in inspection workshop for the convenience of using portable devices?

Mr Huang: There is wired network in inspection workshop. It is possible to include wireless network by the means of setting wireless network interface.

Parkman: Have you thought about providing rest room for maintenance staff for communication, signal, etc.?

Mr Huang: Yes, we have. Rest room for maintenance staff will be located on the ground floor of inspection workshop's outer room, with air conditioner, ensuring them have good environment.

Parkman: 段内变电所设于何处,外电引入手续是否完成?

黄工程师: 段内变电所设于检查库一层,房建设计执行变电所相关规范;外电引入手续正在进行,目前已与吉布提供电公司达成初步协议,请主管部门进一步大力支持。

Parkman: 检查库降温通风设计是如何考虑的?

黄工程师: 检查库采用结构钢柱加轻质砌体墙方案,提高房屋传热系数,有效降低库内温度;同时库内三层作业平台上设有喷雾风机,改善人员作业条件;检查库边跨办公场所均设有空调。

Parkman: What is the location of substation within depot? Have formalities to connect external power been completed?

Mr Huang: Substation within depot is located on the ground floor of inspection workshop, housing construction design conforming to related substation specifications. We are working on formality to connect external power. Now we have reached a preliminary agreement with Djibouti Power Supply Company. The department in charge is kindly requested to provide further support.

Parkman: How about cooling and ventilation design in inspection workshop?

Mr Huang: Inspection workshop adopts constructional steel columns plus lightweight masonry walls to improve housing heat conduction coefficient, effectively reducing temperature indoor; meanwhile spray fan is installed on three-storey working platforms in the workshop, improving working conditions for the staff; offices in the outer room of inspection workshop are equipped with air conditioner.

替换单词 Alternative terms

① 3~5 级修
② 临修作业
   分解检修作业

① grade 3-5 repair
② temporary repair work
   disassembly maintenance work

第十二章 机械
Chapter 12　Mechanics

业务情景：中方黄工程师同业主代表 Blair 讨论设计标准。
Scene: Chinese engineer Mr Huang is discussing design standard with the Employer's Representative Blair.

典型对话 Conversation

黄工程师：我们希望同贵方讨论一下本项目设计采用标准①的问题。

Blair：好的，请讲。

黄工程师：请问贵国有关于铁路固定设施维修方面的标准和规范吗？

Blair：我国目前有部分关于铁路固定设施维修方面的标准，但还不完整，通常参照 UIC 标准和美国标准。

黄工程师：中国是国际铁路联盟的成员国之一，中国标准与 UIC 标准是非常接近的，如果本项目由中国公司承担的话，建议采用中国标准。

Blair：可是我们对中国标准并不了解，我们只熟悉 UIC 标准和美国标准。

Mr Huang: We'd like to discuss with you the design standards① adopted in the Project.

Blair: Yes, please.

Mr Huang: Are there any standards and codes on railway fixed facility maintenance in your country?

Blair: Currently we have some railway fixed facility maintenance standards, but not complete. We usually use UIC standards and American standards.

Mr Huang: China is a member of the International Union of Railways (UIC), therefore Chinese Standards are quite similar to UIC Standards. If the project is undertaken by Chinese company, I suggest using Chinese Standards.

Blair: However, we are only familiar with UIC Standards and American Standards rather than Chinese Standards.

黄工程师：本项目采用中国标准对工程实施会有很大帮助，可以加快设计和施工进度，保证工程按期完工。

Blair：我同意你的观点，但是否采用中国标准我决定不了，需请示我的上级领导。

黄工程师：好的，希望在下一次会谈中能确定。

Mr Huang: Adopting Chinese Standards will be of great help for project implementation, which could speed up design and construction process to ensure that the project could be completed on schedule.

Blair: I agree with you. But I cannot decide whether to adopt Chinese Standards and I need my superior's approval.

Mr Huang: Well, I hope it could be determined in the next discussion.

替换单词 Alternative terms

① 规范
　 规定

① specification
　 regulations

业务情景：中方周工程师同外方代表 Cooper 讨论工程设计范围的问题。
Scene: Chinese engineer Mr Zhou is discussing the design scope of Project with Cooper, the representative of foreign side.

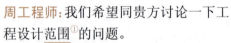

周工程师：我们希望同贵方讨论一下工程设计范围①的问题。
Cooper：好的，请讲。
周工程师：我们仔细阅读了贵方的招标文件，招标文件中没有提到装卸设施，请明确货场装卸设施是否包含在招标

Mr Zhou: We'd like to discuss with you the design scope① of the project.
Cooper: Yes, please.
Mr Zhou: We have carefully read your tender document, while the information concerning handing machinery is not

范围内。

Cooper: 货场装卸设施有哪些设备？

周工程师: 主要包括装卸设备和计量设备。

Cooper: 能否说得具体一点？

周工程师: 装卸设备是指叉车、装载机、门吊等。

Cooper: 那计量设备呢？

周工程师: 计量设备是汽车衡和轨道衡。

Cooper: 汽车衡和轨道衡是计量什么的？

周工程师: 汽车衡是对进出货场汽车所载货物进行计量的仪器。

Cooper: 那轨道衡呢？

周工程师: 轨道衡是对铁路货车所载货物进行计量的。

Cooper: 上述设施是货场运营必不可少的设备，必须含在工程范围内。

周工程师: 好的，那我方将在投标文件中增加货场装卸设施的报价。

mentioned in the document. Please specify whether the loading and unloading facility in freight yard is included in the scope of the Tender.

Cooper: What kind of loading and unloading facility shall be provided in freight yard?

Mr Zhou: It mainly includes handling equipment and measurement device.

Cooper: Can you be more specific?

Mr Zhou: Handling machinery refers to forklift, loader, gantry crane and etc.

Cooper: What about measurement device?

Mr Zhou: The measurement device includes truck scale and track scale.

Cooper: What does the truck scale and track scale measure respectively?

Mr Zhou: Truck scale is an instrument to measure the cargo carried by trucks getting in and out of freight yard.

Cooper: And track scale?

Mr Zhou: Track scale is used for measuring the cargo carried by railway wagon.

Cooper: The above facilities are essential equipment for freight yard operation, which should be included in the project scope.

Mr Zhou: Ok. We will add the quotation of loading and unloading facility in freight yard in the tender document.

替换单词 Alternative terms

① 边界	① border
界线	boundary
接口	interface
分界	boundary

业务情景：中方张工程师同外方代表 Andrew 讨论集装箱装卸设备选型的问题。

Scene: Chinese engineer Mr Zhang is discussing the selection of loading and unloading equipment for container with Andrew, the representative of foreign side.

典型对话 Conversation

张工程师：我们希望同贵方讨论一下集装箱装卸设备选型①的问题。

Mr Zhang: We'd like to discuss with you about the selection① of handing machinery for container.

Andrew：好的，请问集装箱一般采用什么方式进行装卸？

Andrew: Well, what kind of loading and unloading method will be applied?

张工程师：集装箱的装卸方式国际上通常有两种，即采用集装箱正面吊和轨行式集装箱门式起重机。

Mr Zhang: There are two common international methods, namely using reach stacker and rail-mounted gantry crane.

Andrew：两者有什么区别？

Andrew: What's the difference between the two?

138

张工程师：集装箱正面吊是移动设备，作业灵活，不受场地限制；集装箱门式起重机只能在固定的走行范围内进行作业。

Andrew：价格有差别吗？

张工程师：集装箱正面吊的价格较集装箱门式起重机便宜，但是它对货场内道路等级要求较高。

Andrew：中国有无集装箱正面吊生产厂家？

张工程师：有的，比如三一重工就是国际上知名度较高的大型工程机械厂商。

Andrew：那我们要求采用中国产的集装箱正面吊。

张工程师：好的，接下来我们就按集装箱正面吊做方案。

Mr Zhang: Reach stacker is a mobile device with flexible operation, which is not subject to site constraint, while gantry crane operation can be carried out only within a fixed operating range.

Andrew: Is there any difference in price?

Mr Zhang: Compared with gantry crane, reach stacker is much cheaper, but it has a higher requirement on road quality in freight yard.

Andrew: Are there any reach stacker manufacturers in China?

Mr Zhang: Yes. Sany Heavy Industry Co., Ltd. for example. It is a large engineering machinery manufacturer with high reputation at home and abroad.

Andrew: We require using Chinese-made reach stacker.

Mr Zhang: Okay, the reach stacker option will be adopted.

替换单词 Alternative terms

① 选择　　　　　　　　　① selection
　装备　　　　　　　　　　 equipment
　配备　　　　　　　　　　 be equipped with
　配置　　　　　　　　　　 be provided with

业务情景：中方秦工程师同外方代表 Frank 讨论维修体制的问题。
Scene: Chinese engineer Mr Qin is discussing the maintenance system with Frank, the representative of foreign side.

典型对话 Conversation

秦工程师：我们希望同贵方讨论一下铁路固定设施维修体制①的问题。

Frank：好的，请讲。

秦工程师：请问贵国铁路主管部门是哪个部门？

Frank：主管部门是国家铁路局。

秦工程师：铁路局下面有负责维修的部门吗？

Frank：有的，叫基础设施维修部。

秦工程师：基础设施维修部负责铁路哪些设施的维修？

Frank：主要负责铁路固定设施的维修，包括轨道、桥梁、隧道、通信、信号和接触网等。

Mr Qin: We'd like to discuss with you the maintenance system① of railway fixed facility.

Frank: Yes, please.

Mr Qin: Which department is in charge of railway industry in your country?

Frank: National Railway Bureau.

Mr Qin: Is there any department responsible for maintenance?

Frank: Yes, it is called Infrastructure Maintenance Department.

Mr Qin: What kind of facility is maintained by this Department?

Frank: It mainly undertakes the maintenance of railway fixed facility, including track, bridge, tunnel, communication, signal, OCS and so on.

替换单词 Alternative terms

① 机构
　 修程
　 修制

① agency
　 maintenance process
　 maintenance system

第一部分　交通工程情景会话

业务情景：中方万工程师同外方代表 Guy 讨论大型养路机械的问题。
Scene: Chinese engineer Mr Wan is discussing the large track maintenance machinery with Guy, the representative of foreign side.

典型对话 Conversation

万工程师： 我们希望同贵方讨论一下<u>大型养路机械</u>①的问题。

Guy： 好的，请讲。

万工程师： 请问贵国既有铁路线是采用大型养路机械进行维修作业吗？

Guy： 我对大型养路机械不太清楚，大型养路机械主要是指哪些设备？

万工程师： 大型养路机械主要有道砟捣固车、动力稳定车、配砟整形车、钢轨打磨车等。

Guy： 哦，我们的既有线还没有使用过这些设备。

万工程师： 本项目建成后，你们是否打算采用大型养路机械进行线路维修作业？

Guy： 要采用，中国有大型养路机械生产厂家吗？

万工程师： 有，中国有几家大型养路机械生产厂家。

Mr Wan: We'd like to discuss with you the <u>large track maintenance machinery</u>①.

Guy: Yes, please.

Mr Wan: Is large track maintenance machinery applied in the maintenance of existing railways in your country?

Guy: Can you be more specific on what kinds of equipment?

Mr Wan: It mainly includes ballast tamping wagon, dynamic track stabilizer, ballast distributing and regulating machine, rail grinding wagon, etc.

Guy: Oh, we haven't used those equipment in the existing lines yet.

Mr Wan: Do you intend to use large track maintenance machinery for railway maintenance after the project is completed?

Guy: Yes, of course. Is there any large track maintenance machinery manufacturer in China?

Mr Wan: Yes, there are some.

141

Guy：产品的质量如何？

万工程师：产品质量是非常可靠的，它们的产品已经在中国铁路线上可靠地工作了很多年。

Guy：那价格怎么样？

万工程师：价格比欧美产品稍低，而且中国设备厂家的售后服务是非常有保证的。

Guy：非常好，我们可以考虑采用中国生产的大型养路机械。

Guy: How about product quality?

Mr Wan: Product quality is very reliable. Their products have been safely used in Chinese railways for many years.

Guy: How about the price?

Mr Wan: It's lower than European and American products, and Chinese equipment manufacturer's after-sale service is guaranteed.

Guy: Very good, we will consider using Chinese-made large track maintenance machinery.

替换单词 Alternative terms

① 大机　　　　　　　　　　　　　① large track maintenance machinery

业务情景：中方龙工程师同外方代表 Quain 讨论勘测要求的问题。
Scene: Chinese engineer Mr Long is discussing survey requirement with Quain, the representative of foreign side.

典型对话 Conversation

龙工程师：我方于上周一提交的勘测要求，请问您看完没有？

Quain：已经看完了。

龙工程师：是否同意我专业提交的勘测要求？

Mr Long: Have you finished reading the survey requirement we submitted last Monday?

Quain: Yes.

Mr Long: Do you agree with the survey requirement?

第一部分　交通工程情景会话

Quain: 基本同意。另外勘测要求中提到，需要对既有综合工区[①]进行调查，按照我国的工作程序，你们需要提交一份调查申请表。

龙工程师: 有没有申请表的格式呢？

Quain: 我可以提供一份表格供您参考。

龙工程师: 谢谢，申请表提交给哪个部门？
Quain: 交给铁路局。
龙工程师: 申请大概要多少时间能批准下来？
Quain: 一般要1个月左右。
龙工程师: 本项目的工期十分紧张，能否快点批准下来？

Quain: 这个不好办，我们要按工作程序来做。
龙工程师: 有没有其他途径呢？
Quain: 您可以试着去找铁路局局长谈一谈。
龙工程师: 好的，非常谢谢您的建议。

Quain: Basically, yes. Concerning the requirement of making a survey on existing comprehensive work area[①] specified in survey requirement, you need to fill a survey application form in accordance with our working procedures.
Mr Long: What kind of format is applied in application form?
Quain: I will provide a form for your reference.
Mr Long: Thank you. Which department is the application form submitted to?
Quain: The Railway Bureau.
Mr Long: How long does it take to approve the application?
Quain: Generally one month or so.
Mr Long: As the construction period is very tight, could you shorten the time of approval?
Quain: It's very hard, because every step should follow the working program.
Mr Long: Is there any other way?
Quain: You can ask Director of the Railway Bureau for help.
Mr Long: Okay, thank you very much for your suggestion.

替换单词 Alternative terms

① 综合维修工区　　　　　　　　　① comprehensive maintenance work area

业务情景：中方宋工程师同外方代表 Reagan 讨论维修机构和工作流程的问题。

Scene: Chinese engineer Mr Song is discussing maintenance team and workflow with Reagan, the representative of foreign side.

典型对话 Conversation

Reagan: 贵方的概念设计文件我们已经看完了，关于维修机构和工作流程有几个问题请您解释一下。

Reagan: We've read your conceptual design document, but there are several problems on maintenance team and workflow. Could you make a detailed explanation please?

宋工程师：好的，请讲。

Mr Song: Yes, please.

Reagan: 本线设置了两处综合工区，这是怎么确定的？

Reagan: What are the basises that you have designed two comprehensive work areas in the Line?

宋工程师：综合工区设置的数量是根据线路长度、综合工区的管辖范围来确定的。

Mr Song: The number of comprehensive work area is determined by line length and its coverage area.

Reagan: 综合工区的管辖范围与哪些因素有关？

Reagan: What factors are concerned with the coverage area of comprehensive work area?

宋工程师：主要与天窗时间[①]、施工准备时间和生产作业能力有关系。

Mr Song: Such as maintenance time[①], job preparation time and productivity.

Reagan: 本线的天窗时间是几个小时？

Reagan: How long is the maintenance time?

宋工程师：通常天窗时间从凌晨 1:00 开始到 5:00 结束，大约 4 个小时。

Mr Song: Generally, it is from 1:00am to 5:00am for about four hours.

Reagan: 施工准备包括哪些工作内容？

Reagan: What does job preparation include?

宋工程师：准备阶段主要工作内容有工器具准备、进出区间、安全防护等。

Reagan：本线的综合工区的管辖范围按多少考虑合适？

宋工程师：综合考虑本线的具体情况，管辖范围宜取45~60km。

Reagan：本线110km考虑了两处综合工区，我们同意你们的设计方案。

Mr Song: It mainly includes tool & equipment preparation, entering&leaving work area, safety protection and so on.

Reagan: How long does the comprehensive work area cover along the Line?

Mr Song: In consideration of the specific circumstances of the Line, it should cover 45-60km.

Reagan: We agree with your design scheme in which there are two comprehensive work areas along the whole line (110km).

替换单词 Alternative terms

① 施工准备时间　　　　　　　① construction preparation time
　 生产作业能力　　　　　　　　　production operation capability

业务情景：中方黄工程师同外方代表Ramon讨论综合工区选址的问题。
Scene: Chinese engineer Mr Huang is discussing the site selection of comprehensive work area with Ramon, the representative of foreign side.

典型对话 Conversation

Ramon：贵方的概念设计文件我们已经看完了，关于综合工区选址问题需要你解释一下。

Ramon: We've read your conceptual design document. We'd like you to make a detailed explanation on the site selection of comprehensive work area.

黄工程师：好的，请讲。
Ramon：综合工区的选址是怎么考虑的？
黄工程师：综合工区的选址应综合考虑车站规模[①]、站间距、道路、供水、供电等条件，一般设置在较大的中间车站。

Ramon：据上述原则我们认为应将 El Pao 综合工区改到 Tinaco 车站，Tinaco 车站比 El Pao 站的规模要大。

黄工程师：Tinaco 车站虽然较大，但是它位于线路尽头，对于线路中段以后的维修不利，因为进出区间时间较长，缩短了工作时间。

Ramon：我们还是认为在 Tinaco 设置综合工区比较合适，你上面提到的问题有解决办法没有？

黄工程师：可以考虑在 EL Pao 设 1 条停留线。
Ramon：设停留线有什么作用？

Mr Huang: Yes, please.
Ramon: What factors should be taken into consideration in the site selection?
Mr Huang: Station scale[①], distance between stations, road, water supply, power supply and other conditions should be considered in site selection. Generally, the comprehensive work area is located in a large intermediate station.
Ramon: According to the above principles, we suggest that El Pao comprehensive work area should be relocated to Tinaco Station. Tinaco station is much bigger than El Pao Station.
Mr Huang: Although Tinaco Station is much bigger, it is located at the end of the Line which is unfavorable to the maintenance outside the middle section of the Line. Because it takes more time in entering and exiting work area and shortens the working time.
Ramon: We still think that setting comprehensive work area in Tinaco is better. Is there any solution to those problems mentioned above?
Mr Huang: Set a stabling siding at El Pao.
Ramon: What is the stabling siding used for?

第一部分　交通工程情景会话

黄工程师：停留线作为维修车辆的临时停靠线，天窗时间作业时，直接从停留线进入区间，这样可以大大减小进出区间的时间。

Ramon：这个办法太好了，设计文件应按这样做。越行站或会让站可以设置综合工区吗？

黄工程师：由于越行站或会让站车站规模较小且生活条件不方便，一般不在此设置综合工区。

Ramon：本线有没有在越行站设置综合工区？

黄工程师：没有。

Ramon：贵方的综合工区设置方案我们基本同意了。

黄工程师：谢谢，我们按这个方案开展下一阶段工作。

Mr Huang: It serves as a temporary stopping line for maintenance vehicle. Rolling stock could directly get into work area from stabling siding during the maintenance time, which can greatly reduce the entering time.

Ramon: That's great. This method should be applied in design document. Would comprehensive work area be built in overtaking station or passing station?

Mr Huang: No. The scale of overtaking station or passing station is small and its living condition is inconvenient, thus comprehensive work area cannot be set in those stations generally.

Ramon: Is there any comprehensive work area provided in overtaking station in this Line?

Mr Huang: No.

Ramon: We basically agree with your arrangement for comprehensive work area.

Mr Huang: Thank you. Let's get down to the next phase followed by this plan.

替换单词 Alternative terms

① 站间距
　　道路
　　供水
　　供电

① distance between stations
　　road
　　water supply
　　power supply

147

业务情景：中方吴工程师同外方代表 Wilder 讨论综合工区工作流程的问题。

Scene: Chinese engineer Mr Wu is discussing the workflow in comprehensive work area with Wilder, the representative of foreign side.

典型对话 Conversation

Wilder: 贵方的概念设计文件我们已经看完了，关于综合工区工作流程①的一些细节问题需要您解释一下。

吴工程师: 好的，请讲。

Wilder: 我们首先谈一下运输问题，维修人员、材料和机具是怎么进入维修区域的？

吴工程师: 综合工区内配置有轨道车和平板车，维修人员乘坐轨道车进入区间，材料和机具放在平板车上，平板车连挂在轨道车后，随轨道车进入维修区域。

Wilder: 轨道车可以乘坐多少人呢？

吴工程师: 大约 14 人。

Wilder: 平板车上的材料是怎么装卸的？

Wilder: We've read your conceptual design document. Please make a detailed explanation on the workflow① in comprehensive work area.

Mr Wu: Yes, please.

Wilder: Let's talk about transportation first. How to transport maintenance personnel, material and machine & tool to maintenance area?

Mr Wu: Comprehensive work area is equipped with railway trolley and flat wagon for maintenance staff, material and machine & tool respectively. The flat wagon is attached behind railway trolley and enters into maintenance area in sequence.

Wilder: How many passengers may railway trolley accomodate?

Mr Wu: About fourteen passengers.

Wilder: How to load and unload the material carried by flat wagon?

吴工程师：平板车上有起重机，可以对材料、机具进行装卸。

Mr Wu: There is a crane on flat wagon to load and unload materials and machine & tools.

Wilder：维修人员的工作制度是怎么安排的？

Wilder: How to arrange work schedules of maintenance personnel?

吴工程师：维修人员采用一班制，主要在天窗时间内工作。

Mr Wu: Maintenance personnel adopt one-shift operation, mainly in the maintenance time.

Wilder：非天窗时间有无维修人员？

Wilder: Is there any maintenance staff provided in non-maintenance time?

吴工程师：有，我们在车站设有值守人员。

Mr Wu: Yes, we have a duty officer at station.

替换单词 Alternative terms

① 顺序 方式	① sequence method

业务情景：中方郑工程师同外方代表 David 讨论综合工区工种和工作内容的问题。

Scene: Chinese engineer Mr Zheng is discussing the type and content of work in comprehensive work area with David, the representative of foreign side.

典型对话 Conversation

David：贵方的概念设计文件我们已经看完了，文件中对维修人员的工作内容及性质没有说明，有些问题需要你解释一下。

David: We've read your conceptual design document. Please make a detailed explanation on the content and nature of maintenance personnel's work.

郑工程师：好的，请讲。

David：线路维修工作内容有哪些，包括哪些工种？

郑工程师：线路维修有维修①、巡道、探伤和检测等工作，相应把人员分为线路工②、巡道工、探伤工、检测工等。

David：线路工主要干什么工作？

郑工程师：线路工主要进行起道、拨道和捣固作业。

David：巡道工主要是干什么？

郑工程师：巡道工主要是对线路进行巡视、清除线路上的障碍物，以及将线路上的一些紧急情况向车站报告。

David：探伤工人是对钢轨进行探伤吗？

郑工程师：是的。

David：用什么设备进行探伤？

郑工程师：主要是超声波探伤仪。

David：考虑用探伤车吗？

郑工程师：本线相邻的既有线配有探伤车，考虑利用该既有探伤车进行本线的探伤。

David：人工探伤有什么作用呢？

Mr Zheng: Yes, please.

David: What tasks are involved in track maintenance and what types of workers are included?

Mr Zheng: Track maintenance includes mending along the line①, patrolling, flaw detection and inspection, and etc. The workers can be divided accordingly into lineman②, patrolman, flaw detecting man, inspection man and so on.

David: What does a lineman do?

Mr Zheng: He is responsible for track lifting, track lining and tamping.

David: What does a patrolman do?

Mr Zheng: He is responsible for track inspection, obstructions removal, as well as report the urgent events occurred on the line to station.

David: Is a flaw detecting man responsible for flaw detection on rail?

Mr Zheng: Yes.

David: What equipment is used for flaw detection?

Mr Zheng: Ultrasonic flaw detector.

David: Have you thought about using flaw detecting car?

Mr Zheng: The adjacent existing line is equipped with flaw detecting car, which would be used in this Line.

David: What does manual flaw detection do?

郑工程师：人工探伤主要是对探伤车检测的问题进行复核，确认钢轨有无损伤。

Mr Zheng: It could check the problems detected by flaw detecting car to confirm whether the rail is damaged.

替换单词 Alternative terms

① 维修　　　　　　　　　　① track maintenance
　巡道　　　　　　　　　　　 patrolling
　探伤和检测　　　　　　　　 flaw detection and inspection
② 线路工　　　　　　　　　② lineman
　巡道工　　　　　　　　　　 patrolman
　探伤工　　　　　　　　　　 flaw detecting man
　检测工　　　　　　　　　　 inspection man

业务情景：中方郝工程师同外方代表 Fred 讨论综合工区轨道车库设计的问题。

Scene: Chinese engineer Mr Hao is discussing the track depot design in comprehensive work area with Fred, the representative of foreign side.

典型对话 Conversation

Fred: 贵方提交的初步设计文件我们已经看完了，有些问题需要你解释一下。

郝工程师：好的，请讲。

Fred: 综合工区内的轨道车库有何用途？

郝工程师：轨道车库是轨道车组①、接触网作业车、大机的保养和停放场所。

Fred: We've read your preliminary design document. Please make a detailed explanation on some questions.

Mr Hao: Yes, please.

Fred: What is the track depot in comprehensive work area used for?

Mr Hao: It serves as a maintenance and parking place for track car group①, OCS

151

Fred: 轨道车库的长度是怎么计算的？

郝工程师: 轨道车库的长度是按最长的作业车组加上安全距离确定的，最长的作业车组长度是56m，车组前后安全距离是4m，所以轨道车库为60m。

Fred: 我注意到轨道车库内设有一条地沟，地沟长度是怎么确定？

郝工程师: 这条地沟是作为车辆检查用的，地沟长度是按一辆轨道车的长度来确定的。

Fred: 我们认为应按一个车组的长度来确定地沟长度。

郝工程师: 但是车辆保养时每次只能检查一辆车，设置一个车组的地沟长度是没有必要的。

Fred: 那检查下个车怎么办呢？

郝工程师: 只需把车组往前移动就可以检查下一个车。

Fred: 原来是这样，您的这个方案很好，我同意。

郝工程师: 谢谢。

operating vehicle and large track maintenance machinery.

Fred: How to calculate the length of track depot?

Mr Hao: The length of track depot is determined by the length of the longest operating vehicle group plus safe distance, for example, the length of the longest operating vehicle group is 56m, plus the safe distance beyond each vehicle unit of 4m, so the track depot is 60m.

Fred: I noticed that there is a trench in track depot. How to determine the length of trench?

Mr Hao: This trench is used for vehicle inspection, whose length is determined by the length of track car.

Fred: We think that it should be determined by the length of track car group.

Mr Hao: Only one vehicle can be inspected at one time in maintenance, therefore it is not necessary to set the trench length conformed to track car group.

Fred: But how to inspect the next car?

Mr Hao: Just move forward the track car unit.

Fred: I see. I agree with your plan.

Mr Hao: Thank you.

第一部分　交通工程情景会话

替换单词 Alternative terms

① 轨道车组
　接触网作业车
　大机

① track car unit
　OCS operating vehicle
　large track maintenance machinery

业务情景：中方杨工程师同外方代表 Joel 讨论综合工区轨道车库加油设施的问题。
Scene: Chinese engineer Mr Yang is discussing the fueling facility of track depot in comprehensive work area with Joel, the representative of foreign side.

典型对话 Conversation

Joel：贵方提交的初步设计文件我们已经看完了，关于轨道车加油设施①需要同你谈论一下。
杨工程师：好的，请讲。
Joel：维修车辆是电力还是内燃机车？

杨工程师：轨道车、接触网作业车和大型养路机械等维修车辆都是内燃车。

Joel：设计采用什么方式给这些车辆供油？
杨工程师：考虑由当地石油公司的油罐车供油。

Joel: We've read your preliminary design document. I'd like to discuss with you the fueling facility① of track car.
Mr Yang: Yes, please.
Joel: What kind of maintenance vehicle is to be applied, electric or diesel locomotive?
Mr Yang: Track car, OCS operating vehicle and large track maintenance machinery and other maintenance vehicles are all diesel locomotives.
Joel: How to supply oil to those vehicles in your design?
Mr Yang: It is provided by local oil company's oil tank truck.

153

Joel: 油罐车是由承包商提供吗？

杨工程师：不是，由当地石油公司提供。

Joel: 石油公司提供的油有地方存储吗？

杨工程师：有，在综合工区内设有桶装油存放间。

Joel: 桶装油这种加油方式效率低而且自动化程度不高，我们不同意这种方案。

杨工程师：贵方认为应采用哪种方案？

Joel: 采用加油站的方式。

杨工程师：这种方式投资较高，并且合同中没有约定，我们不同意这个方案。

Joel: 那这个问题待下次工作例会的时候集体讨论。

杨工程师：好的。

Joel: Is oil tank truck supplied by the contractor?

Mr Yang: No, it's provided by local oil company.

Joel: Is there any place to store the oil?

Mr Yang: Yes, the comprehensive work area is equipped with a storage room for barreled oil.

Joel: We disagree with this fueling plan of using barreled oil due to its low efficiency and less automation.

Mr Yang: Which plan should be adopted in your opinion?

Joel: Adopt gas station.

Mr Yang: We disagree with this fueling proposal due to more investment needed, besides it is not bonded in the contract.

Joel: We'll leave this issue to the next regular meeting for collective discussion.

Mr Yang: Ok.

替换单词 Alternative terms

① 加油站　　　　　　　　　　① gas station

第一部分　　交通工程情景会话

业务情景：中方彭工程师同外方代表 Justin 讨论大型养路机械的问题。
Scene: Chinese engineer Mr Peng is discussing the large track maintenance machinery with Justin, the representative of foreign side.

典型对话 Conversation

Justin：贵方提交的详细设计文件我们已经看完了，关于大型养路机械的有关问题需要同你谈论一下。

彭工程师：好的，请讲。

Justin：文件中提到了大型养路机械的附属车辆，这些车辆是干什么用的？

彭工程师：附属车辆有宿营车①、餐车、材料车、水槽车、油罐车等，是工作人员的移动生活设施。

Justin：这些车辆是专用车辆吗？

彭工程师：这些车辆主要是通过普通客车改装而成的。

Justin：宿营车、餐车有没有污水处理设施？

彭工程师：宿营车和餐车的污水考虑收集后，排入综合工区的污水处理池集中处理。

Justin: We've read your submitted design document. I'd like to discuss with you the large track maintenance machinery.
Mr Peng: Yes, please.
Justin: What will the auxiliary vehicles of large track maintenance machinery be used for?
Mr Peng: The auxiliary vehicles include boarding cars①, dining cars, material cars, water tank trucks, oil tank trucks, and etc., serving as a moving living facility for railway staff.
Justin: Are they belonging to special vehicles?
Mr Peng: These vehicles are mainly refitted from ordinary passenger train.
Justin: Are the boarding cars and dining cars equipped with sewage treatment facilities?
Mr Peng: The sewage collected from boarding car and dining car would be discharged into sewage treatment pond constructed in comprehensive work area

155

Justin: 请说详细一点，污水是怎么收集的？

彭工程师: 宿营车和餐车都有污水收集箱。

Justin: 那污水收集箱内污水怎么排入综合工区的污水处理池？

彭工程师: 由于宿营车和餐车的污水量不大，是按人工搬运考虑的。

Justin: 从设计总图上看，附属车辆停放线离污水池的距离较远，人工搬运的话劳动强度太大，我们要求采用自动化的搬运设备。

彭工程师: 可以考虑配置一台手推车。
Justin: 好的。

for centralized treatment.
Justin: Could you make a detailed explanation on the procedure of sewage collection?
Mr Peng: The boarding car and the dining car are provided with sewage collection tank.
Justin: How is the sewage in sewage collection tank discharged into sewage treatment pond in the comprehensive work area?
Mr Peng: Manual handling will be considered because of the small sewage quantity from boarding car and dining car.
Justin: We can see from the general design drawing that the stabling siding of auxiliary vehicles is far away from sewage tank. Manual handling requires intense labor, so automated handling equipment will be required.
Mr Peng: Adding a trolley is a way.
Justin: Ok.

替换单词 Alternative terms

① 餐车　　　　　　　　　　① dining car
　材料车　　　　　　　　　　material car
　水槽车　　　　　　　　　　water tank truck
　油罐车　　　　　　　　　　oil tank truck

业务情景：中方李工程师同外方代表 Ken 讨论维修车辆外皮清洗的相关问题。

Scene: Chinese engineer Mr Li is discussing the external cleaning of maintenance car with Ken, the representative of foreign side.

典型对话 Conversation

Ken：贵方提交的详细设计文件我们已经看完了，关于维修车辆外皮清洗有关问题需要同你谈论一下。

李工程师：好的，请讲。

Ken：设计文件没有看到对维修车辆外皮清洗的说明内容，维修车辆的外表面清洗有没有考虑？

李工程师：车辆外皮的清洗是按人工擦洗考虑的。

Ken：人工擦洗这种方式太落后了，我们不同意这样做。

李工程师：像捣固车①、稳定车这些大型养路机械，它们的外表面不适合采用自动洗车机进行清洗。

Ken：那有没有比人工擦洗稍微自动化一点的设备？

李工程师：可以采用冲洗机，像洗汽车的那种冲洗机。

Ken: We've read your submitted design document. I'd like to discuss with you the external cleaning of maintenance car.

Mr Li: Yes, please.

Ken: The description on external cleaning of maintenance car is not mentioned in the design document. Have you ever considered it in your design?

Mr Li: We adopt manual cleaning.

Ken:. We don't agree to use such manual cleaning method. It's so backward.

Mr Li: But the external surface of some large track maintenance machineries like tamping wagon① and stabilizing wagon is not suitable to be cleaned by automatic washing machine.

Ken: Is there any automated equipment better than manual cleaning?

Mr Li: The flushing machine used for car washing is Ok.

Ken: 这倒是一个好办法。另外考虑在哪里洗车？
李工程师: 在轨道车库内。
Ken: 污水能排放吗？
李工程师: 可以，轨道车库内设有地漏，污水通过地漏进入污水处理池。

Ken: 太好了，接下来请按这个方案进行详细设计。
李工程师: 好的。

Ken: That's a good idea. Where can the vehicle be cleaned?
Mr Li: In track depot.
Ken: Can the sewage be discharged?
Mr Li: Yes, the track depot is equipped with floor drain, so that the sewage could be discharged into sewage treatment pond through it.
Ken: Great, the design should conform to this plan.
Mr Li: Ok.

替换单词 Alternative terms

① 稳定车　　　　　　　　　　　① stabilizing wagon

业务情景: 中方郭工程师同外方代表 Barton 讨论大机维修的相关问题。
Scene: Chinese engineer Mr Guo is discussing the maintenance of large track maintenance machinery with Barton, the representative of foreign side.

典型对话 Conversation

Barton: 贵方提交的详细设计文件我们已经看完了，关于大型养路机械的维修的有关问题需要同你谈论一下。

郭工程师: 好的，请讲。
Barton: 请先介绍一下大型养路机械的修程修制。

Barton: We've read your submitted design document. I'd like to discuss with you the maintenance of large track maintenance machinery.

Mr Guo: Yes, please.
Barton: Please make a brief introduction to maintenance system of large track maintenance machinery.

郭工程师：大型养路机械的维修分为<u>日常保养</u>①、年修和全面修理，其修理周期分别是1月、1年和6年。

Barton：大型养路机械的日常保养是在哪里进行？

郭工程师：日常保养是在综合维修中心轨道车库内进行。

Barton：年修和全面修理在哪里？

郭工程师：因为综合维修中心与机车车辆维修基地相邻，大机的年修在机车车辆维修基地进行，全面修理通常委托给设备制造商。

Barton：年修在机车车辆维修基地的哪个位置？

郭工程师：在检修库。

Barton：大机主要配置的<u>维修设备</u>②有哪些？

郭工程师：主要有试验设备、探伤设备和分析仪器等。

Mr Guo: It is divided into <u>routine maintenance</u>①, annual maintenance and comprehensive maintenance, with a maintenance cycle of one month, one year and six years respectively.

Barton: Where is the routine maintenance of large track maintenance machinery carried out?

Mr Guo: In track depot of comprehensive maintenance centre.

Barton: What about annual maintenance and comprehensive maintenance?

Mr Guo: Since the comprehensive maintenance centre is adjacent to the locomotive maintenance base, the annual maintenance of large track maintenance machinery is carried out in locomotive maintenance base, while the comprehensive maintenance is usually commissioned to equipment manufacturer.

Barton: Where is annual maintenance to be performed in locomotive maintenance base?

Mr Guo: In the maintenance depot.

Barton: What is the <u>maintenance equipment</u>② provided for large track maintenance machinery?

Mr Guo: It is provided with testing equipment, flaw detection equipment and analytical instruments.

替换单词 Alternative terms

① 日常保养　　　　　　　　① routine maintenance
　 年修　　　　　　　　　　　 annual maintenance
　 全面修理　　　　　　　　　 comprehensive maintenance
② 试验设备　　　　　　　　② testing equipment
　 探伤设备　　　　　　　　　 flaw detection equipment
　 分析仪器　　　　　　　　　 analytical instrument

业务情景：中方刘工程师同外方代表 Watson 讨论设计文件组成的相关问题。

Scene: Chinese engineer Mr Liu is discussing the composition of the design documents with Watson, the representative of foreign side.

典型对话 Conversation

Watson：贵方提交的详细设计文件我们已经看完了，关于文件组成内容还有一些问题要同你谈论一下。

Watson: We've read your submitted design documents. I'd like to discuss with you some content of the design documents.

刘工程师：好的，请讲。

Mr Liu: Yes, please.

Watson：本次提交的综合维修的初步设计文件只有机械专业的有关内容，还缺少地质①专业的设计内容，应补充这些专业的设计内容。

Watson: The submitted preliminary design document of comprehensive maintenance only specifies the contents of mechanics, but the design on geology① is not mentioned. You should complement relevant geological design contents.

刘工程师：这些专业的设计内容已经完成，各专业已经提交给了各自的咨询工程师。

Mr Liu: The design has been completed and has been submitted to corresponding consulting engineers respectively.

Watson：这不符合我们的审查习惯，你们需要把综合维修的所有专业的设计文件和图纸一起送过来审查。

Watson: It is not consistent with our review procedures. You should submit all disciplines' design documents and drawings of comprehensive maintenance for review.

刘工程师：这点和我国的习惯做法不太一样，请你提供一份综合维修的文件组成内容给我。

Mr Liu: It's quite different from our procedures. Please provide us with a list of design documents on comprehensive maintenance.

Watson：是的，每个国家都有各自的做法和标准，你们来我国做设计请按照我们的做法来。

Watson: Yes, every country has its own practices and standards. Please follow our requirements as you come to our country to do the design.

刘工程师：下次提交的文件就按贵国的文件组成格式来做。

Mr Liu: The next submitted documents would follow the file composition as you required.

替换单词 Alternative terms

① 建筑　　　　　　　　　① building
　结构　　　　　　　　　　 structure
　通信　　　　　　　　　　 communication
　电力　　　　　　　　　　 electric power

业务情景：中方何工程师同外方代表 Eaton 讨论货场粮食装卸的相关问题。
Scene: Chinese engineer Mr He is discussing with Eaton, the representative of foreign side, about issues related to grain loading and unloading in freight yard.

典型对话 Conversation

Eaton: 贵方提交的初步设计文件我们已经看完了，关于粮食和水泥装卸设备今天开个专题会议。

何工程师: 好的。

Eaton: 运量专业的设计文件中提到，本线货场粮食到发量20万t，水泥10万t，粮食和水泥的装卸是怎么考虑的？

何工程师: 粮食和水泥的装卸是按叉车①装卸考虑的。

Eaton: 我们不理解粮食和水泥如何用叉车装卸，它们都是散装的。

何工程师: 粮食和水泥先用袋装，然后用叉车装卸。

Eaton: We have read your submitted preliminary design documents. So we hold a special meeting today on grain and cement loading and unloading equipment.

Mr He: Ok.

Eaton: In the design document of transportation volume, it is mentioned that arrival-departure volume of grain in freight yard is 200000 tons and cement is 100000 tons, what is your design for loading and unloading of grain and cement?

Mr He: Grain and cement will be loaded and unloaded by fork-lifter①.

Eaton: We do not understand how grain and cement are loaded and unloaded by fork-lifter because they are bulk goods.

Mr He: They will be packed in bags firstly, and then loaded and unloaded by fork-lifter.

Eaton: 我们见过的粮食装卸都是采用的自动化设备,本项目也应采用自动化的设备来装卸粮食。

何工程师: 我知道你说的自动化装卸设备,这个设备在中国国内也有应用,但是这个设备不适用于本项目。

Eaton: 为什么?

何工程师: 自动化的装卸设备要求采用专用的底开式车辆,而项目的合同中没有这种车辆。

Eaton: 本项目采用哪种车辆运输粮食?

何工程师: 采用棚车。

Eaton: 采用棚车运输粮食后,用哪种装卸设备最合适?

何工程师: 用叉车最合适。

Eaton: 行,关于粮食的装卸就按叉车装卸、棚车运输这个方案进行下阶段设计。

何工程师: 好的。

Eaton: We have seen automatic equipment used for grain loading and unloading, which shall also be used for this project.

Mr He: I know the automatic handling equipment you're talking about. It is also used in China, but it shall not be applied to this project.

Eaton: Why?

Mr He: Dedicated bottom-open vehicle shall be applicable to this automatic handling equipment, but no such a vehicle is included in the project contract.

Eaton: What type of vehicle is adopted for the project?

Mr He: Box car.

Eaton: What type of handling equipment is the most suitable choice if the grain is carried by box car?

Mr He: Fork-lifter.

Eaton: Ok. For grain loading and unloading, please proceed the design, based on the way in which fork-lifter is used for loading and unloading, boxcar for transport.

Mr He: Ok.

替换单词 Alternative terms

① 吊车　　　　　　　　　① crane
　 半挂车　　　　　　　　　 semi-trailer
　 棚车　　　　　　　　　　 boxcar

业务情景： 中方罗工程师同外方代表 Clarke 讨论货场散装物料装卸的相关问题。

Scene: Chinese engineer Mr Luo is discussing with Clarke, the representative of foreign side, issues related to loading and unloading of bulk materials in freight yard.

典型对话 Conversation

Clarke: 贵方提交的初步设计文件我们已经看完了，关于散装物料装卸设备今天开个专题会议。

罗工程师：好的。

Clarke: 根据经调专业的文件，货场里有矿石①、煤等散装物料，这些物料的装卸是怎么考虑的？

罗工程师：物料的装卸除了和本身的特性有关外，还和物料包装及运输车辆有关系。

Clarke: 请详细解释一下。

罗工程师：矿石和煤是散堆装货物，采用敞车运输。

Clarke: 你刚才说了矿石、煤的包装及运输方式，下面请详细说一下它们的装卸方式。

Clarke: We have read your submitted preliminary design document, and today we are going to hold a meeting on loading and unloading equipment for bulk goods.

Mr Luo: Ok.

Clarke: Document of economic investigation shows that there are bulk materials like ore①, coal, etc. What are you thinking about the loading and unloading of these materials?

Mr Luo: Materials' loading and unloading is relevant not only to their own properties, but also to their packaging and transport vehicles.

Clarke: Could you explain it in detail please?

Mr Luo: Ore and coal are in bulk, carried by open wagon.

Clarke: Just now you talked about how ore and coal are packed and transported. Could you explain their loading and unloading manner please?

第一部分　交通工程情景会话

罗工程师：好的，矿石和煤采用带抓斗的门式起重机②装卸。

Clarke：门式起重机是轨道上行走的，还是轮胎式的？

罗工程师：在固定轨道上行走的，有固定的作业区域。

Clarke：抓斗是干什么用的，它的容积是多大？

罗工程师：抓斗是装卸物料的，容积大约有 $3m^3$。

Clarke：采用抓斗式能把车内的物料卸干净吗？

罗工程师：不能全部卸完，会有一点残留物，大概占货物质量的3%，需要采用人工清除干净。

Clarke：我们同意采用抓斗式起重机对矿石、煤进行装卸，请在文件中添加该设备的照片和详细技术参数。

罗工程师：好的，我会将这部分内容补充进去。

Mr Luo: Ok, ore and coal are loaded and unloaded by portal crane② with grab.

Clarke: Does the portal crane run on track or is it of rubber type?

Mr Luo: It works on fixed track within fixed operating extent.

Clarke: What is the use of grab and how much is its volume?

Mr Luo: The grab is used for loading and unloading materials, with the volume of $3m^3$.

Clarke: Can grab completely unload all materials in the car?

Mr Luo: Not all, a few material will remain, maybe 3% (3 percent) of total weight of the material needs to be cleared by labor.

Clarke: We agree to use crane with grab to load and unload ore and coal. Supplement its picture and detailed technical parameters in the document please.

Mr Luo: All right, we will add this part in.

替换单词 Alternative terms

① 矿粉　　　　　　　① mineral powder
　 磷矿　　　　　　　　 phosphorus ore
　 焦炭　　　　　　　　 coke
　 煤炭　　　　　　　　 coal

② 单梁起重机　　　　　　　　② single girder crane
　双梁起重机　　　　　　　　　 double girder crane
　抓斗防爆起重机　　　　　　　 anti-explosion crane with grab

第一部分 交通工程情景会话

第十三章 信号
Chapter 13 Signal

业务情景：为了顺利开展孟加拉铁路项目工作，李工程师向业主代表Smith先生搜集信号资料。

Scene: In order to carry out the Bangladesh railway project smoothly, Chinese engineer Mr Li is collecting signaling materials from Smith, the Employer Representative.

典型对话 Conversation

李工程师：你好，我是中铁二院信号专业人员。

Smith：你好。有什么需要帮忙的吗？

李工程师：我们现在正从事孟加拉项目，需要贵方提供既有铁路的信号制式，比如<u>闭塞类型</u>[①]。

Smith：没问题。这些资料可能对你们有用。

李工程师：请问有电子版的吗？

Smith：有的，你的<u>邮箱地址</u>[②]是？

李工程师：×××@gmail.com。

Smith：好，我会后发给你。

Mr Li: Hello. I'm a signal engineer from CREEC.

Smith: Hi. Can I help you?

Mr Li: We are now engaged in a project in Bangladesh. We need detailed information of the existing railway signal system, such as <u>block type</u>[①].

Smith: No problem. This information may be helpful for you.

Mr Li: Do you have any soft copies?

Smith: Sure, what is your <u>e-mail address</u>[②]?

Mr Li: ×××@gmail.com.

Smith: Ok, I will email it to you after the meeting.

167

替换单词 Alternative terms

① 联锁类型
　列控系统的制式
　信号显示方式
　运营管理及维护模式

① interlocking type
　train control system
　signal display mode
　operation management and maintenance mode

② ICQ 号
　QQ 号

② ICQ number
　QQ number

业务情景：信号李工程师与业主代表 Robert 先生讨论工程信号系统的初步设计方案，以对主要方案原则和系统总体构成达成一致意见。
Scene: In order to reach consensus on the major schemes and system composition, signal engineer Mr Li is discussing signal system with Robert, the employer's representative.

典型对话 Conversation

李工程师：本次信号工程主要由闭塞系统、联锁系统、行车指挥系统、集中监测等系统构成。各系统的功能及设计方案详见设计文件。

Mr Li: This signal system is mainly composed of block system, interlocking system, train operation dispatching command system and centralized monitoring system. The function and design scheme of each system is described in the design documents in detail.

Robert：各设计方案是否附有图例说明？

Robert: Is the design scheme attached with schematic diagrams and descriptions?

李工程师：每个系统都有原理图及方案说明。

Mr Li: Sure, definitely.

Robert: 另外请提供设计中采用的规范以满足评估要求。

李工程师: 主要的设计规范在附录里已详细列出。

Robert: 除了车站计算机联锁①,贵方是否还能提出别的联锁解决方案?

李工程师: 我方将增加其他方案,供贵方比选。

Robert: 本线各信号系统接口②设计比较复杂,贵方是否有能力完成该部分的设计?

李工程师: 我方在国内外类似项目积累了丰富的经验,顺利开通了诸多长大干线铁路。

Robert: Otherwise, please provide us the codes for design of railway signaling to meet the assessment requirements.

Mr Li: Main design codes have been listed in Appendix in detail.

Robert: Could you please propose any other interlocking solutions except computer interlocking system① applied in station.

Mr Li: We will provide other design schemes for your comparison.

Robert: The signal interfacing② design for this line is rather complicated. Do you have the ability to complete it?

Mr Li: We have accumulated rich experience in similar projects both at home and abroad, and quite a number of long main railways have been opened to traffic.

替换单词 Alternative terms

① 区域计算机联锁
   6502 电气集中联锁
   采用全电子执行单元的计算机联锁

② 站间联系电路
   电码化电路
   特殊信号显示

① area control computer interlocking system
   6502 electrical interlocking
   all-electronic performance units for computer interlocking systems

② connecting circuit between stations
   coding circuit
   special signal indication

业务情景： 在搜集项目资料基础上，编制了项目建议书或初步设计，信号刘工程师与业主代表 Tom 先生一起对技术方案进行澄清和答疑。

Scene: Project proposal or priliminary design have been prepared on the basis of the collected project materials, Mr Liu, engineer of signal, is clarifying and answering questions on technical proposal with Tom, the employer representative.

典型对话 Conversation

刘工程师：方案汇报完毕，我将乐意回答你们的提问。

Tom：第一个问题，本次设计方案文件中，并未看到继电器①数量的内容，请予以解释。

刘工程师：在本阶段的设计过程中，工程数量仅为初步数量，且系统供货商尚未招标，因此，不能提出准确的工程数量。待施工图阶段，将会提出准确的工程数量，所有设备及材料均为贵方采购，贵方应主要审查的是功能是否满足以后贵公司的运营需求。

Tom：但我方还是希望了解工程数量和规模。

刘工程师：在完成施工图后，我们将提供详细的工程数量。

Mr Liu: Our report of the design schemes is completed. I'd be happy to answer your questions.

Tom: The first question, in the design scheme, we did not see any quantities of the relay①, but why?

Mr Liu: At this stage of design process, the BOQ (Bill of Quantity) is only estimated, the bids for suppliers have not started yet. Therefore, we cannot offer the accurate BOQ. The BOQ could be given at the construction stage. Kindly informed that all equipment and materials are purchased by your party, and you should check if the functions could satisfy operation requirement in the future.

Tom: But we still want to know the project scale and BOQ.

Mr Liu: We could provide the detailed BOQ after completing the shop drawing.

Tom: 第二个问题,贵方的设计文件中所提及的除了国际标准外,还有很多中国标准,我方认为应该全部使用国际标准。

刘工程师: 根据合同规定,本工程可以采用中国标准。

Tom: 第三个问题,贵方的设计文件中,对运营人员进行了配属,我方认为有不合理之处,应该考虑到我国的国情。

刘工程师: 关于文件中运营人员的配属,是我方根据我国运营管理的经验提出,供贵方参考。贵方可在组建运营部门时,根据需要配置。

Tom: 好的,我方将就这个问题进行探讨。

Tom: The second question, you have mentioned a number of Chinese standards or codes besides international standards, we assume only the international standards should be applied.

Mr Liu: According to the contract, this project allows Chinese standards.

Tom: The third question, in your design document, operating personnel has been deployed; we think some unreasonable arrangement should be adjusted according to our national conditions.

Mr Liu: The arrangement of the personnel in document stems from the operation and management experience of our country, just for your reference. You could make flexible deployment after operation department are established.

Tom: Ok, we will discuss this issue later.

替换单词 Alternative terms

① 断路器　　　　　　　① fuse(breaker)
　 防雷单元　　　　　　　 lightning arrester
　 转辙设备　　　　　　　 point machine

业务情景：完成了前期设计的阶段性工作后，刘工程师与业主 Tom 先生沟通设计图纸的交付时间安排及后续工作计划。

Scene: After the primary design, Mr Liu, engineer of signal, is communicating with Tom, the Employer's Representative, on the delivery time of design paper and follow-up work plan.

典型对话 Conversation

刘工程师：信号系统设计工作安排主要分为下面几个阶段：资料收集、技术标准确定、前期设计、前期方案审查及讨论、技术设计、技术设计方案审查及讨论、施工图设计、施工图审查及讨论。

Mr Liu: Signal system design mainly includes several stages: data collection, selection of the technical standards, early stage design, review and discussion, technical proposal and review, preparation and review of the shop drawings.

Tom：根据工程的工期安排，我们要求贵公司在两个月时间内完成设计工作。

Tom: According to the schedule of this project, we request you to complete the design work within two months.

刘工程师：目前我们按照该计划开展设计工作，但是信号设计受资料收集、技术标准确定、相关专业资料输入等各方面因素限制，我方将提供一个设计工期计划表给业主审批。

Mr Liu: At present, we are working as scheduled, but the signal design work is constrained by data collection, selection of the technical standards, interactive issues, etc. We will provide a design schedule to the employer for approval.

Tom：希望尽快开展设计工作。

Tom: Hope you could commence the design work as soon as possible.

刘工程师：为了将工程顺利按时推进，需要贵方协调咨询方，及时提出咨询方的审查意见。

Mr Liu: In order to conduct the project smoothly, we need you to coordinate the consultant to give advisory opinion in time.

Tom: 好的，我们将协调咨询方的工作安排。

刘工程师: 我方本次施工设计计划提交咨询公司审查的图纸是信号设备技术图①。

Tom: 贵方请注意按时回复咨询公司的审查意见。

刘工程师: 我方将按照合同的相关规定，按期完成此项工作。

Tom: All right, we'll coordinate the consultant about the work schedule.

Mr Liu: We submit the signal equipment technical drawing① for consulting now.

Tom: Please reply the advisory opinions on time.

Mr Liu: We shall finish the job on time in accordance with the relevant provisions of the contract.

替换单词 Alternative terms

① 电路图
组合内部配线图
系统原理图

① circuit diagram
wiring diagram of the combination relay
system principle diagram

业务情景: 施工图完成后，李工程师与业主、监理、施工单位进行技术交底及澄清，Tom 先生提问。

Scene: After construction drawing is finished, Mr Li, engineer of signal, is carrying technical disclosure and clarification with the Employer, supervisor and construction unit. Tom is asking questions.

典型对话 Conversation

李工程师: 今天就施工图进行技术交底，同时也请到了业主方的监理公司代表参会。施工图是施工单位进行工程实施的依据，施工单位必须严格按照施工图实施，有任何的疑问请及时与设计

Mr Li: Today we plan to make technical clarification on construction drawings, and the consultant's representative for the employer is invited at this meeting. The contractor should construct strictly

单位联系,不可擅自更改设计图纸。

Tom: 同意。

李工程师: 对于进站信号机①的安装,必须满足相关规范中限界的要求。另外,施工图中隐蔽工程需要在业主方的监理代表现场监督后实施,不可擅自实施。

Tom: 好的,我们将会对此类工程进行现场的监理工作。

李工程师: 施工单位在施工过程中如对设计图纸有疑问,须在第一时间与我方联系,由我方对设计方案及图纸进行解释或澄清。

Tom: 已要求施工单位落实施工负责人,牵头与贵方完成施工配合的相关工作。

complying with the construction drawings provided by the design company, and the contractor has to contact the design company if he has any questions for the construction drawings. Moreover, the contractor is not allowed to distort any construction drawings.

Tom: Agreed.

Mr Li: The installation of home signal① must meet the relevant specification for the clearance limit. The covered work in the construction drawing must be conducted under the supervision of the consultant's representative.

Tom: All right, on-site supervision of the project is our work.

Mr Li: The contractor has to contact us timely in case that any question for the drawings needs to be clarified.

Tom: We have already requested the construction director to cooperate with you.

替换单词 Alternative terms

① 出站信号机   ① starting signal
   通过信号机   block signal
   调车信号机   shunting signal
   继电器箱及表示器   relay cabinet and indicator

第一部分　交通工程情景会话

业务情景：咨询工程师Jack完成图纸的审查后，由设计单位李工程师对咨询意见进行答复。
Scene: Mr Li, engineer from design unit, is answering questions from consulting engineer Jack, who has reviewed the drawing.

典型对话 Conversation

Jack: 关于《铁路综合接地系统通用参考图》，我们建议：首先，该参考图以《铁路综合接地系统》为设计依据，其次，全线贯通地线敷设在两侧的通信信号电缆槽内，便于电务部门维修。

Jack: First, we suggest that *The general reference drawing of railway integrated earthing system* should be designed according to the *The Railway Integrated Earthling System*; Second, the earthing wires shall be laid in the specific communication and signal cable trench along both sides of the railway for the convenience of maintenance.

李工程师： 同意咨询意见。

Mr Li: We accept your opinion.

Jack: 文件描述的计费项目与报价表不对应。有关动员/遣散①等费用，是否已经包含在相应的单价中？

Jack: Billing items in the document don't correspond with the quotation sheet. Have the costs such as mobilization/demobilization① been included in the corresponding unit price?

李工程师： 相应单价已包含所有以上费用。

Mr Li: All the above mentioned charges are included in the unit price accordingly.

Jack: 信号设备平面布置图中应标注W1G的股道有效长。道岔及转辙机类型表中应标注60kg/m 18号道岔密贴检查器的设置情况。

Jack: The effective length of the W1G track should be marked in the signal layout drawing. The setting of point detector of 60kg/m (kilograms per meter) in No.18 turnout should be marked in the *Turnout and Switch Machine Type List*.

李工程师： 已经标注了。

Mr Li: We have already revised the drawings.

175

替换单词 Alternative terms

① 保函 ① L/G(letter of guarantee)
  保险   insurance
  备品备件 spare part
  培训   training
  清关   custom clearance

第一部分　交通工程情景会话

第十四章　通信
Chapter 14　Communication

业务情景：为了顺利开展某项目工作，须向业主或代理搜集项目前期的通信资料。

Scene: In order to smoothly carry out a project, Mr Wang is collecting the communication information of the project in the early stage from the owner or the agent.

典型对话 Conversation

王工程师：首先，我们需要既有铁路通信系统的构成情况。

Jones：包括哪些资料呢？

王工程师：通信系统各构成部分所采用的技术标准及功能，各设备的供货商[①]。

Jones：无线通信需要什么资料呢？

王工程师：既有铁路采用的无线通信制式及频率，450MHz[②]频段附近是否有可用的频率。

Jones：没问题，我会将需要的资料整理为文档并发至您邮箱。

Mr Wang: First, we need the compositions of communication system of the existing railway.

Jones: What are they?

Mr Wang: They are technical standards for compositions of communication system, functions of each composition and suppliers[①] of all the equipment.

Jones: What data do you need for wireless communication?

Mr Wang: Could you provide us with the system and frequency for the wireless communication of existing railway and tell us if there are frequencies available near 450MHz[②] frequency band?

Jones: No problem, we will sort the data you want and email it to you.

177

王工程师：新建铁路的附近是否有既有铁路？
Jones：有的。
王工程师：铁路名称和建设标准各是什么呢，是否与本条新建铁路存在交汇点呢？
Jones：好的，我会找相关维护部门收集资料，尽快整理为文档并发至您邮箱。

Mr Wang: Are there any existing railways near the new railway?
Jones: Yes, there are.
Mr Wang: What's the name of the existing railway? And what are the construction standards? Is there any intersection with the new railway?
Jones: Ok, we will collect the information from relevant maintenance departments and email it to you as soon as possible.

替换单词 Alternative terms

① 型号
② 900MHz

① Type
② 900MHz

业务情景：我方做出方案后，王工程师和对方工程师 Jones 进行方案讨论，确定最终设计原则。
Scene: The engineer of design part is discussing the design scheme with the engineer of the owner to determine the final design principle.

典型对话 Conversation

Jones：今天我们开会讨论通信系统的设计方案。在开始讨论方案前，我想强调一下，设计方案必须满足合同的要求。在满足合同的基础上再对细节进行讨论。

Jones: Today we will discuss the design scheme of communication system at this meeting. Before discussion, I'd like to stress that the design must meet the requirements in the Contract. Only after the requirements in the Contract are satisfied we can discuss the details.

王工程师：我们的设计方案是严格按照合同进行设计的。对于合同中没有明确的问题希望在讨论中达成共识。下面我们就按照各个系统进行讨论。

Jones：好的。我们就按照合同中各系统的顺序进行讨论。

王工程师：首先讨论通信中心①的设置地点和规模。

Jones：你们建议设置在哪里？

王工程师：根据铁路走向以及途经城市的规模和重要性，我们建议本条铁路的通信中心设置在 Labu。

Jones：设置在 Labu 非常合理。房屋面积如何考虑呢？

王工程师：通信中心面积按照 500m² 考虑，你觉得可以吗？

Jones：通信中心的房屋结构和面积，我需要和房建专业的负责人沟通后再确定。

王工程师：您确定后请尽快跟我们明确。我们进行下一个系统的讨论：通信光缆及电缆。

Jones：除了主干②光缆，本条铁路是否需要主干电缆呢？

Mr Wang: We design the communication system in accordance with the Contract. In addition, we hope to reach an agreement on the issues not specified in the Contract. Next, let's discuss the design scheme of each system.

Jones: Ok. Let's discuss it following the order of each system in the Contract.

Mr Wang: First, let's discuss the location and scale of the communication centre①.

Jones: Where do you think it shall be set up?

Mr Wang: According to the alignment of the railway and the scale and significance of the city that the railway passes through, we suggest setting up the communication centre in Labu.

Jones: Your suggestion is very reasonable. So how to consider the house size?

Mr Wang: What do you think about the area of 500m² for communication centre?

Jones: The structure and area of communication centre can be determined only after discussion with the head of building profession.

Mr Wang: Please let us know as soon as possible after determination. Next, let's discuss communication cable and optical cable.

Jones: Besides trunk② optical cable, we wonder if the trunk electric cable will be laid for this railway.

王工程师：一般情况下，时速小于200km/h的铁路需要沿铁路线路同沟敷设主干光缆和电缆各一条。

Jones：时速200km/h及以上铁路呢？

王工程师：沿铁路预制电缆沟敷设光缆，不再设置长途电缆。（另设一套GSM-R无线通信系统解决区间通信）。

Jones：主干光缆和电缆各采用什么类型和容量呢？

王工程师：光缆采用$GYTZA_{53}$型32芯，电缆采用$HEYFLT_{23} 7×4×0.9$低频对称充油电缆。

Jones：地区光缆和电缆各采用什么类型和容量呢？

王工程师：地区通信线路主要采用$HYAT_{53}$型填充式全塑电缆。光缆采用$GYTA_{53}$型12芯。

Jones：请问这些型号的光缆是采用什么标准？

Mr Wang: In general, for railway whose speed is less than 200km/h, lay a trunk optical cable and a trunk cable in the same trench.

Jones: How about railway whose speed is equal to or over 200km/h?

Mr Wang: For this case, lay optical cable in the precast cable trench along the railway, no long-distance cable is needed. But we'll set up an additional GSM-R radio communication system to realize the communication between sections.

Jones: What are the type and capacity of trunk optical cable and electric cable respectively?

Mr Wang: Optical cable is 32 cores $GYTZA_{53}$, electric cable is $HEYFLT_{23} 7×4×0.9$ low-frequency symmetric oil-filled cable.

Jones: What are the type and capacity of local optical cable and electric cable?

Mr Wang: For the local communication, we mainly use $HYAT_{53}$ all-plastic cable. The optical cable is 12 cores $GYTA_{53}$.

Jones: Could you tell us what the standards for these cables are?

王工程师：光缆、电缆的生产均采用 ITU-T（ITU for Telecommunication Standardization Sector）标准。由于型号的命名 ITU-T 没有规定，各国均有自己的标准，我们目前是采用中国的命名标准。

Jones：由于资料比较多，我们希望有更多的时间进行研究。现在进行下一个系统的讨论。

王工程师：下面我们讨论传输系统。我们采用的是 SDH 光纤通信技术，满足合同及 ITU-T 相关标准要求。我们在每个车站设置了传输通信设备。

Jones：采用几层组网呢？

王工程师：我们的系统是按两层③结构设计。

Jones：请问传输系统的带宽是多少？

王工程师：骨干层传输带宽是 2.5Gb/s④，接入层传输带宽是 622Mb/s⑤。

Jones：传输设备如何设置呢？

王工程师：在通信中心、车站、调度中心设置骨干层 ADM 设备；在基站、信号、牵引及供电等节点设置接入层 ADM 设备。

Mr Wang: ITU-T standard. But the type naming isn't prescribed in ITU-T standard. So at present we use Chinese naming standard.

Jones: Because there is too much data, we hope to have more time to study it. Now, let's discuss the next system.

Mr Wang: Next, let's discuss transmission system. SDH optical fiber communication technology we use in the design meets the requirements in the Contract and relevant Standards issued by ITU-T. In addition, we have set up the communication transmission equipment in each station.

Jones: How many layers is the network composed of?

Mr Wang: The system is designed according to two-layer③ structure.

Jones: How much is the bandwidth of the transmission system?

Mr Wang: The bandwidth is 2.5Gb/s④ for backbone layer and 622Mb/s⑤ for the access layer.

Jones: How to set up the transmission equipment?

Mr Wang: Set up backbone layer ADM equipment in the communication centre, station and control centre and set up access layer ADM equipment in the base station, signal, traction and power supply nodes.

Jones: 设备是否具备完善的保护机制？

王工程师：通信设备的主要部件都采用主、备用的模式配置，在单板出现故障的情况下也可以保证通信的畅通。在有条件的情况下，可以利用公共通信网络的通道进行保护。

Jones: 是否能提供更详细的说明？

王工程师：本次会议我们先确定系统的框架和技术标准，下次会议我们会给您提供更详细的资料。

Jones: 那我们进行下一个系统的讨论。

王工程师：下面我们讨论数据通信系统。数据通信系统我们采用IP over SDH/裸光纤技术，在各车站和通信中心设置路由器，设备满足合同以及ITU-T 相关的规范。

Jones: 我们要求数据网组网采用IP over SDH/裸光纤组网。

Jones: Is there perfect protective mechanism for equipment?

Mr Wang: Main components of the communication equipment are configured according to master and standby mode. In case one mode is failed, the smooth communication can still be ensured. The equipment can be protected by channel of public communication network if it is available.

Jones: Could you provide us with more detailed descriptions?

Mr Wang: At this meeting, we hope to determine the frame and technical standards for the system. At the next meeting, we will give you more detailed data.

Jones: Then let's discuss the next system.

Mr Wang: Next, let's discuss the data communication system. We use IP over SDH/ bare fiber technology for the data communication system in the design and set up the routers in each station and communication centre. The equipment meets the requirement specified in the Contract and relevant specifications issued by ITU-T.

Jones: We hope to use IP over SDH/bare fiber for data networking.

王工程师：我们可以按照您的要求进行设计，下次方案汇报的时候做进一步讨论，除此以外，您还有别的要求么？

Jones：目前没有。我们进行电话交换系统的讨论吧。

王工程师：好的，电话交换我们采用的是 PBX/IP PBX/Soft Switch 技术。通信中心设置交换中心设备，车站设置接入设备，功能满足合同及 ITU-T 要求。

Jones：我们要求设置电话，并考虑一定的设备扩容能力。

王工程师：没有问题，电话交换设备在满足开通要求的基础上会考虑 30% 的富余量。

Jones：这个很好，请您继续吧。

王工程师：下面我们讨论调度通信系统的设计。

Jones：我们要求列车在区间也能和车站联系。

王工程师：可以满足您的要求，区间我们设置有无线基站/中继台，用于无线信号的覆盖。

Mr Wang: We can do it according to your requirements. Let's discuss it further at the scheme reporting meeting next time. In addition, do you have any other requirements?

Jones: Now, no. Then let's discuss the telephone switching system.

Mr Wang: Ok, we use PBX/IP PBX/Soft Switch technology for the telephone switching system. Set up exchange centre equipment in the communication centre and access equipment in the station whose functions meet the requirements specified in the contract and specifications issued by ITU-T.

Jones: We demand to set up the telephone and reserve capacity for equipment.

Mr Wang: No problem, on the basis of meeting the operating requirements, we will reserve 30% spare equipment capacity for the telephone switching equipment.

Jones: Very good, please go ahead.

Mr Wang: Next, let's discuss the design of dispatching communication system.

Jones: We demand the train can communicate with the station even in the middle of sections.

Mr Wang: No problem. We will set up the wireless base station/relay station for wireless signal to cover the section.

Jones: 那么我们先休息一下，然后再进行下面的讨论。

王工程师: 现在我们讨论一下无线频率使用方面的问题。既有铁路无线通信采用什么频率，在450MHz和900MHz频段附近是否有可用的频率？

Jones: 这需要我们向我国无线电管理部门确认是否有可用的频率资源。

王工程师: 希望你方能尽快落实铁路无线通信频率使用的相关事宜。

Jones: 我们会尽快确定这个事情，并且第一时间电告你们。

王工程师: 谢谢。很高兴今天与您讨论，对部分内容达成了共识。

Jones: 我也很高兴，我们的目标都是一致的。

王工程师: 希望就我们达成共识的内容形成会议纪要并且签署，非常感谢。

Jones: 现在我们就对会议内容进行梳理，并起草会议纪要。

Jones: So let's have a rest, and then discuss the following problems.

Mr Wang: Now let's discuss the use of wireless frequency. What's the wireless communication frequency of the existing railway? Are there frequencies available near 450MHz and 900MHz bands?

Jones: For this problem, we must refer your question to the radio administrative department to confirm whether the frequency resources are available.

Mr Wang: We hope you can clear the relevant matters as soon as possible.

Jones: We will determine this matter and notice you as early as possible.

Mr Wang: Thank you. Glad to discuss with you and we the have reached a consensus on some contents today.

Jones: Me too. We share the same goal.

Mr Wang: We hope the contents we have agreed can be recorded in a meeting minute and signed, thank you very much.

Jones: Now we will sort the meeting contents and draft the meeting minute.

替换单词 Alternative terms

① 通信站
　通信楼
　通信中心

① communication station
　communication building
　communication centre

② 干线
    主干光电缆
	② trunk line
	    trunk optical cable

③ 三层	③ three layers

④ 155Mb/s
    622Mb/s
    10Gb/s
	④ 155Mb/s
	    622Mb/s
	    10Gb/s

⑤ 155Mb/s
    2.5Gb/s
    10Gb/s
	⑤ 155Mb/s
	    2.5Gb/s
	    10Gb/s

业务情景：根据之前方案讨论的设计原则，对设计方案进行修改，并形成最后的设计方案，并对具体方案进行汇报。
Scene: Mr Wang is reporting the final design scheme revised according to design principle determined at the previous discussion meeting to the Owner.

典型对话 Conversation

王工程师：现在我们进行通信系统设计方案的汇报。我将逐一对每个系统设计方案进行汇报。（系统内容以埃塞铁路为例）

Jones：请开始。

王工程师：本线传输系统按干线层传输系统、接入层传输系统两层网构架。干线层传输系统利用沿铁路敷设的 32 芯光缆中的四芯光纤开设 SDH 2.5Gb/s（1+1）MSP 系统；接入层传输系统利用沿铁路敷设的 32 芯光缆中的四芯光

Mr Wang: Now please allow me to report the design scheme of each communicate system to you one by one.

Jones: Ok, please.

Mr Wang: The transmission system is composed of trunk-layer transmission system and access-layer transmission system. For trunk-layer transmission system, four-core optical fiber in the 32-core optical fiber laid along the railway is

纤开设 SDH 622Mb/s（1+1）MSP 系统。

Jones：设备怎么设置呢？

王工程师：Labu、Adama、Metehara、Mieso、Bike、Dire Dawa、Adigala、Dewele、Nagad 车站设置 ADM 设备。在 Labu、Nagad 通信站各设置一套 OLT[①]（optical line terminal，光线路终端）设备，其余各车站设置 ONU（optical network unit，光网络单元）设备。

Jones：网管设备如何设置呢？

王工程师：Labu、Nagad 设置接入网网管终端，负责全线接入网系统的管理。

Jones：请继续。

王工程师：在 Labu、Nagad 通信站各新设 1000L 程控交换机 1 台。新增自动电话用户通过接入网分段接入 Labu、Nagad 通信站程控交换机。

Jones：数据网是按两层组网还是三层组网呢？

王工程师：本线数据网按核心层、汇聚层和接入层三层架构设计，拓扑结构为星型和环型组合结构。

used to set up SDH 2.5Gb/s（1+1）MSP system; for access-layer system, four-core optical fiber in the 32-core optical fiber laid along the railway is used to set up SDH 622Mb/s（1+1）MSP system.

Jones: How to set up the equipment?

Mr Wang: Set up ADM equipment in nine stations, including Labu, Adama, Metehara, Mieso, Bike, Dire Dawa, Adigala, Dewele and Nagad, a set of OLT[①] equipment in Labu communication station and Nagad communication station and ONU equipment in other stations.

Jones: How to set the network management equipment?

Mr Wang: Set up the access network management terminal in Labu station and Nagad station for management of access network system of the whole line.

Jones: Ok, please go ahead.

Mr Wang: Set up a 1000L SPC exchange in Labu communication station and Nagad communication station respectively and new autovon users will access the SPC exchange by access network based on sections they are in.

Jones: Is the data network composed of two layers or three layers?

Mr Wang: The data network is designed as three-layer frameworks, including core layer, convergence layer and access layer.

第一部分　交通工程情景会话

Jones：核心路由器和汇聚层路由器的设置地点呢？
王工程师：在 Labu 通信站设置核心层路由器；Nagad 站为汇聚层节点，设置汇聚层路由器。

Jones：接入层路由器呢？

王工程师：各车站设置 1 台接入层路由器。

Jones：各路由器之间如何互连呢？

王工程师：接入层节点与汇聚层节点之间通过传输系统提供的 POS 155M（O）接口互连，接入层节点之间通过传输系统提供的 FE 接口互连。在 Labu 调度所①、Nagad 通信站新设铁路数字专用通信主设备，各车站设置铁路数字专用通信车站分设备、值班台、录音仪。

Jones：本线是考虑无线列调还是 GSM-R 系统呢？

王工程师：本线新设 450MHz 四频组无线列调系统。

The topological structure is star-ring composite structure.

Jones: Where shall the core-layer router and convergence-layer router be set up?

Mr Wang: Set up the core-layer router in Labu communication station and the convergence-layer router in Nagad convergence layer node.

Jones: Ok, then, how to set up the access-layer router?

Mr Wang: Set up an access-layer router in each station.

Jones: So how to interconnect between routers?

Mr Wang: Access layer node is interconnected with convergence layer node by POS 155M（O）interface supplied by transmission system and with other access layer node by FE interface supplied by transmission system. And then set up the special purposed main equipment of railway digital communication in Labu dispatching office① and Nagad communication station, and subsidiary equipment, duty console and recorder in each station.

Jones: Is radio train dispatching communication system or GSM-R system used for this railway?

Mr Wang: Set up a new 450MHz four-frequency group radio train dispatching communication system for this railway.

Jones: 覆盖范围呢？
王工程师：无线信号仅考虑覆盖车站附近。
Jones: 那具体的设计方案呢？
王工程师：在 Labu 调度中心新设调度总机和监测总机。车站新设车站电台和铁塔天线，机车上安装机车电台。车站助理值班员、运转车长、机车副司机配备便携电台。

Jones: 有平面调车系统吗？
王工程师：根据本线调车作业需求，在吉布提港为调车作业组配备 400MHz 平面调车无线系统。系统由调车固定台、调车机车台及调车便携台组成。

Jones: 含有骨干层[②]传输设备的车站和一般车站电源配置相同吗？

王工程师：不一样的，车站（含骨干层）新设 -48V/100A 高频开关电源设备及 -48V/200Ah 阀控式密封铅酸蓄电池一组；其他车站新设 -48V/75A 高频开关电源设备及 -48V/150Ah 阀控式

Jones: What's the coverage?
Mr Wang: The radio signal only covers the area near the station.
Jones: What's the design scheme?
Mr Wang: The design scheme is to set up a new dispatching switchboard and monitoring switchboard in Labu dispatching centre, a new radio station and tower antenna in the station, and then install a radio station in the locomotive. In addition, the assistant watchman of the station, the train guard and the assistant driver of the locomotive are equipped with portable radio.

Jones: Is there a plane shunting system?
Mr Wang: Yes, there is. According to shunting service requirements of the line, we shall design a 400MHz radio plane shunting system for shunting service group in Djibouti Port. This system is composed of fixed station, locomotive radio station and portable station.

Jones: Is the power supply to the station with backbone-layer[②] transmission equipment the same with that to the ordinary station?

Mr Wang: No, not the same. For the station with backbone layer, set up a new -48V/100A high frequency switching power supply equipment and a set of -48V/200Ah valve control sealed lead

密封铅酸蓄电池一组。

Jones：无线设备的供电方式呢？

王工程师：车站电台采用-48VDC供电。调度总机、监测总机采用220VAC供电。

Jones：工务、电务、车务、水电等专用通信系统怎么解决呢？

王工程师：不构成单独的通信系统，由各车站的ONU设备提供的自动电话解决。新设时钟同步系统，采用主从同步方式。

Jones：时钟信号如何获取呢？

王工程师：骨干传输层SDH设备从Labu通信站BITS设备引接所需定时信号，接入层SDH设备分段从骨干传输层提取线路时钟信号。

acid battery; for other stations, set up a new -48V/75A high frequency switching power supply equipment and a set of -48V/150Ah valve control sealed lead acid battery.

Jones: What's the power supply mode of radio equipment?

Mr Wang: -48VDC for radio station in the train stations and 220VAC for dispatching switchboard and monitoring switchboard.

Jones: Would you like to tell us how to solve the dedicated communication system for permanent way maintenance, maintenance of electrical works, locomotive maintenance and water and electricity maintenance?

Mr Wang: The automatic telephone provided by ONU equipment in each station is used for communication of the above communication systems. They to not constitute a separate communication system. Set up a new clock synchronization system with master-slave synchronization mode.

Jones: How to acquire the clock signal?

Mr Wang: The SDH equipment of backbone transmission layer acquires the required timing signal from BITS equipment in Labu communication station and the SDH equipment of access layer acquires the clock signal of the line by sections from backbone transmission layer.

Jones：需要设置电源及环境监控系统吗？

王工程师：需要的。在Labu、Nagad通信站设电源及环境监控中心设备，各车站通信机械室新设现场监控设备。

Jones：信号和信息机房需要监控吗？

王工程师：需要。在信号机械室及信息机房设置采集器，各综合维修车间、信息中心等设远程客户端。

Jones：光电缆的选型呢？

王工程师：本线选用G652光纤（具备双窗口性能），并且要求在1310nm波长衰减不大于0.36db/km，在1550nm波长衰减不大于0.22db/km。

Jones：光缆的容量选择多少呢？

王工程师：本线新敷设GYTA5332B1光缆1条。

Jones：电缆的容量选择呢？

Jones: Is it necessary to set up the power source and environment monitoring system?

Mr Wang: Yes, it is. Set up the power source and environment monitoring centre equipment in Labu communication station and Nagad communication station and set up the new on-site monitoring equipment in the communication equipment room of each station.

Jones: Is it necessary to monitor the signal and information equipment rooms?

Mr Wang: Yes, it is. Install the collector in the signal and information equipment rooms and set up the remote client in each comprehensive maintenance shop and information centre.

Jones: What's the type of the cable and optical cable?

Mr Wang: The optical fiber for this line is G652 optical fiber with double window performance, and the attenuation is not more than 0.36db/km for 1310nm wave length, not more than 0.22db/km for 1550nm wave length.

Jones: How much is the capacity of the optical cable?

Mr Wang: For this line, lay a new $GYTA_{53}32B1$ optical cable.

Jones: How much is the capacity of the electric cable?

王工程师：根据电气化铁路要求长途电缆屏蔽系数不大于0.1的要求，本线新敷设 HEYFLT237×4×0.9 低频对称充油电缆1条。

Mr Wang: According to the electrified railway's requirement, the shielding factor of the long distance cable shall be less than or equal to 0.1, we shall lay a new HEYFLT237×4×0.9 low frequency symmetric oil-filled cable.

替换单词 Alternative terms

① 调度中心　　　　　　　① dispatching centre
　 调度所　　　　　　　　　 dispatching office
② 干线层　　　　　　　　② trunk layer
　 骨干层　　　　　　　　　 backbone layer

业务情景：方案汇报通过后，积极展开各阶段设计。
Scene: After reporting the scheme, Mr Wang will carry out works of each design stage actively.

典型对话 Conversation

王工程师：目前我们的通信设计已经完成了资料收集、技术标准确定、前期设计、前期方案审查阶段①的工作。

Mr Wang: At present, we have completed the data collection, determination of technical standards, preliminary design and review of preliminary scheme①.

Jones：根据工程的工期要求，要求在3个月时间完成设计工作。

Jones: According to construction duration, you shall complete the design within 3 months.

王工程师：目前我们按照该时间计划开展设计工作，但是通信设计工作会受其他因素影响。

Jones：有哪些因素呢？

王工程师：资料收集、技术标准确定、无线频率申请、相关资料等各方面因素限制。

Jones：需要我们提供怎样的支持？

王工程师：我们需要在以上工作按期完成的情况下，才能顺利推进通信的设计工作，我们将提供一个设计工期计划表给业主审批。

Jones：希望尽快开展设计工作，为后期施工设计提供实施条件。

王工程师：好的，我们将在近期开展设计工作②。

Mr Wang: We are carrying out the design according to schedule, but the communication design may be affected by other factors.

Jones: What are those factors?

Mr Wang: Such as data collection, determination of technical standards, application of radio frequency and data of related professions and so on.

Jones: What can we do for you?

Mr Wang: We can only promote the design work of the communication after completing the above works on schedule and we will submit a design schedule to the owner for approval.

Jones: We hope you can carry out the design work as soon as possible so as to provide the implementation conditions for later construction design.

Mr Wang: Ok, we will begin to design② soon.

替换单词 Alternative terms

① 技术设计阶段
　技术设计方案审查阶段
　施工图设计阶段
　施工图审查阶段

① technical design stage
　technical design review stage
　construction drawing design stage
　construction drawing review stage

② 通信线路敷设
　通信设备安装
　通信单系统调试

② laying of communication line
　installation of communication equipment
　single communication system debugging

业务情景：设计完成后，进行文件图纸的技术交底。
Scene: After completion of the design, Mr Wang will carry out the technical disclosure of documents and drawings.

典型对话 Conversation

Jones：维护部门和施工单位根据设计内容和图纸内容提出了意见和问题。

Jones: According to the contents of design and drawing, the maintenance department and construction contractor have presented their ideas and issues.

王工程师：好的，我们会结合工程情况、设计原则及所提的意见和问题修改设计方案。

Mr Wang: Ok, we will revise our design according to engineering conditions, design principle and above ideas and issues.

Jones：希望能在两个月时间内完成修改。

Jones: We hope you can complete the revise within two months.

王工程师：我们会按时完成。

Mr Wang: No problem. We will finish it on time.

Jones：通信工程静态验收前，应完成施工图配套文件，并提供给建设单位。

Jones: Before static acceptance of communication work, a complete set of construction drawing documents shall be finished and provided to contractor.

王工程师：已经将配套文件提供给了建设单位。

Mr Wang: We have done that.

Jones：还需要将本工程I类变更①设计文件、施工配合中的工作联系单②更正说明等资料整理完毕，并提供建设单位。

Jones: In addition, you shall sort the change descriptions of Class I change① design document and contact list② for coordinating construction and provide them to contractor.

王工程师：好的，我们会尽快整理完毕并提供给建设单位。做变更设计的内容需要向我们单位发送相关信函。

Jones：好的，我们会尽快整理并发送。

Mr Wang: Ok, we will do it as soon as possible. But please send relevant letters on design change contents to our company.

Jones: Ok, we will sort and send it to you as soon as possible.

替换单词 Alternative terms

① II 类变更
② 施工图

① Class II change
② construction drawing

第一部分　交通工程情景会话

第十五章　信息
Chapter 15　Information

业务情景：为了顺利开展某项目工作，须向业主搜集信息资料。
Scene: In order to carry on the project, Mr Wang is gathering information from the owner.

典型对话 Conversation

王工程师：Jones 先生，我们正在从事某项目的工作，需了解既有铁路信息系统的构成情况。

Jones：请稍等。相关材料都在这里。

王工程师：请问既有信息系统包括哪些系统？
Jones：包括售检票系统、旅客服务信息系统、办公信息系统、货运信息系统等。

王工程师：请问信息系统主要网络设备和服务器设备采用哪个品牌的产品，设备使用了多少年呢？

Jones：信息系统的三层交换机基本采用的是Cisco的，服务器采用的是IBM Power系列的，都已经用了4年了。

Mr Wang: Jones, we hope to know something about composition of the information system of existing railway for the project we involved.

Jones: Ok. Here are the related materials.

Mr Wang: What systems are included in the existing information system?
Jones: It includes systems of automatic fare collection, passenger services information, office information freight information, and etc.

Mr Wang: Which brand of products is adopted for the main network devices and server of information system? How long have the devices been used?

Jones: Cisco is basically used for three layer switches① in information system and IBM Power series for the server, The devices have been used for four years.

195

王工程师：请问售检票系统② 采用哪种组网方式？

Jones：目前采用环型组网③ 的方式。

王工程师：我们还想了解一下目前信息系统的运营维护管理体制、机构设置、定员设置及各机构的职责和管理范围。

Jones：这个内容比较多，我们会根据要求，找相关运营、维护管理部门汇集资料，尽快整理提供给您。

Mr Wang: Which networking mode is adopted for automatic fare collection system② ?

Jones: Ring-type networking③ is adopted currently.

Mr Wang: Furthermore, we'd like to know operation, maintenance and management structures for current information system, institution and staff quota and the responsibility and management scope of each organization.

Jones: As a lot of information is involved, we'll collect it from the related departments of operation, maintenance and management and offer it to you as soon as possible.

替换单词 Alternative terms

① 路由器
   二层交换机
   网络设备
② 旅客服务信息系统
   办公信息系统
   防灾安全监控系统
   客票系统
   自动售检票系统
   货物运输管理信息系统

③ 星形组网
   树型组网

① router
   two-layer switch
   network equipment
② passenger services information system
   office information system
   disaster prevention and safety monitoring system
   ticketing and reservation system
   automatic fare collection system
   freight transportation management information system

③ star type networking
   tree shape networking

第一部分　交通工程情景会话

业务情景： 王工程师与 Jones 讨论信息系统的设计方案。
Scene: Mr Wang and Jones are discussing the design plan of information system.

典型对话 Conversation

王工程师： Jones 先生您好，今天我们开会主要讨论信息系统的设计方案，希望会议中能够达成共识。

Jones： 好的，设计方案必须满足合同的要求，在满足合同的基础上再对细节进行讨论。

王工程师： 我们的设计方案是严格按照合同进行设计的，对于合同中没有明确的问题希望在讨论中达成共识。下面我们就按照各个系统进行讨论可以吗？

Jones： 可以，我们就按照合同中各系统的顺序进行讨论。

王工程师： 首先我想讨论客票系统①的设置地点和规模。

Jones： 好的。

王工程师： 根据铁路走向以及途经城市的规模和重要型，我们建议在吉布提设置本线的客票系统中心，客票系统中心面积按照 400m² 考虑，你觉得可以吗？

Jones： 我同意您的建议。

Mr Wang: Hello! Jones. Today we'll mainly discuss the design plan of information system, and I hope we'll reach a consensus.

Jones: Ok. The design plan must meet the requirements of contract. On this base, the details shall be discussed.

Mr Wang: Our scheme is designed in strict accordance with the contract. For the questions not clearly defined in the contract, I hope an agreement will be reached by discussion. Shall we begin now?

Jones: Yes, let's discuss according to the sequence of each system in the contract.

Mr Wang: First, we'll discuss the location and scale of ticketing and reservation system①.

Jones: Ok.

Mr Wang: From the railway alignment, scale and importance of the cities which railway passes through, we suggest the ticketing and reservation system centre with area of 400m² to be set at Djibouti. Do you think so?

Jones: Yes.

王工程师：我们在每一个办理客运作业的车站设置车站级客票系统。

Jones：车站级客票系统设计的依据是什么？

王工程师：根据车站旅客最高聚集人数②来确定客票系统的设置规模。

Jones：车站系统由哪些设备构成？

王工程师：包括服务器、管理工作站、业务管理终端、维护终端、票务安全设备及现场设备。

Jones：现场设备包括哪些设备？

王工程师：现场设备包括窗口售票机、自动售票机、补票机、进站闸机、出站闸机等。

Jones：本线采用哪种票制？

王工程师：采用磁介质纸票③。

Mr Wang: The station-level ticketing and reservation system shall be set at each station which serves the passenger.

Jones: What's its design basis?

Mr Wang: The scale is determined according to maximum gathered station passengers②.

Jones: What equipment constitutes the station system?

Mr Wang: Server, management workstation, business management terminal, maintenance terminal, safe ticketing equipment and field devices.

Jones: What's included in field devices?

Mr Wang: Ticket booth, ticket vending machine, fare adjustment machine, train brake machine and outbound brake machine and so on.

Jones: What kind of ticket system shall be adopted for this line?

Mr Wang: Magnetic medium paper tickets③ shall be adopted.

替换单词 Alternative terms

① 票务系统
   自动售检票系统
② 高峰小时上下车人数
③ 二维码纸票
   非接触式 IC 卡

① ticketing system
   automatic fare collection system
② number of passengers getting on or off the train at peak hour
③ QR code paper tickets
   contactless IC card

第一部分　交通工程情景会话

业务情景：王工程师与工程师 Jones 讨论旅客服务信息系统。
Scene: Mr Wang is discussing the passenger service information system with Jones.

典型对话 Conversation

Jones：本工程在哪些地方设置旅客服务信息系统？
王工程师：每一个办理客运作业的车站均设置车站级旅客服务信息系统。
Jones：旅客服务信息系统设计的依据是什么？
王工程师：根据车站站房面积来确定旅客服务信息系统的设置规模。
Jones：系统采用什么架构？

王工程师：本线采用中心—车站两级系统架构。
Jones：旅客服务信息系统的中心在哪里？
王工程师：本次设计，我们暂时考虑在吉布提设置本线的旅客服务信息系统中心。
Jones：旅客服务信息系统由哪些子系统构成？
王工程师：旅客服务信息系统包括综合显示系统、广播系统、视频监视系统、入侵报警系统、门禁系统、时钟系统、信息查询系统、旅客携带物品安全检查设施等。

Jones: Where shall the passenger service information system be set?
Mr Wang: At each station servicing passengers .
Jones: What's the design basis of passenger service information system?
Mr Wang: Its scale is determined according to the station building area.
Jones: What framework shall be adopted for the system?
Mr Wang: Two-grade system of centre-station framework shall be adopted.
Jones: Where is its centre?

Mr Wang: Temporarily, we consider to set it at Djibouti for this line.
Jones: What subsystems make up the passenger service information system?
Mr Wang: It includes integrated display system, broadcasting system, video monitoring system, intruder alarm system, access control system, clock system, information service system and safety inspection facilities for luggage carried by passengers, etc.

Jones: 综合显示系统采用哪些终端设备？

王工程师: 综合显示系统终端设备包括 LED 显示屏[①]、PDP 显示屏。

Jones: 请介绍一下视频监视系统方案。

王工程师: 视频监视系统在各楼层办公区域走道、机房入口、票据室、售票室、候车区域、检票区域、站台等地设置前端摄像机[②]。在综合监控室、值班室设置视频终端，完成以上区域视频图像的调用查看。

Jones: 是否能提供更详细的说明。

王工程师: 本次会议我们先确定系统的框架和主要技术标准，下次会议我们会给您提供更详细的资料。

Jones: What terminal equipment shall be used for integrated display system?

Mr Wang: It includes LED panel[①], PDP panel.

Jones: Please describe video monitoring system scheme.

Mr Wang: The places such as office aisle of each floor, computer room entrance, billing room, booking office, waiting area, check-in area and platform shall be set with front-end cameras[②]. The video terminal shall be set in comprehensive monitoring room and duty room to review and monitor the video image of the above areas.

Jones: Can you provide us more details?

Mr Wang: This time we'll first confirm the framework and major technical standards of the system, and we'll offer you more detailed data at next meeting.

替换单词 Alternative terms

① 全彩 LED 显示屏
　室内高亮双基色显示屏
　室外超高亮双基色显示屏
② 固定半球摄像机
　一体化快球摄像机
　固定枪机
　带云台枪机

① full color LED panel
　indoor highlight two basic color panel
　outdoor super-bright two basic color panel
② fixed dome camera
　integrated fast ball camera
　fixed bolt
　tilt head video cameras

第一部分　交通工程情景会话

业务情景：王工程师与工程师 Jones 讨论货物运输管理信息系统、防灾安全监控系统等方案。
Scene: Mr Wang is discussing the schemes of cargo transportation management information system and disaster prevention and safety monitoring system with Jones.

典型对话 Conversation

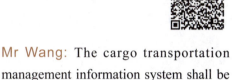

王工程师：我们在每一个办理货运作业的车站设置货物运输管理信息系统。

Jones：货物运输管理信息系统设计的依据是什么？

王工程师：根据车站每天货物的装车卸车量来确定系统的设置规模。

Jones：货物运输管理信息系统的中心在哪里？

王工程师：考虑在吉布提设置本线的货物运输管理信息系统中心。

王工程师：现在我们讨论一下防灾安全监控系统①方案。

Jones：防灾安全监控系统设计的依据是什么？

王工程师：根据沿线地质地貌、气候及主要自然灾害情况和车站②分布情况及性质，设置相应的子系统。

Jones：包括哪些子系统？

Mr Wang: The cargo transportation management information system shall be set at each handling freight station.

Jones: What's the design basis of the system?

Mr Wang: The scale of system is determined according to the loading and unloading quantity of station per day.

Jones: Where's the centre of the system?

Mr Wang: It's considered to be set at Djibuti.

Mr Wang: Let's go on to the disaster prevention and safety monitoring system① scheme.

Jones: What's its design basis?

Mr Wang: Corresponding subsystems are set according to the geology, geomorphology, climate, and conditions of main natural disasters, stations'② distributions and their characters along the line.

Jones: What subsystems are included?

201

王工程师：包括风监测子系统、雨量监测子系统、地震监控子系统、异物侵限监控子系统。

Jones：很好，谢谢！

王工程师：很高兴今天与您讨论，对部分内容达成了共识，对于我方开展下阶段的工作起到了积极的作用，同时我方希望就我们达成共识的内容形成会议纪要并且签署，非常感谢。

Jones：我也很高兴，我们的目标都是一致的，希望把工作做好，现在我们就对会议内容进行梳理，并起草会议纪要。

Mr Wang: It includes four monitoring subsystems of wind, rainfall, earthquake and foreign invasion.

Jones: Quite good, thank you.

Mr Wang: Very glad to discuss with you and some contents are agreed. It is positive for our works in the next stage. I hope the meeting minutes will be recorded and signed, thank you.

Jones: I am glad too. We have the same goal. I'll draft the meeting minutes right now.

替换单词 Alternative terms

① 然灾害及异物侵限监测系统　　① natural disaster and foreign invasion monitoring system

② 段　　② depot
　 所　　　 point

业务情景：为了顺利开展某项目工作，王工程师向业主代表 Jones 搜集信息资料。

Scene: Mr Wang is gathering information from Jones, the owner's representative, in order to carry out the project smoothly.

典型对话 Conversation

王工程师：本项目信息系统主要由以下几个系统构成：客票发售与预订系统、旅客服务信息系统、货物运输管理信息

Mr Wang: The information system of the project consists of the following systems: ticketing and reservation, passenger service

第一部分　交通工程情景会话

系统。接下来,我将逐一对每个系统设计方案进行汇报。

Jones: 好的。

王工程师: 客票发售与预订系统采用中心—车站的分级结构设计。Labu 调度楼设置客票发售与预订系统中心,各客运车站设置客票发售与预订系统车站级设备。

Jones: 中心包括哪些设备?

王工程师: 中心包括服务器[①]、管理维护终端、网络及电源设备等。

Jones: 车站设置哪些设备?

王工程师: 车站设置窗口售票终端、网络及电源设备等。

Jones: 本线采用什么票制?

王工程师: 车票票制采用磁介质纸质车票[②]。

Jones: 系统网络构成方案是如何考虑的?

王工程师: 客票发售与预订系统采用独立组网方式。车站客票系统以两个 2Mb/s 通道接入 Labu 调度楼的售票中心。

information and cargo transportation management information system. Here's the design scheme report of each system.

Jones: Ok.

Mr Wang: The ticketing and reservation system shall adopt centre-station graded structure. The centre of the system shall be set at Labu dispatch building. The station-level ticketing and reservation system shall be set at each passenger station.

Jones: What equipment are included in centre?

Mr Wang: Server[①], maintenance and management terminal, network and power unit, etc. are included.

Jones: What equipment shall be set in the station?

Mr Wang: The window ticketing terminal, network, power unit and so on.

Jones: Which ticket system shall be adopted for the line?

Mr Wang: Magnetic medium paper tickets[②].

Jones: How is the constitution scheme of system network?

Mr Wang: The ticketing and reservation system adopts independent networking mode, with two 2Mb/s channels accessing the ticket centre of Labu dispatch building.

Jones: 系统有哪些主要功能？

王工程师: 主要包括交易处理、检票处理、业务管理、收入管理、统计管理、系统管理监控等功能。

Jones: What functions does the system mainly possess?

Mr Wang: Such functions as transaction processing, checking in, business management, revenue management, statistical management, system management and monitoring are included.

替换单词 Alternative terms

① 小型机
   PC 服务器
② IC 卡
   非接触式 IC 卡

① minicomputer
   PC server
② IC card
   contactless IC card

业务情景: 王工程师与工程师 Jones 讨论旅客服务信息系统。
Scene: Mr Wang is discussing passenger service information system with Jones.

典型对话 Conversation

王工程师: 旅客服务信息系统包含综合显示系统、客运广播系统、时钟系统以及综合布线系统。

Jones: 综合显示系统包括哪些终端？

王工程师: 售票屏、进站屏、到发通告显示终端等。

Mr Wang: The passenger service information system includes integrated display system, broadcasting system for passenger, clock system and premises distribution system.

Jones: Which terminals are included in the integrated display system?

Mr Wang: The ticketing screen, entrance screen, arrival-departure announcement display terminal and so on.

Jones: 广播系统是如何考虑的?

王工程师: 客运车站设置小型铁路车站<u>模拟广播系统</u>①。系统由主控设备、人工呼叫站、噪声探测、功率放大器、扬声器和音频调节器等设备构成。

Jones: 广播分区是如何设置的?

王工程师: 车站的广播负荷分区按照售票厅、候车厅、检票口、站台、办公等区域进行划分。

Jones: 扬声器采用哪些规格型号?

王工程师: 采用吸顶式② 5W 扬声器。

Jones: 请介绍一下时钟系统的设计方案。

王工程师: 车站设置 GPS 天线及二级母钟,接收统一时钟源,对整个站区内的子钟和相关系统进行时钟同步,并驱动本站所有子钟同步。客运车站的基本站台和中间站台各设两个双面指针式子钟。

Jones: 综合布线系统是如何设计的?

Jones: How is the broadcasting system considered?

Mr Wang: The passenger station shall be set with <u>analog broadcasting system</u>① for small railway stations. The system consists of main control equipment, manual calling station, noise detection, power amplifier, loudspeaker and tone control, etc.

Jones: How is the broadcasting section divided?

Mr Wang: The station broadcasting section is divided based on ticketing hall, waiting hall, fare gate, platform and administrative area, etc.

Jones: Which type of the loudspeaker shall be used?

Mr Wang: 5W <u>ceiling type</u>② loudspeaker.

Jones: Please tell me about the design scheme of clock system.

Mr Wang: The station shall be set with GPS antenna and level II master clock, receiving the unified clock source, synchronizing all the secondary clocks and related systems of the whole station area. The basic platform and intermediate platform in passenger station shall be set with 2 secondary clocks with pointers on double dials.

Jones: How is the premises distribution system designed?

王工程师：本工程采用超五类非屏蔽双绞线、光缆、信息插座、配线架等对整个站房进行布线，满足用户对语音、数据的通信需求。

Mr Wang: The wiring in the whole station building shall adopt UTP, optical cable, telecommunications outlet and distribution frame, etc. to meet the communication requirements of voice and data for users.

替换单词 Alternative terms

① 数字广播系统
② 壁挂式
　　线阵式

① digital audio broadcasting system
② wall-mounted
　　linear array

业务情景：王工程师与工程师 Jones 讨论货物运输管理信息系统。
Scene: Mr Wang is discussing the freight transportation management information system with Jones.

典型对话 Conversation

王工程师：系统采用中心—车站的分级结构设计。在 Labu 调度中心设置货物运输管理信息系统中心设备，在本线各货运车站设置车站级设备。

Mr Wang: The system shall adopt centre-station graded structure design. The centre equipment of the system shall be set at Labu dispatch centre. The station-level equipment shall be set at each freight station.

Jones：中心包括哪些设备？

Jones: Which devices are included in the centre?

王工程师：中心包括服务器、管理维护终端、网络及电源设备等。

Mr Wang: Server, maintenance and management terminal, network and power unit, etc.

Jones: 车站设置哪些设备？

王工程师: 车站设置作业终端、网络及电源设备等。

Jones: 系统网络构成方案是如何考虑的？

王工程师: 系统采用<u>独立组网</u>①方式。Sebetta、Indode、Mojo、Adama、Mieso 站分别设置 1 台路由器，通过传输系统提供 2Mb/s 通道接入 Labu 调度中心，接口采用 E1（FE 电口）。

Jones: 局域网方案是如何考虑的呢？

王工程师: 货物运输管理信息系统局域网由两层构建，核心汇聚层设置 1 台二层交换机，接入层设置二层交换机接入各现场设备。

Jones: 系统有哪些主要功能？

王工程师: 货物运输管理信息系统满足运输组织、货运营销的需要。系统主要包括货运计划、货运制票、列车确报三大模块。

Jones: What equipment shall be set in the station?

Mr Wang: The operation terminal, network, power unit and so on.

Jones: How is the system network constitution scheme considered?

Mr Wang: The system adopts <u>independent networking</u>① mode. One router is set respectively at such stations as Sebetta, Indode, Mojo, Adama and Mieso, providing 2Mb/s channel accessing Labu dispatch centre via transmission system, with E1 (FE) adopted for the interface.

Jones: How about LAN scheme?

Mr Wang: LAN of the system is constructed with two layers: the core convergence layer is set with one two-layer switch, and the access layer is set with a two-layer switch to connect each field device.

Jones: What functions does the system mainly possess?

Mr Wang: The system satisfies the requirements of transportation organization and freight marketing. The system mainly includes such three modules as freight transport plan, freight transport bills printing and train list information after departure.

替换单词 Alternative terms

① IP 数据网   ① IP data network

业务情景：王工程师与工程师 Jones 讨论设计工作安排。
Scene: Mr Wang is discussing the arrangement of design work with Jones.

典型对话 Conversation

王工程师： 信息系统设计工作安排主要分为下面几个阶段：资料收集、技术标准确定、前期设计、前期方案审查及讨论、技术设计、技术设计方案审查及讨论、施工图设计、施工图审查及讨论。

Mr Wang: The information system design work is mainly divided into the following stages: data collection; technical standards definition; earlier stage design, earlier stage scheme review and discussion; technical design; scheme review and discussion for technical design; construction drawing design; scheme review and discussion for construction drawing design.

Jones： 根据工程的工期要求，需在一个月时间完成设计工作。

Jones: According to the time limit of the project, the design work must be completed in one month.

王工程师： 目前我们按照该时间计划开展设计工作，但是信息设计工作会受资料收集①等方面因素限制。我们将提供一个设计工期计划表给业主审批。

Mr Wang: Currently, we're carrying on the information system design work according to the schedule, but maybe restricted by factors such as data collection①. We'll provide a design schedule to the owner for approval.

Jones: 希望尽快开展设计工作，为后期施工设计提供实施条件。

王工程师：信息的建设工期主要包括以下几个阶段：进场准备、熟悉施工图纸、设备及材料招标采购、信息系统设备安装、信息系统调试、验收及相关资料准备。

Jones: 维护部门和施工单位根据设计内容和图纸内容提出了意见和问题。

王工程师：我们会结合工程情况和设计原则修改。

Jones: 希望能在一个月时间内完成修改。

王工程师：好的，我们会按时完成。

Jones: I hope you can carry out your design as soon as possible so as to supply conditions to implement the construction design at the next stage.

Mr Wang: The construction period includes mobilization, getting familiar with construction drawings, equipment & material purchase by public bidding, information system equipment installation, debugging, acceptance inspection and related data preparation.

Jones: The maintenance department and construction party have put forward opinions and problems according to the design content and drawings.

Mr Wang: We'll make alterations based on engineering conditions and design principles.

Jones: I hope alterations shall be completed in a month.

Mr Wang: We'll complete it on time.

替换单词 Alternative terms

① 技术标准确定
　相关专业资料提供

① technical standard determination
　related specialty data supplying

业务情景：王工程师与工程师 Jones 讨论配合施工。
Scene: Mr Wang is discussing the construction coordination with Jones.

典型对话 Conversation

Jones: 信息工程静态验收前，应完成施工图配套文件，并提供给建设单位。

王工程师: 我方已经将配套文件提供给了建设单位。

Jones: 还需要将本工程Ⅰ类变更设计文件①、施工配合中的工作联系单、施工图更正说明等资料整理完毕，提供给建设单位。

王工程师: 好的，我们会尽快整理完毕并提供给建设单位。做变更设计的内容需要向我们单位发送相关信函。

Jones: 我们会尽快发送。

Jones: The supportive documents of construction drawing shall be completed and provided to the construction party before static acceptance of information engineering.

Mr Wang: Our party has already provided the supportive documents to the construction party.

Jones: Such data as Type Ⅰ altered design document① of the project, liaison bills to coordinate construction and discription on construction drawing's correction also need to be organized and provided to the construction party.

Mr Wang: Yes, we will. The related letter about altered design content needs to be sent to our party.

Jones: Ok. We will send it soon.

替换单词 Alternative terms

① Ⅱ类变更设计文件　　　　① Type Ⅱ altered design document

第一部分　交通工程情景会话

业务情景：王工程师与工程师 Jones 参加咨询大纲审查会。
Scene: Mr Wang and Jones are attending the consultation outline review meeting.

典型对话 Conversation

王工程师：今天对本次咨询大纲进行汇报。
Jones：请介绍一下咨询大纲内容。
王工程师：咨询大纲主要包括咨询重点和咨询内容。
Jones：咨询重点有哪些？
王工程师：信息系统[①]设计方案的完整性、系统构成、网络结构设计等。

Jones：咨询内容包括哪些？

王工程师：对信息系统的设计原则、方案、说明、投资进行审核。

Mr Wang: I'd like to report about the consulting outline.
Jones: Please.
Mr Wang: It mainly includes the consulting focuses and consulting content.
Jones: What are the consulting focuses?
Mr Wang: Integrity of the designing scheme for information system[①]; system composition; network structure design, etc.
Jones: What are included in consulting contents?
Mr Wang: The design principles, scheme, instruction and investment for the information system shall be approved and verified.

替换单词 Alternative terms

① 旅客服务信息系统
　办公自动化系统
　公共安全管理信息系统

　综合维修管理信息系统

　防灾安全监控系统

① passenger services information system
　office automation system
　public security management information system
　comprehensive maintenance management information system
　disaster prevention and safety monitoring system

业务情景：王工程师参加咨询会议，与相关方代表 Jones 沟通，提出咨询意见。
Scene: Mr Wang is attending the consulting meeting, communicating with Jones, the interested party representative, and putting forward the advisory opinion.

典型对话 Conversation

Jones: 请介绍一下现场核对情况。

王工程师: 主要是既有中心系统配合工程①，如本线信息系统的网络接入。

Jones: 既有车站需要现场核对哪些内容呢？

王工程师: 包括既有车站信息系统组成、既有信息系统前端设备数量及安装位置等。

Jones: 目前有哪些咨询意见？

王工程师: 请在接口说明中补充旅客服务信息系统与票务系统的接口内容。请补充与通信②专业的接口界面。

Jones: 好的，请设计方根据咨询意见修改文件。

Jones: Please describe the site verification.

Mr Wang: It mainly focuses on subsidiaries① of the existing central system, such as network access of information system.

Jones: What needs to be verified at site for the existing station?

Mr Wang: The existing station information system's composition, quantity and installation locations of front-end equipment, etc. are included.

Jones: What advisory opinions are there at present?

Mr Wang: Please supply the content of interface between passenger service information system and ticketing system in the interface description; supply the interface to communication② specialty.

Jones: Ok. The designer shall alter the documents according to the advisory opinions.

替换单词 Alternative terms

① 既有车站信息系统设置情况　　① existing station information system settings
② 电力　　② electric power
　结构　　　structure
　暖通　　　heating and ventilation
　信号　　　signal
　桥梁　　　bridge
　路基　　　subgrade
　隧道　　　tunnel
　牵引变电　traction power transformation

业务情景：王工程师汇报咨询成果，并回答业主代表 Jones 提出的问题。
Scene: Mr Wang is giving the consulting result report, answering questions from the owner's representative Jones.

典型对话 Conversation

王工程师： 今天我将信息专业的咨询成果给各位进行汇报，包括咨询概述、重大咨询意见及关键技术、优化意见、咨询意见执行情况及取得的成绩四个方面。

Mr Wang: Now I'd like to give a report on consultation result of information specialty including four aspects of consulting introduction, major advisory opinions and executive condition of key technologies, optimizing opinions, advisory opinions and achieved results.

Jones： 好的，请讲。

Jones: Please go on.

王工程师： 专业咨询概述包括三方面：（1）审核施工图对初步设计批复意见的执行情况。是否有重大变更及其相应的批文和说明。设计内容和系统方案

Mr Wang: The consulting introduction includes: firstly, to verify executive conditions of official opinions from preliminary design on construction drawing,

是否符合相关标准和设计规范。
（2）审核信息系统设计采用的技术方案是否合理①。
（3）审核信息系统设计方案的完整性，以及本专业与其他专业及系统之间的接口、分工界面是否清晰。

Jones：有哪些重大咨询意见及关键技术？

王工程师：首先请设计单位确认各车站客运服务信息系统是否包含综合布线系统。其次请核实各车站是否设置自助查询系统。最后建议在接口说明中补充旅客服务信息系统与票务系统的接口。

Jones：有何优化意见？

王工程师：我们建议每个站台敷设至少两根广播线。补充窗口屏的线缆型号及走线方式。建议统一采用相同芯数的单模光缆。总之，设计单位基本按照咨询意见进行修改，取得良好效果。

whether there is a major alteration and its corresponding approval and instruction, whether the design content and system scheme meet the relevant standard and design codes; secondly, to verify whether the technical proposal adopted for information system is rational①; thirdly, to verify the integrity of design scheme and whether the interface between information and other specialties or systems is clear.

Jones: What major advisory opinions and key technologies are there?

Mr Wang: First, the design party should confirm whether the passenger service information system of each station includes premises distribution system; second, please verify whether the self-help enquiry system is set in each station; at last we suggest to supplement the interface between passenger service information system and ticketing system in the interface instruction.

Jones: Any optimizing opinions?

Mr Wang: We suggest that each station should be laid with at least 2 broadcasting lines. The cable model and wiring mode of window screen should be supplemented. The unified single-mode optical cable with same cores is suggested to be used. Design party has basically revised its design according to advisory opinions and achieved a better result.

替换单词 Alternative terms

① 可靠   ① reliable
  经济   economic

第十六章　牵引供电
Chapter 16　Tractive Power Supply

业务情景： 中方李工程师到埃塞俄比亚国家电网公司收集资料，Richard 先生接待。

Scene: Chinese engineer Mr Li is going to the Ethiopian Electric Power Corporation (EEPCO) to collect data. Richard is receiving him.

典型对话 Conversation

李工程师： 我们正在进行埃塞埃塞铁路的设计工作，需要收集贵国电网的一些资料，包括埃塞电网现状及规划地理接线图。

Richard： 我们国家电网频率为 50Hz，电压等级分为 400kV、230kV、132kV 等，电源构成主要以水力发电为主，占电网总装机容量的 70%，剩余火电①占 30%，电网总装机容量为 350 万 kW。

李工程师： 请根据这张铁路线路示意图介绍一下沿线电网现状。

Mr Li: As we are working on the design of a railway project in this country, we need electrical grid data from your company, such as the current situation and planned geographical wiring diagram of Ethiopian electrical grid.

Richard: In Ethiopia, the grid frequency is 50Hz, voltage classes are 400kV, 230kV and 132kV. Hydroelectricity is the main component of power sources, accounting for 70% of the gross installed capacity of electrical grid, while the rest 30% is provided by thermal power①. The gross installed capacity is 3.5million kW.

Mr Li: Here is the railway alignment diagram. Could you please explain the situation of electrical grid along this railway?

216

第一部分　交通工程情景会话

Richard: 沿线电源点有一水电站，分布有 3 座 230kV 变电站，以 230kV 单回线路为主干，132kV 线路辐射构成。

李工程师: 沿线规划情况呢？

Richard: 根据 2020 年电网建设规划，电厂将增加 50 万 kW 装机容量，达到 100 万 kW 装机容量，沿线将新建 1 座 400kV② 变电站，形成 230kV 双回输电线路。

李工程师: 请预测一下目前电网承担铁路牵引供电负荷的能力。

Richard: 目前电网运行情况比较良好，在丰水季有部分剩余电量出口邻国，能否承担铁路牵引负荷需要贵公司正式提供铁路负荷需求资料，经过详细分析、论证后，才能得出相应结论。

李工程师: 你这里有沿线变电站的系统短路容量资料吗？

Richard: Hydropower station is a the power source and three substations of 230kV are distributed along the line. Single circuit of 230kV is the main cable and lines of 132kV are radiated from it.

Mr Li: How about the planning for areas along the railway?

Richard: According to the electrical grid construction planning in 2020, the installed capacity of a power plant will be increased by 500000kW and then the gross installed capacity will be 1million kW by that time. And there will be a new substation of 400kV②, forming double circuit power supply of 230kV.

Mr Li: In your estimation, is the load capacity in current grid capable for railway traction power?

Richard: The current situation seems fine. We have extra power for export in wet season. If you need my further comment on load capacity for railway traction power, I need an official railway load demand data from your side. The conclusion will be based on detailed analysis and demonstration.

Mr Li: Do you have system short circuit capacity data of substations along the line?

Richard：系统短路容量随着电网的建设和发展在不断发生变化，每年我们都需要进行重新计算，更新资料。去年的数据是沿线230kV（132kV）变电站230kV系统短路容量最大为8000MV·A，最小为4000MV·A，132kV系统短路容量最大为1200MV·A，最小为600MV·A。

李工程师：我们还想了解一下贵国电网建设的工程造价的大致情况。

Richard：一般情况下，建设1座230kV（132kV）变电站③大约需要1亿本地货币。

李工程师：请问贵国对于牵引变电所外部电源的建设及管理模式是怎样的？

Richard：外部电源工程应包括在贵方的合同范围内，由贵方负责建设，建成后移交给我方，由我方负责管理。

李工程师：那你们电网公司，与铁路公司在管理和维护上的分工和界面是怎样的？

Richard: The system short circuit capacity is constantly changing with construction and development of electrical grid. We have to re-calculate and update the data every year. Last year, for 230kV (132kV) substation with the short circuit capacity of 230kV system is 8000MV·A in maximum and 4000MV·A in minimum, while the short circuit capacity of 132kV is 1200MV·A in maximum and 600MV·A in minimum.

Mr Li: How about the construction cost of the grid in your country?

Richard: Generally, the cost to build a substation of 230kV (132kV)③ is about 100 million Birr.

Mr Li: How about the construction and management codes of external power supply for traction substations in your country?

Richard: Generally, the external power supply will be provided by you according to the agreement. You build it, and we take over and take care of it.

Mr Li: Could you specify the respective responsibilities of your company and Ethiopian Railway Company for maintenance and management?

第一部分　交通工程情景会话

Richard：管理和维护的界面以牵引变电所进线的最后一个杆塔为分界，杆塔（包括杆塔）以外的线路、间隔、变电站等由电网公司负责管理和维护；杆塔（不包括杆塔）以内的牵引变电所由铁路公司负责管理和维护。

李工程师：请问电网公司对铁路用户的收费政策如何？

Richard：电网公司对铁路牵引用电按大工业用户收费，实施两部制电价政策，其中基本电费为每月30元本地货币（比尔）/(kV·A)，电度电费为0.6比尔/kW·h。

Richard: The last tower of the traction substation incoming line is the interface between us and Ethiopian Railway Company. We only maintain and manage the lines, intervals and substations beyond the tower. The tower itself is also our responsibility. Substations within the tower will be the railway company's reasonability.

Mr Li: How do you charge railway customers?

Richard: We charge large industrial customers for basic usage which is 30 Birr per kV·A per month and actual usage which is 0.6 Birr per kW·h. This policy applies to railway traction power supply.

替换单词 Alternative terms

① 水电
　风能
　潮汐能
② 230kV
　132kV
③ 增加1个230kV（132kV）出线间隔

　建设1公里230kV（132kV）输电线路

① hydroelectricity
　wind energy source
　tidal power
② 230kV
　132kV
③ add one outgoing line interval of 230kV (132kV)

　build one kilometer of 230kV (132kV) electric transmission line

业务情景：中方李工程师到埃塞俄比亚铁路公司收集既有电气化铁路资料，Richard 先生接待。
Scene: Mr Li is going to Ethiopian Railway Company to collect data about railway electrification. Richard is receiving him.

典型对话 Conversation

李工程师：请问贵国电气化铁路采用的主要技术标准是什么？

Mr Li: Could you please tell me about the main specification of railway electrification in Ethiopia?

Richard：这条 A 到 B 的双线干线铁路，全长 300km，设计最高运行速度为 140km/h，最大坡度为 15‰，采用 C 型电力机车，双机牵引 3500t，信号采用自动闭塞，最小追踪间隔时分是 10min。

Richard: This double track trunk railway, 300km long from A to B with the highest design running speed of 140km/h and the maximum slope of 15‰. Type-C electric locomotives are used on this line with two engines generating traction power of 3500 tons. Automatic blocking system with minimum train trace interval of ten minutes is applied.

李工程师：请介绍一下改线牵引供电系统的主要技术标准。

Mr Li: How about the specification of traction power system for the reconstructed line?

Richard：牵引供电系统采用<u>单相工频（50Hz）交流</u>[①]供电方式，牵引网额定电压为 <u>25kV（3000V、1500V、750V）</u>，供电方式采用<u>带回流线的直接供电方式</u>[②]。

Richard: Traction power system adopts single-phased AC power supply with 50 Hz <u>industrial frequency</u>[①]. Rated voltage for traction grid is 25kV (3000V, 1500V, 750V). The power supply mode is <u>direct feed with return cable (T-R-NF)</u>[②].

李工程师：这是该线的牵引供电设施分布示意图[③]吗？

Mr Li: Is this the <u>distribution diagram of traction power facilities</u>[③]?

Richard: 是的。全线共有 7 座牵引变电所、7 座分区所和 1 座开闭所。这是各所的<u>牵引变压器</u>④安装容量，这是馈线分布情况，每个所都由电力系统引入两路 132kV 电源供电。

李工程师：这条线路的牵引负荷情况怎么样？牵引变压器的接线形式是怎样的、容量利用率怎么样？

Richard: 这条铁路于 2010 年开通，单个机车电流大约是 400A，牵引变压器是<u>单相接线</u>⑤，容量利用率大约为 10%。

李工程师：A 牵引变电所有预留和扩建的条件吗？

Richard: 有一定条件，我建议你们最好能到 A 牵引变电所现场看一看，以便收集和了解情况。另外，我们有一个调度中心，负责牵引供电系统的调度指挥。

Richard: Yes, it is. There are totally 7 traction substations, 7 section post and 1 switching station. This is the installed capacity of <u>traction transformer</u>④ in each station, and this is distribution diagram of feeder line. Each station has two power sources of 132kV supplied by electric power system.

Mr Li: How about the traction load of this line? What's the connection mode for traction transformer? What about the rate of capacity utilization?

Richard: This railway has started operation since 2010. Current for single locomotive is about 400A. Traction transformer adopts <u>single-phase connection</u>⑤. The rate of capacity utilization is around 10%.

Mr Li: Are there any reservation or extension conditions for traction substation A?

Richard: To some degree, yes. I suggest you pay a visit to the site. You can check by yourself and gather more information you need. Besides, we have one dispatching centre for traction power supply.

替换单词 Alternative terms

① 直流
② AT 供电方式
　BT 供电方式
　直接供电方式

① direct current
② power supply mode of AT
　power supply mode of BT
　direct power supply mode（T-R）

③ 供电分段示意图	③ power supply sectionalizing diagram
④ 自耦变压器	④ auto-transformer
所用变压器	house transformer
⑤ 三相 VV 接线	⑤ three-phase VV connection
平衡接线	balanced connection
星-三角接线	star-delta connection
斯科特接线	scott connection

业务情景： 中方李工程师与外方工程师 Richard 讨论牵引变电所接入电力系统的相关问题。

Scene: Mr Li is discussing with the foreign engineer Richard about incoming power supply system for traction substations.

典型对话 Conversation

李工程师： 每个牵引变电所的安装容量近期（远期）大约是 32MV·A，近期（远期）电量需求大约是 4000 万 kW·h/（所·年），结合贵国电网情况，初步考虑采用 132kV 电压等级供电。

Mr Li: The installed capacity for each substation in short term (long term) is about 32MV·A. The demand for power supply in short term (long term) is about 40 million kW·h per station per year. Our preliminary plan is to adopt 132kV voltage class for power supply considering the current situation of this country.

Richard： 采用 132kV 电压等级供电是经济、合理的。

Richard: This configuration is economical and reasonable.

李工程师：我们初步考虑采用三相VV接线牵引变压器①。我们会提供一个关于不同接线牵引变压器的对照比较资料。希望贵方收到资料后，尽快组织专家分析、讨论，确定牵引变压器接线形式，以保证工程设计的进度要求。

Mr Li: Traction transformer of three-phase VV connection① is the option we came up with first. We will compare traction transformers with different connection modes and compile a document for you. To make sure we can follow the time schedule for engineering design, we hope you will organize an expert panel to analyze and discuss it upon receiving our document.

Richard：我们收到资料3天后，会召集相关会议，尽快就牵引变压器接线形式给出明确意见。

Richard: We will gather our experts for a meeting to determine the connection mode of traction transformer in three days after we receive your document.

李工程师：贵国是否有电能质量方面的相关规程、规范？

Mr Li: Do you have any specifications or regulation for the quality of electric energy?

Richard：目前还没有，主要遵照IEC（国际电工委员会）的相关规程、规范。

Richard: Not yet. We usually follow the regulation and specification of IEC (*International Electrotechnical Commission*).

替换单词 Alternative terms

① 单相牵引变压器
　 平衡牵引变压器
　 星-三角牵引变压器

① Single-phase traction transformer
　 balancing traction transformer
　 star-delta traction transformer

业务情景：中方李工程师与外方工程师 Richard 讨论牵引供电系统设计方案问题。

Scene: Mr Li is discussing with the foreign engineer Richard about design proposals for traction power supply system.

典型对话 Conversation

李工程师：我们今天要讨论的牵引供电系统方案，包括牵引网供电方式、牵引变电所进线电压等级、牵引变压器接线形式、牵引变电所分布方案等。

Mr Li: Today we will discuss traction power supply proposals, including power supply mode of traction grid, voltage class of incoming line in substation, connection mode of traction transformer and substation distribution plan.

Richard：我们很乐意就这几个问题与贵方进线讨论。

Richard: It would be our pleasure to discuss with you on those subjects.

李工程师：首先我们推荐采用带回流线的直接供电方式，初步设计①中已对几种供电方式进行了详细的比较。

Mr Li: First, we recommend adopting direct power supply with return feeder （T-R-NF）. We have already made detailed comparison among several proposals in preliminary designs①.

Richard：我们认为采用带回流线的直接供电方式对本线而言是经济、合理的，但需要注意的是远期运量增加、速度提高后，牵引网的供电能力能否满足要求，是否应在初期建设中对相关补强措施进行一定的预留。

Richard: Your suggestion is economical and reasonable. However, we must pay attention to issues such as whether the capacity of traction grid could meet demand after speed and ridership being increased in long-term period, whether we should make more reservation in reinforcing measures in preliminary construction period.

李工程师：在我方的设计中，牵引供电系统能力是按照满足远期运能、运量和运行速度要求配置的。

Richard：那就确定采用带回流线的直接供电方式。

李工程师：我们接着讨论牵引变电所进线电压等级和牵引变压器接线形式。牵引变压器进线电压等级是132kV，牵引变压器接线形式是VV接线。

Richard：我们没意见。

李工程师：请大家看这张牵引变电所分布方案示意图，上面是全线线路纵断面图，中间的文字和数据是车站名称和相邻车站间距离，下面是牵引变电所分布方案图，这个图例表示牵引变电所，这个图例表示分区所，这是开闭所。全线共新建5座牵引变电所、5座分区所和1座开闭所。

Richard：我们总体上同意，但需要注意的是A城市是沿线最为重要的城市，是本地区经济和文化中心，根据规划，还将有两条线路引入，而本线将要建设的车站将会成为衔接其他两条线的枢纽

Mr Li: The power supply capacity could meet the demand in context of ridership increase and speed change in long-term period. We took all these factors into consideration while working on the design.

Richard: Then we decide to adopt direct power supply with return feeder.（T-R-NF）

Mr Li: Let's move on to the topic of voltage class of traction substation incoming line and traction transformer connection mode. Our suggestion is to adopt voltage class 132kV, and the transformer will adopt VV connection.

Richard: No objection.

Mr Li: May I have your attention here on this traction substation distribution diagram? This is the profile of the whole line on the top. The words and data in the middle represent station name and intervals between stations. In the bottom, you can see the distribution plan of substations. This legend represents traction substation, this is section post, and this is switching station. There are totally five substations, five section posts and one switching station.

Richard: We generally agree. But you have to consider city A that is one of the most important cities along the line, the economic and cultural centre in local area. According to the plan, two more lines are proposed.

车站。我们也注意到了你们的方案中,在该车站附近设置了牵引变电所,可以兼顾未来其他线的供电,最大限度地利用牵引变电所的供电能力,但请你们做好相关预留设计,避免将来大的废弃和改造工作。

Therefore, stations on this line will become the hub connecting these two. We notice that you proposed traction substations besides this station, which is good for the power supply of other lines in the future. Your effort to maximize the power supply capacity is admirable, but we also hope you pay attention to reservation in your design to avoid waste and reconstruction in the future.

李工程师:我们将结合相关路网规划方案,做好统筹研究和预留设计工作。

Mr Li: We will work on the integration study and reservation design considering the relevant network planning.

替换单词 Alternative terms

① 方案设计
可行性研究
施工图设计

① project design
feasibility study
construction drawing design

业务情景:中方李工程师与外方工程师 Richard 讨论牵引供电系统对沿线电力系统的影响。
Scene: Mr Li and Richard are discussing the impact of traction power supply system on electric system along the line.

典型对话 Conversation

李工程师:牵引供电系统对沿线电力系统的影响主要分为下面几个问题:负序问题、谐波问题、功率因数①问题。牵

Mr Li: The impact of traction power supply system on electric system along the line is mainly divided into the following

引变压器将采用三相 VV 接线，以改善对沿线电力系统的负序影响，同时，牵引变电所采用相序轮换方式接入电力系统，以降低对沿线电力系统的负序影响。

Richard：采用上述措施[②]后，相关指标是否满足 IEC61000-2-12 的相关规定？

李工程师：根据我方提供的资料，贵国电力部门对相关变电站母线上的负序电压不平衡度进行了分析计算，结果表明，牵引供电系统对沿线电力系统的负序影响能够满足 IEC61000-2-12 规定的指标。

Richard：那我们接着谈谈其他几个问题吧。

李工程师：对于谐波问题，我们提供的机车将采用目前最为先进的交流传动技术，通过采用 PWM（脉宽调制）等技术，使电源侧的交流电波形比较平滑，大幅度降低谐波含量。

aspects: negative sequence, harmonic wave and power factor[①]. The traction transformer will adopt three-phase VV connection to improve the impact of negative sequence on the power system along the line, while the traction substation adopts the mode of phase sequence rotation to access the power system, so as to reduce the impact of negative sequence on power system along the line.

Richard：After adopting the above measures[②], can the relative index meet the specification of IEC61000-2-12?

Mr Li: According to the information & data provided by us, the power supply department of your country has analyzed and calculated the unbalance degree of negative sequence voltage on busbar of related transformer substations, which turns out that the negative sequence impact of traction power supply system on electric system along the line can meet the specified index of IEC61000-2-12.

Richard：Ok, let's talk about some other problems.

Mr Li: As to harmonic wave problem, our locomotives will adopt the most advanced AC drive technology. By the use of PWM technology, the AC waveform on mains side will be smoothed so that the harmonic content will be greatly reduced.

Richard：那么对电网的谐波影响是否低于 IEC61000-3-2 的限值？

李工程师：根据我方提供的谐波频谱和负荷电流等资料，贵国电力部门对相关变电站母线上的谐波电压畸变率进行了分析计算，计算结果表明，牵引供电系统对沿线电力系统的谐波影响能够满足 IEC61000-3-2 规定的指标。

Richard：我们国家对于 132kV 电压等级的功率因数，要求不低于 0.9。

李工程师：我们提供的机车采用先进的技术，牵引负荷的功率因数比较高，实测数据能够达到 0.97 左右。

Richard：希望你们提供关于牵引供电系统对沿线电力系统影响的专题报告，你们可以把电网公司研究报告一并作为附件提供给我们。

Richard: Is the harmonic impact on power grid below the limiting value of IEC61000-3-2?

Mr Li: According to the information & data of harmonic spectrum and load current provided by us, the power supply department of your country has analyzed and calculated the distortion factor of harmonic voltage on busbar of related transformer substations, which turns out that the harmonic impact of traction power supply system on electric system along the line can meet the specified index of IEC61000-3-2.

Richard: The requirement for power factor of 132kV voltage in our country is no less than 0.9.

Mr Li: Since advanced technology is adopted for our locomotives, the power factor of traction load is relatively high. On-the-spot measured data can reach about 0.97.

Richard: I want you to provide a special report about the impact of traction power supply system on electric system along the line, and you can also provide the research report of grid company as an attachment.

替换单词 Alternative terms

① 电压波动
② 无功补偿装置
　SVC 装置
　滤波装置

① voltage fluctuation
② reactive power compensation device
　SVC device
　filtre device

业务情景：设计方李工程师和业主方工程师 Richard 就牵引供电系统设计工作安排进行讨论。

Scene: Mr Li from the design unit and the Employer's engineer Richard are discussing the working schedule for the design of traction power supply system.

典型对话 Conversation

李工程师： 我们安排的牵引供电系统总的设计工期是6个月。

Richard： 希望你们提供一个设计流程图，便于我们认识和掌握设计过程和内容。

李工程师： 好的。具体安排为相关专业提供设计基础资料大约安排1个月，在这1个月的时间里，牵引供电系统专业将完成电网和既有牵引供电设施等资料的收集工作；牵引供电专业根据相关资料，开展方案设计和供电计算安排2个月；提供相关专业和电力部门设计资料并配合他们完成设计工作安排1个月；完成文件编制和图纸的绘制安排1个月；剩余1个月为监理和业主审查，以及根据审查意见进行修改的时间。

Mr Li: In our plan, the total design time of traction power supply system is six months.

Richard: I want you to provide a design flow chart, so that we can know about the design process and design content.

Mr Li: Okay. The specific arrangement is as follows: basic information and data for design will be provided within one month. During this period, the traction power supply engineer shall complete the information & data collection for traction power supply facilities; the engineer shall carry out scheme design and power supply calculation in two months according to the related materials about traction power supply, provide design materials for relative disciplines and electric power department, and then cooperate with them to complete design work in one month. Documents and drawings' preparation will be completed within one month. The

Richard：希望你们提供一个准确到具体日期的时间流程图。有些工作是可以交叉进行的，希望你们抓紧时间、合理安排，高效地完成高质量的设计。

李工程师：好的。如果对时间安排没有其他意见，我们就继续讨论一下设计工作开展的沟通、协商制度。

Richard：好的。

李工程师：我们建议每周五 15:00 召开一次有设计和监理人员参加的工作会，工作会主要讨论设计进度执行情况、存在的问题、解决的办法，同时，对相关技术问题进行讨论。每个月第一个星期五召开的工作会，希望业主参加，便于掌握设计情况并协调解决具体问题。

Richard：这样的安排非常合理和周到。今天会议所涉及的内容将记录在会议纪要中。请你们下周二前将设计流程图①提供给我们。

last month is reserved for review by the Consultant and the Employer, as well as for variation according to the review comments.

Richard: I want you to provide a time flow chart with specific date. As some works can be done simultaneously, I hope you will arrange the time reasonably so as to complete high-quality design effectively.

Mr Li: Okay. If you don't have any other opinion about the time arrangement, we can go on to discuss the communication and coordination system for design work.

Richard: Ok.

Mr Li: We suggest that the designers and consultants hold a working meeting at 15:00 every Friday to discuss the execution of design schedule, the existing problems and solutions. Meanwhile related technical problems will be discussed at the meeting. I hope the Employer will join the meeting held on the first Friday of each month to know the design status and coordinately solve specific problems.

Richard: It's very reasonable and considerate. The details of today's meeting will be recorded in the minutes of meeting. We hope you can provide the design flow chart① to us before next Tuesday.

第一部分　交通工程情景会话

替换单词 Alternative terms

① 时间流程图　　　　　　　　　　① time flow chart

业务情景：设计方李工程师就牵引供电系统设计向业主方工程师 Richard 进行技术交底。

Scene: Technical disclosure for the design of traction power supply system is being carried out between design unit's engineer Mr Li and the Employer's engineer Richard.

典型对话 Conversation

李工程师：我先介绍一下牵引供电系统设计情况。（略）

Richard：请问每个牵引变电所的牵引变压器安装容量是多少？

李工程师：A 所是两台（25+25）MV·A 的，具体请见书面交底资料。需要重点关注 3 个技术问题：第一，电网对牵引供电系统的相关要求和规定引起的工程问题还需进一步落实，具体为计量准确度和电量信息传输的要求；继电保护和整定时限的要求；电力部门电源工程和铁路牵引供电系统工程工期的衔接要求；电能质量检测的要求；调度信息①等信息沟通和传输的要求。

Mr Li: Firstly, I want to introduce the design condition of traction power supply system. (omitted)

Richard: What is the installed capacity of each traction substation transformer?

Mr Li: Substation A has two(25+25) MV·A trans formers. The details can be referred to the written technical disclosure materials. Three technical problems shall be taken into account: firstly, the engineering problems caused by related requirements and specifications of power grid to traction power supply system shall be further put into practice, which are as follows: requirements for accuracy of measurement and electric quantity information transmission; requirements

231

Richard: 这几个问题我们牵头向相关部门落实后以书面形式提交给设计方。

李工程师: 第二，牵引变电所接入电力系统的相序问题。我们已经将各牵引变电所牵引变压器的套管相序和电力系统接引的相序以示意图的方式进行了说明，为了避免出现差错，在牵引变电所接入电力系统前，双方应对相序进行认真核查，并确认无误。

Richard: 施工前我们将组织电力部门、设计、施工、监理等单位一起到现场确认。

李工程师: 第三，与既有线衔接部分的<u>正常供电</u>[②]方案，我们已经完成了正式报告，并于10天前提交给了铁路公司。

for relay protection and setting time limit; requirements for connection between construction periods of power source engineering of the power sector and railway traction power supply system; power quality testing requirements; requirements for information communication and transmission, such as <u>scheduling information</u>[①].

Richard: We will take the lead to solve these problems with relevant departments and submit it to the design party in written form.

Mr Li: Secondly, phase sequence for traction power substation to link to the electrical power system. We have provided the sketch diagrams showing the phase sequence of transformer sleeving of traction substation and electrical power system connection. To avoid errors, both parties shall carefully check the phase sequence before connecting traction substation to the electrical power system.

Richard: We'll organize power sector, design unit, construction unit and supervision unit to visit the site for confirmation before construction.

Mr Li: Thirdly, we have finished the formal report for <u>normal power supply</u>[②] of the section linking to the existing line, and submitted the report to railway corporation ten days ago.

第一部分　交通工程情景会话

Richard：这份报告我们已收到。这个问题除了涉及供电能力问题外，还涉及馈线相序的配合、保护整定的配合、开关倒闸作业程序、运营维护和检修配合等诸多方面的问题，需要多方、多部门共同商定。

Richard: We have received the report. Besides the power supply capacity, this issue also involves coordination of feeder phase sequence, coordination of protection setting, and operation procedures for switch back brake, as well as operation maintenance and service coordination etc., which requires common agreement of all the parties and sectors.

替换单词 Alternative terms

① 开关量信息
② 事故情况下供电
  非正常情况供电
  越区供电

① switching value information
② power supply in emergency
  non-normal power supply
  over-zone feeding

业务情景：业主方工程师 Richard、设计方李工程师和咨询方工程师 Ryan 对牵引供电系统咨询意见进行讨论。
Scene: Designer Mr Li, the Employer's engineer Richard and the Consultant Ryan are discussing the consultant comments for traction power supply system.

典型对话 Conversation

Ryan：我们一共提出了 60 条咨询意见，主要咨询意见有 5 条。第 1 条：供电方案建议补充采用带加强线直接供电方式的方案。

Ryan: We have provided sixty consulting opinions, five of which are our main consulting opinions. The first is, for the power supply scheme, it is suggested to adopt the mode of direct power supply with line feeder.

233

Richard: 请问提出该条意见的理由是什么？

Ryan: 主要是考虑本线为城际铁路，牵引负荷具有很强的时效性，采用带加强线的直接供电方式，能够提供供电能力，具有较好的经济性和适应性。

李工程师: 经供电计算，设置加强线能够提高列车运行时牵引网的<u>电压水平</u>①。

Ryan: 第 2 条: 建议研究采用全并联供电的可行性。

李工程师: 供电计算结果同第 1 条，采用全并联供电对于改善越区供电能力效果不明显，同时还增加了牵引网的复杂性。

Ryan: 第 3 条: 设计原则中提出牵引网平均有效电压不低于 22.5kV，建议进行相应计算。

李工程师: 我们将利用供电仿真软件进行相关计算，以确定牵引网平均有效电压是否满足不低于 22.5kV 的要求。

Ryan: 第 4 条: 建议补充采用 132kV 单相牵引变压器的论证分析。

Richard: Please specify the reason for this opinion.

Ryan: Since the line is interurban railway, the traction load is highly occasional, adopting mode of direct power supply will be a solution and is also economical and adaptable.

Mr Li: After calculating by power supply, the setting of line feeder will improve the <u>voltage level</u>① of traction network when the train is running.

Ryan: The second opinion is suggesting to make research on adopting wholly parallel operation mode.

Mr Li: The calculating result of power supply is the same as the first opinion. Adopting wholly parallel operation mode has little effect on the over-zone feeding capacity but it increased the complexity of traction network.

Ryan: The third, the average effective voltage of traction network shall not be below 22.5kV specified in the design principle. It is suggested to calculate it correspondingly.

Mr Li: We will use the power supply simulation software for relevant calculation, so as to determine if the average effective voltage of traction network can meet the requirement of 22.5kV.

Ryan: The fourth, it is suggested to supplement the demonstration and analysis

Richard：本线沿线电网很发达，单相牵引变压器具有诸多优点，有必要对采用单相牵引变压器进行论证。

Ryan：第 5 条：建议尽快完善牵引变电所接入电力系统方案设计工作。

李工程师：第 4 条与第 5 条意见是相关联的，我建议业主方催促承担牵引变电所接入电力系统方案设计的电力设计部门，尽快完善设计工作。

Richard：很感谢大家提出的非常专业的解释和说明。请设计方就越区供电的能力问题完成一个补充报告。对于第 3 条意见，我同意设计方的建议，完成一个专题计算工作。对于第 4 条和第 5 条意见，我们将给电力设计部门发函，提出具体时间和工作内容等要求。

for adopting 132kV single phase traction transformer.

Richard: The grid is developed along the line. Single-phase traction transformer has many advantages. It is necessary to demonstrate the adoption of single-phase traction transformer.

Ryan: The fifth, it is suggested to complete the design of the traction substation linking to the electrical power system.

Mr Li: The fourth and the fifth opinions are relevant, so I suggest that the Emloyer shall urge the power design department to complete the design of traction substation linking to the electrical power system.

Richard: I appreciate your professional explanations and demonstrations. Please provide the supplementary report for over-zone power supply capacity. As to the third opinion, I agree with the suggestion by the design party to complete special calculation. As to the fourth and fifth opinions, we will send letter to electrical power design department, and present requirements such as the specified time and work content.

替换单词 Alternative terms

① 牵引网载流能力　　　　　　　① current-carrying capacity of traction network

第十七章　牵引变电
Chapter 17　Traction Substation

业务情景: 中方王工程师与外方工程师 Jones 讨论某项目牵引变电所情况。

Scene: Mr Wang, an engineer from Chinese side is discussing with Jones, a foreign engineer, about traction substation of a project.

典型对话 Conversation

Jones: 请介绍一下本项目既有牵引变电所的情况,包括电压等级、设备配置等情况。

王工程师: 这个工程牵引变电所外部电源电压为 110kV,牵引侧电压等级为 27.5kV。110kV 设备采用室外布置,27.5kV 侧设备采用室内布置。

Jones: 本次工程准备如何进行改造?

王工程师: 根据用电负荷的需要,我们计划在这个牵引变电所增加两条馈出线,牵引变压器的容量需要增大,同时更新相应的导流回路、设备和材料。

Jones: Would you please tell us about the existing traction substation of the project, such as voltage class, equipment configuration and so on?

Mr Wang: The voltage of external power supply of the traction substation is 110kV, and the voltage class of the traction side is 27.5kV. Outdoor layout is adopted for 110kV equipment, and indoor layout is adopted for equipment at the side of 27.5kV.

Jones: How will the project be upgraded?

Mr Wang: According to the demand of electric load, we plan to add two feeders for the traction substation. The capacity of traction transformer should be expanded and the corresponding diversion circuits, equipment and materials will be replaced.

Jones: 本项目除了改建刚刚提到的牵引变电所外,还有没有考虑新建的供电设施?

王工程师: 我们计划在甲车站新建一座牵引变电所,同时在乙车站新建一座分区所。

Jones: 新建供电设施所的设备配置准备如何考虑?

王工程师: 为了便于维护和管理,我们认为应该与既有牵引变电所的设备标准一致。

Jones: 考虑到一致的设备标准,对于设备①供货商方面如何选择?

王工程师: 设备的技术标准只要满足中国标准②就可以了,供货商方面应该交由工程承包商来选择。

Jones: Are there any new power supply facilities in the project in addition to the upgrading of traction substation mentioned above?

Mr Wang: We plan to build a new traction substation at station A and a new section post at station B.

Jones: How is the equipment's configuration in the newly-built power supply facility room?

Mr Wang: For the purpose of maintenance and management, the standards of equipment should be in consistency with those of the existing traction substation.

Jones: In consideration of the same equipment standards, how about equipment[①] suppliers?

Mr Wang: The Contractor of the project will be responsible for selecting of equipment suppliers and the technical standards of equipment shall meet Chinese standards[②].

替换单词 Alternative terms

① 牵引变压器　　　　　① traction transformer
　 开关设备　　　　　　　 switch gear
　 互感器　　　　　　　　 mutual inductor
　 避雷器　　　　　　　　 lightning protector
　 二次设备　　　　　　　 secondary equipment
② IEC 标准　　　　　　② IEC Standard

业务情景: 中方王工程师与外方工程师 Jones 讨论设施、建筑物改造。
Scene: Mr Wang is discussing with Jones about reconstruction of facilities and structures.

典型对话 Conversation

Jones: 根据地形图,既有的牵引变电所周围有很多建筑物,如果要改造这个变电所,这些建筑物要拆除才能满足改造需要。

Jones: According to topographic map, there are many buildings around the existing traction substation. If the substation will be upgraded, these buildings should be demolished to meet the demand of upgrade.

王工程师: 是的,我们已经通过业主与这些建筑物的物主就拆迁和补偿达成了一致,工程开工后,这些建筑物将统一到铁路用地中进行拆除。

Mr Wang: That's right. With the help of the Employer, we have made agreements with owners of these buildings on relocation and compensation. These buildings will be demolished on railway land after the commencement of the project.

Jones: 同时也要考虑从变电所到接触网的供电线路走廊,如果没有走廊,对工程的实施将会产生一定影响。

Jones: Power line corridor from the substation to OCS should also be taken into consideration. If there is no corridor, the implementation of the project will be affected.

王工程师: 牵引变电所到铁路线路之间的用地,都属于铁路公司的用地范围,供电线路可以走得通。

Mr Wang: As the land between the traction substation and railway line is within the scope of railway company, power lines are able to get connected.

Jones: 按照图纸来看,这个车站还需要新建其他供电设施吗?

Jones: According to drawings, it seems that other power supply facilities should also be built for the station?

王工程师:这个车站既有的机务段要增加股道①,需要牵引变电所单独出馈线来供电。

Jones:这样一来,牵引变电所改造的工程量就会比较大,27.5kV 设备间房屋的大小估计不能满足需要了。

王工程师:如果不足,就在既有房屋旁边扩建,变电所的场坪足够。

Jones:是的,不新建开闭所②的方案,也易于运营管理。

Mr Wang: Tracks① should be added to the existing locomotive depot of the station, requiring separate feeders from the traction substation for power supply.

Jones: Then the traction substation will be largely reconstructed; and 27.5kV equipment room cannot meet the demand.

Mr Wang: Expansion work will be carried out near the existing room if it is insufficient.

Jones: That's right. New subsectioning post② will not be built for benefiting operation management.

替换单词 Alternative terms

① 挂网
② 改建牵引变电所

① steel bar net
② reconstruction of traction substation

业务情景:中方王工程师与外方工程师 Jones 就外部电源配合进行交流。
Scene: Mr Wang is discussing with Jones about external power supply.

典型对话 Conversation

Jones:关于牵引变电所外部电源问题,我们认为牵引变电所围墙以外 110kV 输电线路及电力变电站的相关工程由贵方来主导工作。

Jones: As for external power of the traction substation, you are supposed to undertake relevant works for 110kV transmission lines and electrical substation outside the wall of the traction substation.

王工程师：这个工作上次你们也谈到了，外部电源的设计由我方来做。

Jones：我们将本次工程的牵引变电站分布，以及需用电负荷①的要求提供给你们，便于你们做外部电源方案的设计工作。

王工程师：我们还需要一些具体接口②方面的资料。

Jones：最好有一个书面的分工界面，详细设计时我们还需要贵方提供相关的保护整定值配合的资料。

王工程师：没有问题，我们尽量去做。

Mr Wang: You've mentioned this issue last time. We will undertake the design of external power supply.

Jones: We'll provide requirements to the traction substation distribution and electrical load① of the project for your design on external power scheme.

Mr Wang: We also need some information on specific interface②.

Jones: A written report on the interface is preferred. Materials on protection setting value will be needed for detail design.

Mr Wang: No problem, we'll try to make it.

替换单词 Alternative terms

① 供电质量
② 电力计费
　 架构类型
　 架构位置

① power supply quality
② electricity charging
　 structure type
　 structure location

业务情景：中方王工程师与外方工程师 Jones 讨论收集资料。
Scene: Mr Wang is discussing with Jones about data collection.

典型对话 Conversation

王工程师：本次工程需要对既有的牵引变电所进行改造，希望你们能够提供既有变电所的图纸。

Mr Wang: As upgrade of the existing traction substation will be carried out in the project, we hope that you can provide drawings of the existing substation.

Jones：没有问题，请你们将需要的图纸内容，列出一个目录①。

王工程师：这是需图纸的目录，我们需要牵引变电所的主接线图②及架构的相关图纸。

Jones：这些图纸都有，但你们不能带走，如果需要可以拍照。

王工程师：太感谢了，变电所的设备都是哪些工厂生产的呢？

Jones：供货商比较多，我这里没有统计，只有看了实际的设备才知道。

王工程师：那我们能不能参观一下这个牵引变电所。

Jones：可以，我本周五下午有时间，我带你们一起去参观变电所。

Jones: No problem. Please make a catalog① of drawings you need.

Mr Wang: This is the catalog. We need main wiring drawing② of the traction substation and relevant drawings of structure.

Jones: We have these drawings. You can take pictures if you need.

Mr Wang: Thank you very much. Would you please tell us about the equipment manufacturers of the substation?

Jones: We have a lot of suppliers, but I do not have the specific information right now. I can tell only when I come to the actual equipment.

Mr Wang: Can you show us around the traction substation?

Jones: Of course. I will be available this Friday afternoon, and then I will show you around.

替换单词 Alternative terms

① 清单
② 设备平面布置图
　设备安装图
　控制系统图
　保护配置图
　房屋图

① list
② equipment plane layout drawing
　equipment installation drawing
　control system drawing
　protection configuration map
　house map

业务情景：地勘外方分包商（外方工程师 Jones）与牵引变电专业设计人员（中方王工程师）就变电所的土壤电阻率勘测资料进行交接。
Scene: Foreign subcontractor of geological survey Jones is exchanging ideas with Chinese traction substation designer Mr Wang on survey data of soil resistivity of the substation.

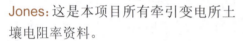

Jones: 这是本项目所有牵引变电所土壤电阻率资料。

王工程师: 好的，是否按照我们所要求的测量条件进行物探？

Jones: 是的，你们要求在场坪的海拔高程以下 1m、3m、5m 分别测量，而且要求是要在三个晴天后进行测量。

王工程师: 牵引变电所所在位置是否有不良地质地段？

Jones: 地质情况在地质说明书里有描述，场地大部分条件比较好，是黏土①。

王工程师: 那就太好了，我们一直担心变电所场地中有软土②，现在有了这些地质资料，我们就可以进行变电站接地系统的设计工作。

Jones: This is all soil resistivity data of the traction substation of the project.

Mr Wang: Ok. Was the geophysical prospecting carried out according to survey conditions we require?

Jones: Yes. As your request, survey was conducted respectively at 1m, 3m and 5m below sea-level elevation of the field, and the survey was carried out after three sunny days.

Mr Wang: Are there any unfavorable geological conditions at the place where the traction substation is located?

Jones: As stated in geological description, most of the field is covered with clay①, the favorable geological conditions.

Mr Wang: That's great. We have been worried if there is soft soil② within the substation area. Now we can carry out the design of grounding system of the substation with these geological data.

第一部分　交通工程情景会话

替换单词 Alternative terms

① 红黏土　　　　　　　① red clay
　　粉质黏土　　　　　　　 silty clay
② 松散的粉砂　　　　　② loose silt
　　细砂　　　　　　　　　 fine sand

业务情景： 水文外方分包商工程师 Jones 同中方牵引变电专业设计人员王工程师就某变电所的洪水位勘测资料进行交接。

Scene: Jones, foreign subcontractor of hydrology is exchanging ideas with traction substation designer Mr Wang (from Chinese side) on flood level survey data of the substation.

典型对话 Conversation

Jones： 大罗河在 DK388+100 处的水文资料已经整理好了。

王工程师： 感谢，这个工点是全线剩余的最后一个工点了，也是我们最担心的一个工点，因为距离变电所所址 200m 处有一条河流。

Jones： 牵引变电所距离大罗河很近，我们调查了 1954 年以来的洪水情况，分别在 1958 年和 1999 年发生过 1 次洪水。根据当年的观测数据，我们测量了河流的汇水面积，并做了相关计算。

Jones: Hydrological data of Daluo River at DK388+100 have been collected.

Mr Wang: Thanks a lot. This is the last remaining work site of the whole line, and is most concerned, because there is a river 200m away from the substation.

Jones: The traction substation is much closer to Daluo River. There were two floods respectively in 1958 and 1999 as we investigated since the year of 1954. According to the observation data of those two years, we surveyed the catchment area of the river and made relevant calculations.

243

王工程师：看到了，这个工点的百年洪水位①是海拔 392.15m。

Jones：百年洪水位是通过计算得出来的，但这个工点既有地形只有388m左右。

王工程师：这就是说，场坪在施工时，需要抬高 4m 多，才能达到躲避洪水位的要求。非常感谢您提供这么详细的资料。

Mr Wang: I see. The one-hundred-year flood level① of the work site is elevation 392.15m.

Jones: We can get the one-hundred-year flood level through calculation, but the existing terrain level of the work site is only 388m in height.

Mr Wang: That is to say, 4m-elevation should be made during field construction, so as to meet the demand of avoiding flood. Thank you very much for providing such detailed information to us.

替换单词 Alternative terms

① 五十年洪水位　　　　　　　　① fifty-year flood level

业务情景：中方王工程师与外方工程师 Jones 讨论变电所主接线方案。
Scene: Mr Wang is discussing with Jones about main wiring scheme of the substation.

典型对话 Conversation

Jones：牵引变电所主接线图中，1号和2号132kV电源进线间，为什么通过两组隔离开关连接起来了？

王工程师：采用这种132kV侧接线方式①后可以使变电所的运行更加灵活。

Jones: I don't know why two sets of isolation switches are adopted for connection between 132kV power line 1 and 2 in the main wiring drawing of the traction substation.

Mr Wang: Because the mode of 132kV side wiring connection① will make the operation of substation more flexible.

Jones: 举个例子呢？

王工程师：比如 1 号进线的 1 号变压器发生故障后，1 号进线可以通过跨条向 2 号变压器供电。

Jones: 为什么有些隔离开关是采用手动操作，有些隔离开关采用电机操作？

王工程师：用于改变变电所运行方式的隔离开关，一般采用电动操作；而手动隔离开关是用于变电所检修时。

Jones: 27.5kV 出线侧，为什么设置了 3 台断路器？

王工程师：这 3 台断路器，其中左、右侧两台是正常情况下，向接触网的上、下行分别供电用的；中间的那 1 台，是给另外两台作备用的。

Jones: 这台 63kV•A 的变压器是做什么用的？

王工程师：这台变压器是所用电源的变压器，是给变电所内的一些交流负荷进行供电的。

Jones: 虚线部分是表示什么意思？

王工程师：虚线部分表示预留的电气设备，本次工程不会实施，是为今后本项目扩能准备的。

Jones: To give an example?

Mr Wang: For example, if transformer 1 of power line 1 fails, transformer 2 can be powered by power line 1 through connection strap.

Jones: Why are some isolation switches manual-operated, while others are motor-operated?

Mr Wang: The isolation switches used to change operating mode of the substation are usually motor-operated, while manual isolation switch is used for substation maintenance.

Jones: Why are there three circuit breakers at 27.5kV outlet side?

Mr Wang: The two circuit breakers on the left and right will provide power for uplink and downlink of OCS under normal circumstances. The one in the middle is used as backup.

Jones: What is this 63kV•A transformer used for?

Mr Wang: Served as the transformer for the power source, it will provide power for some AC load in the substation.

Jones: What does dotted line mean?

Mr Wang: The dotted line means reserved electrical equipment which will not be implemented in the project. It is prepared for future expansion of the project.

Jones: 为什么会设有4台变压器？
王工程师：牵引供电是两台，一主一备，还有两台是沿线车站、贯通线② 用的。

Jones: Why are there four transformers?
Mr Wang: Two for traction power supply: one is the main transformer and the other is for backup. The other two are used for stations along the line and link lines② .

替换单词 Alternative terms

① 带跨条的分支接线
② 电力配电所

① branch wiring with connection strap
② electricity distribution substation

业务情景：中方王工程师与外方工程师Jones讨论变电所平面布置的相关方案。
Scene: Mr Wang is discussing with Jones about plane layout scheme of the substation.

典型对话 Conversation

Jones: 整个变电所的排水设计，你们是怎么考虑的？

王工程师：沿着变电所的南北方向，变电所的场坪有1%的排水坡度，场坪的水可以顺着这个坡度排向车站的排水系统中。

Jones: 雨季的时候，雨量会比较多，雨水会不会进入电缆沟里面呢？

Jones: Would you please tell us about the drainage design of the whole substation?

Mr Wang: There is 1% of drainage slope on the field in north-south direction along the substation. Therefore, water on the field can be discharged to drainage system of stations along the slope.

Jones: As there will be more rainfall in rainy season, will the rain water go into cable trench?

王工程师：电缆沟上面有盖板，可以阻止一部分水进入电缆沟，同时，电缆沟里面有0.5%的排水坡度，在电缆沟的尽头，会有几根排水管，将沟内的水排出变电所。

Jones：变电所内没有设备安装的地方，比如围墙附近，场坪怎么处理？

王工程师：我们建议采用水泥硬化①。因为这样做可以尽量避免植物在泥土中的生长，植物长高后，可能威胁变电站运行的安全。

Jones：图纸上显示，变电所的室外设备都是安装在钢材质支柱上，为什么不考虑采用混凝土支柱？

王工程师：钢材防腐处理后，较混凝土材质的支柱更加耐用，而且贵国盛产钢材，混凝土价格较高也需要进口。

Jones：这些支柱为什么有的2.5m高，有的3m高，还有的4m高？

王工程师：我们在变电所的平面设计中，要考虑设备间、设备和导线间的带电距离，也要考虑导线走向尽量平顺，所以设计出了不同的杆型以供选择。

Mr Wang: There will be a cover above the cable trench, so as to prevent water from entering. Moreover, 0.5% of drainage slope will be set in the cable trench and a few drains are set at the end of the cable trench to discharge water out of the substation.

Jones: How to treat places of non-equipment area in the substation, such as places near the wall?

Mr Wang: It is suggested to harden the ground by cement①, so as to avoid plants' growing in the soil. If the plants grow taller in the soil, they may threaten the safety of the substation.

Jones: As it is shown on the drawings, all outdoor equipment of the substation are installed on steel pillars, why not concrete pillars?

Mr Wang: Steel after anti-corrosion treatment is more durable than concrete pillar. Besides, your country is rich in steel, and concrete is much more expensive and need to be imported.

Jones: Why are some pillars 2.5m high, some 3m high and others 4m high?

Mr Wang: In the plane design of the substation, spaces for equipment room, and between equipment or wires should be considered. Also, the wires should be laid smoothly. There are different types of pillars for selection.

Jones: 铁路和电力公司的分界在哪里？

王工程师: 在这里，这是变电所 132kV 电源的进线架构，这个架构以外部分属于电力公司负责设计、施工和运营维护。

Jones: 这个变电所土质不好，比较松软，设计的时候请注意。

Jones: Where is the boundary between the railway and electric power company?

Mr Wang: Here it is. This is the structure of 132kV power line of the substation, and the parts outside the structure will be undertaken by the electric power company in terms of design, construction and operation maintenance.

Jones: The soil within the substation is relatively soft, so more attention should be paid when conducting design.

替换单词 Alternative terms

① 铺上道砟　　　　　　　　　　① ballast pavement

业务情景: 中方王工程师与外方工程师 Jones 讨论变电所生产房屋布置的相关方案。
Scene: Mr Wang is discussing with Jones about production house layout scheme of the substation.

典型对话 Conversation

Jones: 变电所送电后，我们是否需要安排值班人员？

王工程师: 是的，需要安排值班员，合同中约定的设计方案没有采用远动系统，需要值班人员在变电所完成变电运营中需要的所有操作。

Jones: Do we need to arrange on-duty personnel after power transmission is realized in the substation?

Mr Wang: Yes. Remote control system is not adopted as agreed in the contract, so personnel to be on-duty should be arranged to complete all operations required by substation's operation.

第一部分　交通工程情景会话

Jones：图纸中显示有两个用于值班员休息的房屋,够用吗?

王工程师：变电所内日常一人值班,一人待班,两间房屋够用了。另外,我们在这里还配置了<u>厨房</u>①。值班人员的生活条件可以满足。

Jones：值班人员在哪些地方可以对电气设备进行操作呢?

王工程师：在三个地方,一是用于监控变电所的工控机上,二是在控制保护屏的<u>开关</u>②或按钮上,三是在设备处进行就地操作。

Jones：如何让房屋内的设备处于能够正常运行的环境条件下?

王工程师：设计中,在主控室设置了空调,在高压室设置了排风扇。这些空调或排风扇都是根据电气设备的具体情况,暖通专业通过计算后进行配置的。

Jones：房屋内的照明是如何考虑的?

王工程师：按照功能区的不同,进行了照度的人性化设计,在不同的房间内配

Jones: There are two rooms for on-duty personnel on the drawing, are they enough?

Mr Wang: Yes, two rooms are enough. One is for personnel on duty and the other is for stand-by personnel in the substation. In addition, we also arrange a <u>kitchen</u>① so as to satisfy living conditions of the personnel.

Jones: What parts can the on-duty personnel do operation to electrical equipment?

Mr Wang: At three parts, one is industrial personal computer for monitoring the substation, the second is <u>switch</u>② or button of control protection screen, the third is on the equipment itself.

Jones: How to create an environment for normal operation for equipment inside the house?

Mr Wang: According to the design, air conditioners are set in main control room and exhaust fans are set in high-voltage room. These air-conditioners or exhaust fans will be set based on the specific conditions of electrical equipment and calculations by HVAC discipline.

Jones: Would you please tell us about lighting inside the house?

Mr Wang: According to different functional areas, user-friendly design is

249

置了不同型号和数量的灯具。同时，我们还设置了用于变电所交流停电后，自动启动的直流照明系统。

conducted in terms of illumination. Different types and quantities of lamps are set in different rooms. Besides, we also set up automatically activated DC lighting system in case AC power is off in the substation.

替换单词 Alternative terms

① 卫生间　　　　　　　　　① Bathroom
② 按钮　　　　　　　　　　② button

业务情景：中方王工程师就外方工程师 Jones 提出的关于牵引变电专业设计方案的问题进行答复。
Scene: The Chinese engineer Mr Wang is giving reply on questions of design scheme in traction substation discipline raised by foreign engineer Jones.

典型对话 Conversation

Jones：您提及的这些设备的型号，在贵国应用的情况如何？

Jones: As for the model you mentioned for the equipment, how about its application in China?

王工程师：这些变压器、断路器、开关等设备，在我们国家有着广泛的应用，都属于技术成熟产品。

Mr Wang: These transformers, breakers and switches, etc. are all mature technology products and are broadly applied in our country.

Jones：你们在设备设计及制造方面，采用的是什么标准？

Jones: Which standards have you adopted for the equipment's design and manufacturing?

王工程师：按合同约定，本项目的标准是中国标准，中国的设备标准一般是在IEC标准的基础上进行修正，有些标准比IEC标准略高。

Jones：是否可以给我提供一些你们国家标准的相关资料。

王工程师：由于标准太多，我只能摘录或者提供一些主要技术参数给你。

Jones：你们在设计中考虑了哪些环境条件？

王工程师：我们收集了该项目沿线的气象条件，所有的设计都适应沿线气象条件的要求。我们设计中也考虑到了沿线的污染程度①等因素。

Jones：每个变电所的占地面积是多少？设备运输怎么考虑？

王工程师：变电所长度为75m，宽度为70m，在变电所内、外部均设计了公路，电气设备通过汽车运输。

Mr Wang: In accordance with the Contract, we adopt China Standard for this project, and generally, China standard is amended from IEC standard. Some of them are higher than IEC.

Jones: Can you provide me some related materials of Chinese standards?

Mr Wang: As we have too many standards, I can only excerpt and supply you some main technical parameters.

Jones: In your design, what environmental conditions have you considered?

Mr Wang: We have collected meteorological conditions along the line, and make sure all the design could fulfill the requirements of these conditions. And also, we have considered other factors such as degree of contamination① along the line.

Jones: What's the floor space for each substation? How do you consider the transportation of equipment?

Mr Wang: Each substation is 75m in length and 70m in width. We have designed road inside and outside of the substation. The electrical equipment will be truck transported.

替换单词 Alternative terms

① 海拔高度
   地震参数

① altitude height
   seismic parameters

业务情景：中方王工程师向外方工程师 Jones 汇报牵引变电专业的计划和进度。
Scene: Mr Wang is reporting to Jones on the plan and progress of traction substation.

典型对话 Conversation

Jones: 这次准备提供的图纸有哪几类？

王工程师: 我们变电专业这次提交的设计图纸是变电所布置图、变电所控制保护图[①]等。

Jones: 这些什么时候可以交给我，我想尽快看到图纸。

王工程师: 我们也想尽快把图纸交给您，但现在设备的详细参数还没有确定，我们希望待参数确定后，再提交图纸。

Jones: 您说的对，那请您给我一个图纸交付的时间计划表。

王工程师: 好的，我们先确定设备详细参数吧，变电所布置图在参数确定后 2 个月内交付，变电所控制保护图为 5 个月内交付，其他的图纸在 6 个月内交付完毕。

Jones: 我觉得没有问题，你们还是尽快与承包商一起确定设备参数吧。

Jones: How many kinds of drawings have you prepared this time?

Mr Wang: The design drawings of submitted by our substation discipline this time are the substation layout plan and substation control protection drawing[①] and so on.

Jones: When can you give me these drawings? I can't wait to see.

Mr Wang: How I wish I could, but equipment's detail parameters haven't been decided yet. Thus, the drawings can't be provided until the parameters are determined.

Jones: You're right, so please supply me a schedule for drawing delivery.

Mr Wang: No problem. Let's ascertain the specific parameters first. The substation layout plan will be delivered in two months and substation control protection drawing in five months, and the rest drawings will be completed and delivered in six months, after the parameters are determined.

Jones: I think it's Ok. So you may decide the equipment parameters jointly with the contractor as soon as possible.

第一部分　交通工程情景会话

替换单词 Alternative terms

① 设备安装图
　自用电系统图

① equipment installation drawing
　auxiliary power supply system drawing

业务情景： 中方王工程师向外方工程师 Jones 汇报牵引变电专业的建设进度。
Scene: Mr Wang is reporting to Jones on the construction progress of traction substation.

典型对话 Conversation

Jones：一座牵引变电所的施工需要多少时间？

王工程师：合理的工期是在变电所场坪建好的情况下，四个月以内完成。

Jones：一座分区所呢？

王工程师：分区所的设备数量少一些，需要两个月就能够完成。

Jones：距离合同规定的交付时间只有一年时间了，希望能够抓紧一些。

王工程师：时间确实有点紧张，变电所和分区所施工完毕后，还需要调试三个月，才能够交付使用，我们会尽快的。

Jones：在工程建设过程中，还存在什么问题？

Jones: How long dose it take to build a traction substation?

Mr Wang: In the case of substation yard completed, the reasonable period is four months.

Jones: What about a section post?

Mr Wang: As the section post has less equipment, two months will be enough.

Jones: There's only one year left according to the Contract. I hope you could make it hurry.

Mr Wang: That' true, time is a little bit tight. After the completion of substations and section posts, we still need three months more to debug before delivery. But we will speed up.

Jones: Does any problem exist during the construction?

王工程师：没有什么问题，现在所有的电气设备[1]都已经到货了，设备的基础已经完成，一切都按照计划在进行。

Mr Wang: So far no problem, and all the electrical equipment[1] have arrived and their bases have been available. Everything is under schedule.

替换单词 Alternative terms

① 材料　　　　　　　　　　　　　① material

业务情景：中方王工程师向外方工程师 Jones 技术交底。
Scene: Mr Wang is doing technical disclosure to Jones.

典型对话 Conversation

Jones: 对于避雷针及其接地装置，设计中是如何考虑安全运行的？

Jones: As for lightening rod and other earthing devices, how do you consider safe operation in your design?

王工程师：独立的避雷针及其接地装置与道路或建筑物出入口等的距离应大于3m。避雷针与主接地网的地下连接点至变压器接地线与主接地网的地下连接点，沿接地体的长度不得小于15m。

Mr Wang: The distance between independent lightening rods and/or their earthing devices and road and/or structure's entrance-exit should be over 3m. The length of the grounding system between two underground connection points on main grounding network that separately connected lighting rod and transformer earthing wire should be no less than 15m.

Jones: 室内不同材质的母线连接时，需要注意什么？

Jones: When two indoor busbars made of different materials are connected, what should be noted?

王工程师：铜和铜连接时，必须搪锡；铝和铝可直接连接；钢和钢必须搪锡或镀锌，不得直接连接。铜和铝，应采用铜铝过渡措施，并在铜的一端搪锡。

Jones：高压室网栅的网孔大小和高度有什么要求？

王工程师：配电装置的网栅高度不应低于1.7m，网栅的网孔不应大于40mm×40mm。

Jones：地网采用的是铜材质，能否考虑采用钢材质？

王工程师：为了提高地网的防腐能力，延长使用寿命，设计要求地网采用铜材质。

Jones：地网敷设完毕后，如果接地电阻达不到图纸的要求，如果处理？

Mr Wang: Copper-copper connection must be enameled tin ; aluminum-aluminum connection could be connected directly ; steel-steel connection must be enameled tin or galvanized and connecting directly is not allowed. As for cooper and aluminum, we should adopt cooper-aluminum transition measures and enameled tin should be set at one end of the cooper.

Jones: Are there any requirements on mesh size and height of high-pressure chamber mesh?

Mr Wang: The mesh height of power distribution unit should be no less than 1.7m, and the mesh size should be no larger than 40mm×40mm.

Jones: The earth screen is of copper, how about steel?

Mr Wang: In order to improve the anti-corruption ability of earth screen and lengthen its service life, the earth screen should adopt copper in compliance with design requirements.

Jones: After earth screen is laid, if earthing resistance can't reach the requirements of drawings, how do we deal with it?

王工程师：处理的方式很多，可以将接地网外引至变电所外接地电阻较低的地方，可以采用接地深井①。具体的降低接地电阻措施，应该根据每个工点的实际情况来确定。

Mr Wang: There are many ways to handle. We can lead earth screen to relatively low earthing resistance area that is outside of the substation or adopt earthing deep well①. The specific lowering earthing resistance measures should be ascertained by actual situation of each site.

Jones：变电所内的安全监控用摄像机的数量是多少？

Jones: How many safe monitoring cameras are set within substations?

王工程师：在132kV设备区有4台；在高压室有两台；在主控制室有两台；在27.5kV出线侧有两台；变电所一共设置了10台。

Mr Wang: We have four in 132kV equipment zone, two in high-pressure chamber, two in main control office and two at 27.5kV outlet side, totally ten sets.

替换单词 Alternative terms

① 离子接地体　　　　　　　　　① ion grounding body

业务情景：中方王工程师向外方工程师Jones技术交底。
Scene: Mr Wang is doing technical disclosure to Jones.

典型对话 Conversation

Jones：我们牵引供电远动系统的通信通道是怎么构成的？

Jones: How does the communication channel of traction power supply's remote action system constitute?

王工程师：在每个牵引变电所①、分区所、AT所等供电设施控制室内，通信专业均设置了通信接入设备。这些设

Mr Wang: At each traction substation①, section post and AT post. etc. within power supply facility control room,

备可以满足调度电话、自动电话和远动的需求。远动通道采用光纤传输，连接牵引供电设施和电力调度中心。

Jones: 我们与通信专业的接口在什么位置？

王工程师: 接口在主控制室的通信机柜上,从通信机柜到我们的控制保护屏之间的光纤,是我们电气化施工单位负责采购和施工。在调度中心也是一样的情况,接口在通信机柜上。

Jones: 房屋的室内给排水和消防工程由谁来负责？

王工程师: 室内给排水[②]、消防以及通风,均由设计单位的暖通专业负责设计工作,工程中应该由房建的施工单位来完成。

Jones: 那我们一定要注意一下接口的处理了。

the communication discipline has been equipped with communication access device. All the equipment could satisfy the demands of dispatching phones, automatic phones and remote-control. The remote-control channels adopt optical fiber transmission for connecting traction supply facility and electric dispatching centre.

Jones: Where do we set the interface with communication discipline?

Mr Wang: The interface is set at the communication cabinets in main control room. Our electrical construction party takes charge of procuring and constructing the optical fiber used between communication cabinets and control protection screens. It's the same in dispatching centre. The interface is installed on communication cabinets.

Jones: Who will be in charge of indoor water supply and drainage and firefighting engineering?

Mr Wang: Indoor water supply and drainage[②], fire-fighting and ventilation will be all designed by HVAC principals, and the construction will be completed by the building construction party.

Jones: Then, we must pay close attention to the treatment of interfaces.

王工程师：是的，房建施工时需要注意房屋上、下水管的材质，消防设备的位置以及用电需求，通风设备与电气设备之间的安全距离等。

Mr Wang: Yes, when we implement housing construction, we should have an eye on the material quality on plumbings, the location of fire-fighting equipment, electricity demands and safe distance between ventilation equipment and electric equipment.

替换单词 Alternative terms

① 分区所　　　　　　① section post
　 AT 所　　　　　　　 AT post
② 消防　　　　　　　② fire-fighting
　 通风　　　　　　　　ventilation

业务情景：牵引变电专业设计人员张工程师对牵引变电所施工中出现的一些问题向监理单位技术人员 Jones 进行说明、答复。
Scene: Mr Zhang, the designer of traction substation discipline, is explaining and giving reply to Jones on some problems arised in the process of traction substation construction.

典型对话 Conversation

张工程师：现在整个变电所的工程进度如何？
Jones：地网已经敷设完毕，生产房屋修建和设备基础已经完成，准备进行设备安装。

Mr Zhang: How about the process of the whole substation?
Jones: Till now, we have completed earth screen layout, production house construction and equipment foundation, and we are preparing to conduct equipment installation.

第一部分　交通工程情景会话

张工程师：我们到变电所现场去看看吧。
Jones：地网敷设完毕后,我们进行了接地电阻的测量,现在是 0.35Ω,满足设计要求。

张工程师：是的,变电所这块地是黏土,对于降低接地电阻比较有利。

Jones：请您看看这里,这根支柱顶部安装了一支避雷器,它受到了来自导线的力,容易使避雷器的接线端子变形。

张工程师：我们建议在避雷器旁边安装一根支持绝缘子,用来代替避雷器接受来自导线的力,因此需要增加绝缘子和一些钢材。

Jones：高压电缆采用 $N+1$ 的备用方式后,从牵引变压器到开关柜 A 相的电缆需要 3 根,原设计图纸中开关柜内的电缆接线端子尺寸偏小。

张工程师：我们会尽快落实这些尺寸[①]。设备安装过程中,存在什么问题吗？

Jones：有一些问题,主要是有些设备接线端子是铝质材料[②],连接这些设备的线夹类型很多。

Mr Zhang: Let's pay a visit to the site.
Jones: After the completion of earth screen layout, we carried out the measurement of earthing resistance, which is 0.35Ω. The result satisfies the design requirements.

Mr Zhang: Yes, the earth where this substation is located is clay, which is in favor of lowering earthing resistance.

Jones: Please look, an arrestor is installed at the top of this pillar. It is under the press of the wire, thus its earthing end will be distorted easily.

Mr Zhang: We suggest to set up one supportive insulator next to this arrestor, to support the wire instead of the arrestor. Thus, we need to increase insulators and some steel.

Jones: After we adopt $N+1$ standby mode for high-voltage cable, we need three A-phase cables to connect traction transformer and switch cabinet. But, the size of cable terminals are relative small as designed in the switch cabinets according to the original design drawings.

Mr Zhang: We shall quickly confirm these dimensions[①]. Are there any problem during the equipment installation?

Jones: Yes, there are. Some equipment terminals are made of aluminous materials[②], but there are many types of cable clamps for connection.

259

张工程师：铝材质连接端子应采用设备线夹，铜材质接线端子应采用铜铝过渡设备线夹，必须注意，不能混淆。

Jones：是的，以后在设备采购时应该注意，统一设备接线端子的材质。

张工程师：开关柜和控制保护屏前方铺设的绝缘胶垫，是否已经采购？

Jones：根据施工图，我们已经采购了控制保护屏前面的绝缘胶垫。开关柜使用的绝缘胶垫，等到开关柜到货后，我们根据开关柜的尺寸再去采购。

张工程师：这是安全运营所必需的，可在操作设备时保护值班人员。

Jones：前面是通信专业设置的机柜，现在还不知道变电专业的控制保护设备如何与这面机柜相连接。

Mr Zhang: The aluminous terminals should adopt equipment cable clamps while copper terminals should adopt copper-aluminum transitional equipment cable clamps. We must be careful not to misuse them.

Jones: You're definitely right, we must pay attention to it when we procure the equipment in the future. The materials for equipment terminals should be unified.

Mr Zhang: Have you procured the insulating rubber pad laid in front of switch cabinets and control protection screen?

Jones: In accordance with the construction drawing, we procured the insulating pad in front of control protection screen. As soon as the arrival of switch cabinets, we will measure them first and then procure the insulating pad based on measured results.

Mr Zhang: That is necessary for safe operation, to protect duty staff from potential dangers during the equipment operation.

Jones: The equipment cabinet in front of us is set up by communication discipline. Up to now, we have no idea how to connect the control protection equipment of substation discipline with this equipment cabinet.

第一部分　交通工程情景会话

张工程师：所有的接口和通信协议，我已经与通信专业协商好了，并告知了双方的供货商，我想他们很快会找到您来处理这个问题的。

Mr Zhang: All the protocols for interface and communication have already been well negotiated with communication discipline, and been understood by both party's suppliers. I think they will communicate with you soon to deal with the problem.

替换单词 Alternative terms

① 方案
② 铜质材料

① scheme plan
② copper material

业务情景：牵引变电专业设计人员张工程师就牵引变电所咨询图中出现的一些问题向监理单位技术人员Jones进行说明、答复。
Scene: Mr Zhang, the designer of traction substation discipline, is explaining and giving reply to Jones on some problems incurred in the consulting drawings of traction substation.

典型对话 Conversation

Jones：贵公司就这个项目的施工图，我们已经咨询完毕，现在将几个可能存在的问题与您讨论一下，以便确定最后的咨询意见。

Jones: As for the construction drawing of this project, we have done our consultation for you. Now, I wish I can discuss with you about some problems which may appear in the future, so as to ascertain the final consulting opinions.

张工程师：非常感谢你们对设计图纸提出的诚恳意见，我们看过后，受益匪浅。

Mr Zhang: We really appreciate the honest opinions on the drawings you made for us, and we really benefit a lot.

261

Jones: 我们建议在牵引变电所内的控制电缆均采用阻燃型控制电缆。

张工程师：同意您的咨询意见。

Jones: 因本项目所在地区的环境比较潮湿，端子箱设计中是否考虑了这些因素？

张工程师：考虑了。我们在端子箱的整体技术要求中，已经明确了当地的环境条件。

Jones: 为了避免<u>断路器</u>[①]、隔离开关位置信号与设备本体位置不对应，建议控制保护屏上的开关位置信号灯自<u>断路器</u>本体上的辅助触点引出。

张工程师：同意您的咨询意见。

Jones: 部分图纸中，设备的高度和宽度标注有误，请你们要仔细核对并修改。

张工程师：好的。

Jones: 在图纸中，我们建议为便于上、下行分开运行，在分区所和 AT 所的主接线中，上、下行并联的母线上设置电动隔离开关。

Jones: We suggest flame-retarded control cables should be adopted within traction substations.

Mr Zhang: I agree.

Jones: Because of the wet environment, have you considered about this factor during the terminal box design?

Mr Zhang: Yes, we have. We have already clarified local environment conditions among our integrated technology requirements for terminal boxes.

Jones: To avoid non-corresponding of positions between the signal and equipment such as <u>breakers</u>[①] and insulating switch, we suggest to lead the signal light of switch positions on control protection screen from the auxiliary contact in the body of self-circuit breaker.

Mr Zhang: I agree.

Jones: On part of the drawings, the equipment's heights and widths are wrongly marked. Please check and correct them carefully.

Mr Zhang: Fine.

Jones: In this drawing, we suggest to set up motor isolating switch on the up-down direction parallel busbar among the main connection lines at section post and AT post to ease the separate operation of up-down busbar.

王工程师：同意,但目前设备已经采购完成,我得征求建设单位的同意后方可实施。

Mr Zhang: Ok, but the procurement of equipment has been finished. I have to ask for the construction party's consent before the implementation.

Jones：建议在高压室中增设SF6气体浓度监测装置,与通风系统联动,并纳入变电所安全监控系统中。

Jones: We recommend adding SF6 gas concentration monitoring device in high-pressure room, which could be coordinately operated with ventilation system and be incorporated into substation safety monitoring system.

王工程师：好的,我们会在施工图中,增加这项要求。

Mr Zhang: No problem. We will add this requirement in our construction drawing design.

Jones：接触网用的隔离开关控制图,缺少电缆联系表,需要你们补充完善。

Jones: The cable contact table is absent from the isolating switch control drawing used for the OCS, so we need you to add it up.

王工程师：同意您的咨询意见,这些电缆我们重新统计一下。

Mr Zhang: Totally agree, and we will recount the cables.

Jones：部分图纸中,字体的大小和类型没有统一,虽然影响不大,但还是希望能够统一。

Jones: The fonts in some drawings are not uniform. Although it is not a big deal, we still want them to be uniformed.

王工程师：好的,我们将咨询版的图纸认真再核对一次。

Mr Zhang: Ok, we will carefully recheck the consultive-version drawings.

替换单词 Alternative terms

① 隔离开关　　　　　　　　　① isolating switch

第十八章　接触网
Chapter 18　Overhead Catenary System

业务情景：中方张工程师与业主方工程师 John 讨论规范等资料的收集。

Scene: Mr Zhang and John are discussing collection for specification and other data.

典型对话 Conversation

张工程师：为了便于我方开展设计，我们需要您提供设计所需的基本资料。

John：请说你需要哪些资料。

张工程师：主要资料有贵国有关接触网、结构方面的<u>标准规范</u>①。

John：我方将提供相关的资料供您参考，不过，由于规范涉及知识产权，请您自行购买。

张工程师：能否请您提供一个规范清单以及出版社的联系方式以便我们购买？

John：这是出版社的电话，请您联系。规范清单我会以电子邮件的方式发送给你。

Mr Zhang: To facilitate our design, we kindly request you to provide us with the basic data necessary for the design.

John: Please specify the data you need.

Mr Zhang: The specific data are <u>standards or specifications</u>① of OCS and structure in your country.

John: We will provide you with related data for reference; however, since the specifications are protected by intellectual property rights, you have to buy them yourself.

Mr Zhang: Could you please provide us with a specification list and contact information of the publishing house for the convenience of our purchase?

John: This is the phone number of the publishing house. I will send the specification list to you by e-mail.

第一部分　交通工程情景会话

替换单词 Alternative terms

① 规章制度　　　　　　　　　① rule and regulation
　标准图集　　　　　　　　　　 standard schematic handbook

业务情景：中方张工程师与业主方工程师 John 讨论气象资料的收集。
Scene: Mr Zhang and John are discussing collection of meteorological data.

典型对话 Conversation

张工程师：为了便于我方开展设计，我们需要您提供本线经过地区的气象资料①。

John：有些资料我方没有，请你们到国家气象局、国家铁路局去收集，必要时，你们可以去现场收集。

张工程师：能否请贵方出具支持函件，以便我方顺利地在国家气象局，以及沿线的气象台站收集到所需资料。

John：我们将出具函件支持你们的工作。

张工程师：请问我什么时候可以拿到函件？
John：5个工作日后。

Mr Zhang: To facilitate our design, we request you to provide us with meteorological data① of the region where this line passes by.

John: Some data are not available. Please go to State Meteorological Administration and State Railway Administration to collect them. If necessary, you may collect those data on site.

Mr Zhang: Could you please send us the supporting letter so that we can easily collect the required data from the State Meteorological Administration and the Meteorological Stations along the line?

John: We will issue the supporting letter in favor of your work.

Mr Zhang: When could you give us the supporting letter?
John: Five working days later.

替换单词 Alternative terms

① 水文　　　　　　　　　　　① hydrological
　 地质　　　　　　　　　　　　 geological
　 外部环境资料　　　　　　　　 external environment data

业务情景：中方张工程师与业主方工程师 John 讨论改造既有铁路项目①的资料收集。
Scene: Mr Zhang and John are discussing data collection of the existing railway reconstruction project.①

典型对话 Conversation

张工程师：为了便于我方开展设计，我们需要您提供一些关于既有铁路的资料。

John：请问具体是哪些资料？

张工程师：主要是既有铁路的接触网悬挂类型②等资料。

John：请你提供一份清单，以便我方查找。

张工程师：好的，这是清单。

John：大部分资料我们这里都可以提供。但是有些资料我们这里也没有，需要你去现场找接触网工区、变电所工作人员收集。

张工程师：请你给一个他们的地址和联系方式，我下周就去找他们。

John：请等一下，我马上写给你。

Mr Zhang: To facilitate our design, we kindly request you to give us some data related to the existing railway.

John: Please specify the data you need.

Mr Zhang: We would like to have some data related to the OCS suspension type② of the existing railway.

John: Please give us a list.

Mr Zhang: Ok, here is the list.

John: We can provide most of the data. However, for those not available here, you can collect them from the engineers in the OCS workshop and substation on site.

Mr Zhang: Would you please give us their address and contact information? I will go to find them next week.

John: Wait a moment. I will give it to you right away.

替换单词 Alternative terms

① 增建二线铁路项目 　　　　　① second line railway additional project
② 支柱类型　　　　　　　　　② pole type
　基础类型　　　　　　　　　　 foundation type
　下锚方式　　　　　　　　　　 anchor type
　零部件主要尺寸及性能参数　　　 main sizes and performance parameters of OCS components
　供电分段示意图　　　　　　　 schematic diagram of power supply section
　接触网悬挂高度　　　　　　　 OCS suspension height
　结构高度　　　　　　　　　　 structure height

业务情景：中方张工程师与业主方工程师 John 初步设计方案讨论。
Scene: Mr Zhang and John are discussing preliminary design plan.

典型对话 Conversation

张工程师：John，今天我们开会讨论接触网初步设计方案，希望我们能达成共识，双方能形成会议纪要，以便我们后期设计工作能顺利开展。

Mr Zhang: John, today we are going to hold a meeting to discuss OCS preliminary design plan. I hope we can reach a consensus and take minutes of meeting, so that we could do our design better in the later period.

John：好的，在开始讨论方案前，我想强调一下，你们的设计方案必须满足技术合同要求及相关标准规范要求。

John: Ok. Before discussing the plan, I want to emphasize that your design plan must meet the requirements of both technical contract and related standard specifications.

张工程师：我们的方案是严格按照技术合同进行设计的，但是对于合同中一些地方，我们存在一些疑问，需要您给予解释。另外，本线接触网是采用哪国标准？我们建议采用欧洲标准①。

John：你们采用的所有标准都必须提供给我正式出版的英文版本。

张工程师：这个没有问题。我们还有一些技术要求在合同中没有明确，如本接触网系统是否采用双重绝缘②，希望您能在这次会上将其明确下来，我们纳入会议纪要后，就可以开展设计工作了。

John：关于您提的这个技术标准我们需要召开一个专题技术讨论会后才能决定。

张工程师：那我们就合同内的各条款进行讨论吧。首先，对于合同中关于机车车辆限界③问题，请您给予明确。

John：本线机车车辆限界目前还没有确定下来，是因为机车车辆正在招标，可能要等到明年3月份才会有招标结果，到时我会把相关参数提供给你们。

Mr Zhang: Our plan is designed in strict accordance with the technical contract; however, your clarification is needed in some parts of the contract where we have questions. Besides, which standard do you adopt for the OCS of this line? We recommend you to adopt European Standard①.

John: English version of official publication is required for all the standards you adopt.

Mr Zhang: No problem. Some technical requirements are not determined in the contract, for example, whether the OCS adopts double insulation②. We hope you will determine them in the meeting and record them in the minutes so that, we will be able to carry out the design works.

John: The technical standard you mentioned cannot be determined until we hold a technical meeting to discuss about it.

Mr Zhang: Then let's discuss each clause in the contract. First of all, please clarify the rolling stock clearance③ issue in the contract.

John: The rolling stock clearance of this line has not been decided yet, because the rolling stock is on bidding and the bidding result will not be disclosed until March of next year. At that time we will provide you with related parameters.

第一部分　交通工程情景会话

张工程师：那么，受电弓类型及参数是否也要等到那个时候才能明确下来？

John：对于这点我们很抱歉。

张工程师：这样的话，由于缺少最基本的外部输入资料，会导致接触网设计无法开展，设计时间会相应推迟。

John：你们可以致函我公司，说明要求延长设计时间的原因。我们会开会讨论此事的。

张工程师：好的。

Mr Zhang: Does it mean the type and parameter of pantograph cannot be confirmed until that time?

John: We are very sorry about that.

Mr Zhang: In this case, the lack of basic external input data will make the progress of OCS design impossible, therefore the design period will be delayed accordingly.

John: You may send a letter to our company, indicating the reason for the extension of design period. We will hold a meeting to discuss about it.

Mr Zhang: Ok.

替换单词 Alternative terms

① UIC 标准　　　　　　　　　　① UIC standard
　　中国标准　　　　　　　　　　　Chinese standard
② 单绝缘　　　　　　　　　　② single insulation
③ 货物装载高度　　　　　　　　③ cargo loading height

业务情景：中方张工程师与业主方工程师 John 讨论详细设计方案。
Scene: Mr Zhang and John are discussing detailed design plan.

典型对话 Conversation

工程师：现在我代表接触网专业进行接触网设计方案的汇报。根据上阶段的审查意见，结合本线线路工程的技术标准，本线接触网采用全补偿简单链形悬

Mr Zhang: Now I would like to present you the OCS design scheme. According to the assessment opinions of the previous stage and the technical standards of this

269

挂①。接触网线材规格及张力选择见这个表。

John：对于规格及张力的选择，你们的依据什么？

张工程师：对于接触网线材规格及张力选择，我们是做了仿真研究的，研究结果表明，表中的接触网线材规格及张力选择能满足本线运营速度要求。

John：好的，请继续。

张工程师：接触线悬挂点悬挂高度按6000mm设计，结构高度一般为1.6m，跨线建筑物或其他困难区段可适当降低结构高度，但最短吊弦长度不得小于0.5m，特殊困难区段根据具体情况确定。全线按重污区②设计，绝缘子优先采用瓷质绝缘子③。

John：因为全线按重污区设计，所以是否应考虑采用复合绝缘子④。

张工程师：是的，与接触网连接的绝缘子、隧道内绝缘子采用复合绝缘子。

line, OCS adopts completely compensation simple catenary①. The selection of OCS conductor's specification and its strength are shown on the list.

John: What is your basis for the selection of specification and strength?

Mr Zhang: As for the selection of OCS conductor specification and strength, we have made simulation study which shows OCS conductor's specification and strength on the list could meet the requirement of operating speed for this line.

John: Ok, go ahead please.

Mr Zhang: The height of suspension point of contact line is designed as 6000mm. The structure height is usually 1.6m. In the rail structure or other difficult sections, an appropriate reduction of height is allowed, but the minimum dropper height shall be no less than 0.5m. Special difficult section shall be determined according to its actual condition. The whole line is designed as heavy polluted area②. Porcelain insulator③ shall be the priority.

John: Since the whole line is designed as heavy polluted area, will it be possible to adopt composite insulator④ ?

Mr Zhang: Exactly. Composite insulator is adopted for insulators which connected with OCS lines and which is inside the tunnel.

John: 请继续。

张工程师: 长度大于300m 路基区段腕臂柱采用<u>圆形钢筋混凝土支柱</u>⑤, 桥梁及其他路基区段采用<u>H 型钢柱</u>⑥。车站内一般采用线间立腕臂柱方案, 咽喉区等跨越多股道时, 采用<u>硬横梁</u>⑦。

John: 这样的方案我们同意, 那么关于接触网锚段划分及跨距是怎么考虑的呢?

张工程师: 正线接触网锚段长度一般不大于 2×700m, 锚段关节一般采用 5 跨形式。支柱跨距一般不大于 65m。

John: 对于跨距的选用, 请您补充一个跨距选用表。

张工程师: 我们在设计中会补充这个跨距选用表的。

John: 那么请继续介绍关于道岔处接触网的布置方案吧。

张工程师: 道岔处接触网悬挂安装方式, 与正线相交的道岔采用无交叉方式, 非正线交叉的道岔采用交叉线岔方式。

John: Go on please.

Mr Zhang: <u>Circular reinforced concrete post</u>⑤ is adopted for cantilever post in the subgrade section whose length is over 300m, and <u>H-type steel post</u>⑥ is adopted in the bridge and other short subgrade sections. The post across the tracks is adopted inside the station. <u>Rigid beam</u>⑦ is adopted in the place crossing multi-track such as the turnout zone.

John: We agree with this plan. What do you think of the anchor segment dividing and span of OCS?

Mr Zhang: The tension length of the main line is usually no more than 2×700m, and overlap section adopts five-span form. The span between posts is no more than 65m.

John: As for the selection of span, please supplement a span selection list.

Mr Zhang: We will supplement it in our design.

John: Please continue with the OCS layout plan at the turnout.

Mr Zhang: For the OCS overhead crossing installation at the turnout, turnout connected to main line adopts non-crossing installation; turnout irrelevant to the main line adopts crossing installation.

电分相采用带空气绝缘中性段的绝缘锚段关节形式。电分相位置应满足行车需要,避免设置在大坡道及列车出站加速区段和线路限速低速区段。

John: 请问您所指的大坡道是指千分之几的坡道?

张工程师: 6‰,接触网分相装置不宜设在大于6‰的大坡道地段。

John: 好的,请继续。

张工程师: 供电线上网可采用架空或电缆的方式。正馈线及保护线一般设于田野侧。

John: 这点我们完全同意。

张工程师: 关于工区设置问题,我们的方案如下:牵引供电设施运营由A站综合维修车间及B、C、D站的综合工区内设置接触网工区进行维护管理。E站综合维修车间内设置供电抢修车间。

以上就是关于接触网设计方案的汇报,谢谢。

Electrical phase separation adopts insulated overlap type with air insulated neutral section. The position of electrical phase separation shall meet the requirement of train's running. It shall avoid to be set in the steep slope, acceleration areas of train departure and low-speed sections with speed limit.

John: As for the steep slope you mentioned, which grade does it mean?

Mr Zhang: 6‰, OCS phase separation shall not be set in the steep grade section over 6‰ (6 perimil).

John: Ok, go on please.

Mr Zhang: Power supply line may adopt overhead or cable type. Positive feeder and protective wire are often set on the sides of the field.

John: We totally agree with this point.

Mr Zhang: As for the setting of OCS workshop, our proposal is as follows: for the operation of traction power supply facilities, OCS workshop is set in the comprehensive maintenance workshop of the A Station and comprehensive workshop of the B, C and D Stations. Emergency maintenance workshop for power supply is set in the comprehensive maintenance workshop of the E Station.

This is the presentation of OCS design plan, thank you.

第一部分　交通工程情景会话

替换单词 Alternative terms

① 全补偿弹性链型悬挂　　　　① completely compensation elastic chain suspension
　简单悬挂　　　　　　　　　　 simple suspension
② 轻污区　　　　　　　　　　　② light polluted area
③ 复合绝缘子　　　　　　　　　③ composite insulator
④ 瓷质绝缘子　　　　　　　　　④ porcelain insulator
⑤ 格构式钢柱　　　　　　　　　⑤ lattice type steel pole
　H 型钢柱　　　　　　　　　　 H-type steel pole
　横腹式预应力混凝土支柱　　　　 transversal pre-stress steel reinforced concrete pole
⑥ 格构式钢柱　　　　　　　　　⑥ lattice type steel pole
⑦ 软横跨　　　　　　　　　　　⑦ headspan suspension

业务情景： 中方张工程师与业主方工程师 John 讨论设计工作及时间安排。
Scene: Mr Zhang and John are discussing design work and schedule arrangement.

典型对话 Conversation

张工程师：请问 5 年的总工期是从什么时候开始计算的？

John：从本项目开工开始计算，开工将在设计图纸完成后一个月开始。

张工程师：5 年工期包括了接触网的联调联试①和动态检测②时间吗？

Mr Zhang: When does the total five-year construction period start?

John: It starts from the commencement day of this project. The construction begins in a month after the design drawings are completed.

Mr Zhang: Does the five-year construction period include the time for OCS integrated test① and dynamic test②?

John: 包括了。

张工程师: 目前, 我们的设计进度有所滞后, 是由于贵公司一直没有对技术标准进行明确。

John: 请你们发一个正式的函给我们, 我们研究此事后会给予书面答复。

John: Yes.

Mr Zhang: At present, our design schedule is a little bit lagging behind, because your company does not specify the technical standards.

John: Please send us an official letter and we will give you a written reply after studying on the matter.

替换单词 Alternative terms

① 试运行
② 试运营

① trial run
② trial operation

业务情景: 中方张工程师与外方工程师John就接触网详细设计进行技术交底
Scene: Mr Zhang and John are discussing technical disclosure of OCS detailed design.

典型对话 Conversation

张工程师: 现在我们就我方设计的接触网图纸、接触网文件进行一次技术交底, 如果你们有任何疑问, 请随时提出来, 我们会给出详细解答。

John: 好的, 我们对于施工图内的有些地方有点疑问。首先, 接触网基础预留施工的误差控制要求存在疑问, 请对这些误差名称及采用数据的理由逐一解

Mr Zhang: Now we will give the technical disclosure of OCS drawings and data designed by us. If you have any question, please put forward. We would like to make detailed clarification.

John: Ok. We have some questions about certain parts in the construction drawing. First, there are some questions about error control requirement of pole

释一下。另外,接触网基础施工时,是否必须采用机械钻孔①施工,能否采用人工开挖基坑②方式?

张工程师:你们必须严格按照设计图纸及文件施工。

John:施工图内写的地质承载力是什么意思?有何作用?

张工程师:图纸内的地质承载力是指接触网支柱基础底面处的路基地质承载力,基础设计强度跟地质承载力有很大的关系。

John:有些桥上的接触网基础在预留施工时如果位置搞错了,有什么补救措施吗?

张工程师:对于这个问题,请你们到时给铁路公司去函,让铁路公司决定如何处理。

foundation reserved in construction. Please explain one by one the error meanings and reasons for the adopted data. Besides, during the construction of OCS foundation, does it require to adopt machine drilling ① for construction? Will it be possible to adopt manual excavation ② ?

Mr Zhang: You have to construct it in strict accordance with design drawings and documents.

John: What does the geological bearing capacity in the construction drawing mean? What is used for?

Mr Zhang: The geological bearing capacity in the construction drawing refers to subgrade geological bearing capacity at the bottom of OCS pole foundation. It is strongly related with geological bearing capacity.

John: If misplacement of the OCS foundation on some bridges occurs when reserved in construction, what remedial measure can we adopt?

Mr Zhang: As for the question, you shall send a letter to the Railway Corporation at that time. The Corporation will handle the matter.

替换单词 Alternative terms

① 人工开挖基坑 ① manual excavation
② 机械钻孔 ② machine drilling

业务情景：中方张工程师与外方工程师 John 讨论配合施工中存在的问题。
Scene: Mr Zhang and John are discussing existing problems during construction guidance.

典型对话 Conversation

张工程师：130~131 号接触网支柱的实际跨距已经超过了设计要求，请你们重新施工，调整支柱位置。

Mr Zhang: The actual span between pole No.130 and No.131 OCS exceeds the design requirement. Please reconstruct to adjust the pole position.

John：这个地方由于现场新增了涵洞①，支柱位置无法调整。另外，个别地方支柱基坑开挖后，发现现场实际地质承载力与设计图纸不符，我们如何处理？

John: The pole position cannot be adjusted since a new culvert① is added on site. Furthermore, what can we deal with the unconformity between the actual geological bearing capacity on site and that in the design drawing, after the pole foundation is excavated at certain place?

张工程师：请你们以书面方式加盖公章后发给我，我将以变更设计方式处理这个事情。

Mr Zhang: Please send us a letter in written form with the official seal. I will deal with this matter by the mode of changing the design.

第一部分　交通工程情景会话

替换单词 Alternative terms

① 跨线桥　　　　　　　　　① overpass bridge
　 框架桥　　　　　　　　　　 frame bridge

业务情景：中方张工程师与业主方工程师 John 对接触网设计文件进行咨询讨论。
Scene: Mr Zhang and John are having a consultancy discussion of OCS design documents.

典型对话 Conversation

John： 贵公司提供的设计文件，我们已经咨询完毕，现在就其中的几个问题与您沟通一下。

张工程师： 谢谢您提出的咨询意见。

John： 承力索采用 JTMH120、接触线采用 CTS150，建议动车所①的承力索采用 JTMH95、接触线采用 CTS120。

张工程师： 经过我方核算，可以优化，我方同意承力索采用 JTMH95、接触线采用 CTS120。

John： 部分图纸中，接触网零件的尺寸标注有误，请仔细核对并修改。

John: We have completed consultation on the design documents provided by your company. Now we would like to discuss with you about some of the questions.

Mr Zhang: Thank you for your comment.

John: Messenger wire adopts JTMH120 and contact line adopts CTS150. Messenger wire of the EMU depot① is suggested to adopt JTMH95 and contact line is to adopt CTS120.

Mr Zhang: Optimization can be carried out after our estimation. We agree that the messenger wire adopts JTMH95 and contact line adopts CTS120.

John: In some drawings, there are mistakes in the marked size of OCS components. Please carefully check and revise.

277

张工程师:好的,我们将再一次核对并修改,感谢您提出的宝贵意见。

Mr Zhang: Ok. We will check again and revise. Thank you for your comment.

替换单词 Alternative terms

① 机务段　　　　　　　　　　① locomotive depot
　车辆段　　　　　　　　　　　 rolling stock depot
　停车场　　　　　　　　　　　 parking lot

第一部分　交通工程情景会话

第十九章　供电段
Chapter 19　Power Supply Section

业务情景：中方王工程师向外方工程师 Jones 了解相关资料。
Scene: Mr Wang, the engineer from Chinese side, is learning relevant data from Jones, the engineer from foreign side.

🔊 典型对话 Conversation

王工程师：请问贵国现有电气化铁路按什么标准进行设计①？

Jones：按欧洲标准②进行设计。
王工程师：那么运营维护是采用哪国标准呢？
Jones：也是采用欧洲标准。
王工程师：您现在能否为我们提供最近完工的电气化铁路竣工图？

Jones：您要哪个专业的？
王工程师：电气化专业。
Jones：有的，您看，这就是最近完工的东干线竣工图的电子文档。我可以发给您。

Mr Wang: Would you please tell me which standards are adopted for the design① of the existing electrified railway of your country?
Jones: European Standards②.
Mr Wang: How about the standards for operation & maintenance?
Jones: The same.
Mr Wang: Can you provide us with the as-built drawings of electrified railway completed recently?
Jones: Which specialty do you want?
Mr Wang: Electrification.
Jones: All right. Look, this is the soft copy of the as-built Drawing of the east trunk line completed recently.

替换单词 Alternative terms

| ① 施工 | ① construction |
| 验收 | acceptance |

279

② 中国标准　　　　　　　　② Chinese Standards
　俄罗斯标准　　　　　　　　　Russian Standards

业务情景: 中方王工程师要求外方工程师 Jones 提供相关资料。
Scene: Mr Wang is requesting Jones to provide relevant data.

典型对话 Conversation

王工程师: 您好,请提供贵国电气化铁路牵引供电设施及维护管理机构设计和施工规范以及验收标准。

Mr Wang: Please provide us with the specification and acceptance standards for design and construction for traction power supply facilities and their maintenance organization of the electrified railways in your country.

Jones: 好的。

王工程师: 能否提供贵国电气化铁路近期①发展规划?

Jones: All right.

Mr Wang: Can you give us the short-term① development planning for the electrified railway of your country?

Jones: 要经过上级有关部门批准。

Jones: Sorry, that requires approval from superior departments.

王工程师: 请提供贵国现有电气化铁路牵引供电维护机构设置、机具设备配置情况。

Mr Wang: Please give us the information of maintenance organization as well as facilities and equipment configuration for traction power supply in your existing electrified railways.

王工程师: 请问贵国现有的电气化铁路接触网供电设施零部件是自制②吗?

Mr Wang: As for the components and parts of OCS currently used in your electrified railways, are they domestically-made②?

Jones: 不,是采用招标采购。

Jones: No, by tendering procurement.

替换单词 Alternative terms

① 远期
② 外购

① long-term
② outsourcing

业务情景：中方王工程师向外方工程师 Jones 了解相关信息。
Scene: Mr Wang is learning from Jones about relevant information.

典型对话 Conversation

王工程师：现在运营的牵引变电所主变压器的绝缘油是采用何种标准进行化验、分析及处理的？

Jones：采用欧洲标准，只考虑简化分析和绝缘耐压试验。

王工程师：贵国对电气化牵引供电设施的牵引变电所①是按何种标准、周期进行试验，能提供吗？

Jones：采用欧洲标准定期对设备检测、试验。

王工程师：可否提供采用何种方法和手段测试接触网技术状况？

Jones：有综合检测车，由德国提供，测试车最高结构速度 90km/h。

Mr Wang: What kind of standards have you followed for the test, analysis and treatment on the insulating oil of main transformer in the operating traction substations?

Jones: European Standards. Only consider simple analysis and insulation voltage test.

Mr Wang: What kind of standards and periods do you apply to test traction substations① in your country? Can you provide them?

Jones: European standards are adopted for equipment inspection and test at fixed period.

Mr Wang: Would you please tell us about the methods you apply to test OCS technical conditions?

Jones: We have comprehensive inspection car, provided by Germany with highest structural speed of 90km/h.

王工程师：贵国电气化铁路是否配备接触网带电水冲洗车？

Jones：是的。

王工程师：贵国电气化铁路按什么标准配备接触网供电设施抢修车组？

Jones：接触网供电设施抢修车组由架线车、放线车、25t 轨道吊车、60t 平车、牵引轨道车组成。80～100km 配备一组接触网供电设施抢修车。

王工程师：现有电气化铁路是否采用信息化管理手段？

Jones：是的，已经采用了。

王工程师：目前现有的电气化铁路牵引供电维护设施的设置有无标准，比如设施<u>占地面积</u>[②]？

Jones：还没有。

王工程师：目前现有的电气化铁路接触网牵引供电设施实施带电检修作业吗？

Jones：没有。

Mr Wang: Have you been equipped with charged water washing car on your electrified railway?

Jones: Yes. We have.

Mr Wang: What kind of standards have you applied for the OCS power supply facilities to rescue vehicles division in your electrified railway?

Jones: The rescue vehicles division of OCS power supply facilities includes wiring car, wire-barrow, 25t gantry crane, 60t flatcar, and traction rail car. For every 80 to 100km, we will provide one division of rescue vehicles of OCS power supply facilities.

Mr Wang: Do you use information management for the existing electrified railways?

Jones: Yes, we do.

Mr Wang: Do you have any standards for the configuration of traction power supply maintenance facilities in your existing electrified railway, for example, <u>floor area</u>[②]?

Jones: No, we don't.

Mr Wang: Do you perform live line inspection and maintenance on the OCS traction power supply facilities?

Jones: No, we don't.

第一部分　交通工程情景会话

王工程师：牵引供电维护机构采用什么标准或方法，对牵引供变电所一二次设备进行试验、检测？

Mr Wang: For the test and examination on primary and secondary equipment of substations, what kinds of standards or methods do the traction power supply maintenance organization adopt?

Jones：我们采用欧洲标准。

Jones: We adopt European Standards.

替换单词 Alternative terms

① 开闭所
　分区所
② 房屋面积
　检修定员
　主要大型机具

① switching post(SP)
　coupling post(CP)/section post
② building area
　inspection personnel quota
　main large machinery

业务情景：王工程师在气象局和铁路公司收集资料，分别由工作人员 Eric 和 Allen 先生接待他。

Scene: In the Bureau of Meteorology and the Railway Company, Mr Wang is collecting data, and Eric and Allen are receiving him.

典型对话 Conversation

王工程师：为便于开展设计，请问您能够提供贵国的气象资料①吗？

Mr Wang: For a better design, would you please provide us with meteorological data① of your country?

Eric：没问题。

Eric: No problem.

王工程师：您好，恳请贵国提供一条电气化铁路牵引供电维护设施机具设备详细清单以便开展设计。

Mr Wang: Well. Please provide a list of maintenance machineries and equipment for traction power supply of an electrified railway in your country.

Allen：好的。

Allen: Ok.

283

替换单词 Alternative terms

① 地质资料

50年及100年洪水位资料

① geological data

50-year and 100-year flood level data

业务情景：王工程师向铁路公司工程师 Jones 了解情况。
Scene: Mr Wang is communicating with Jones, the engineer of the Railway Company.

典型对话 Conversation

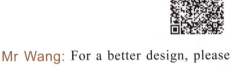

王工程师：您好，为便于开展设计，要求贵国提供电气化铁路牵引供电维护机构①分布图，以及各牵引供电维护机构规模②、运营维护方式以及检修机具等资料。

Mr Wang: For a better design, please provide such data like the layout plan for the traction power supply maintenance organization① of electrified railway, the scale② of each organization, operation and maintenance method and the inspection machineries.

Jones：请出示您的授权信。

Jones: Authorization letter, please.

王工程师：好的，这是贵国铁路公司的授权信。

Mr Wang: All right, this is the letter from the railway company.

Jones：您需要的各类资料目前还不完备，但我们会在最短的时间里收集完毕并发送给您方。

Jones: The data you want are not well prepared, but we will collect and send them to you very soon.

王工程师：多长时间内可以收集完毕？一定不能误了工期！

Mr Wang: How long will it take? Just don't risk the delay of construction period.

Jones：半个月内一定完成，请您放心。

Jones: Don't worry. We will make it within half a month.

第一部分　交通工程情景会话

王工程师：我想搜集关于道路和规划的一些资料。

Jones：请问您要什么资料？

王工程师：贵国对城市轨道交通平交道口接触网净空的要求的资料。

Jones：好的，这些就是您需要的相关资料，请参考。

王工程师：谢谢，我回去会仔细研究，净空高度确定后会发函给您方确认，然后再展开设计。

Mr Wang: I'd like some data about road and planning.

Jones: More specific, please?

Mr Wang: I want the OCS clearance requirement at level crossings for urban rail transit.

Jones: Ok, these are the relevant data you require.

Mr Wang: Thanks, I will study them carefully and send you a letter for approval after the confirmation of clear height. And then we will design.

替换单词 Alternative terms

① 供电段　　　　　　　　　　① power supply section
　供电车间　　　　　　　　　　　power supply workshop
　接触网工区　　　　　　　　　　OCS work zone
② 设备　　　　　　　　　　② equipment
　定员　　　　　　　　　　　　　personnel quota
　房屋面积配备　　　　　　　　　building area preparation
　占地面积　　　　　　　　　　　floor area

业务情景：中方王工程师与外方工程师 Jones 讨论设计计算问题

Scene: Mr Wang is discussing the calculation issues related to design with the foreign engineer Jones.

典型对话 Conversation

Jones：您好，请问接触网采用 JTMH

Jones: Excuse me. Do we need proof

120+CTMH150 的导线组合是否需要验证过程？

王工程师：当然需要。您看，这是从供电的载流量的角度进行验算的资料，这是从悬挂张力与导线拉断力之间的关系进行验算的资料。

Jones：好的，谢谢你们做的这方面的工作。另外今天我还想就接触网带电部分和结构体、车体之间的最小净距进行一次讨论。

王工程师：好的，请讲。

Jones：贵方的设计文件我已经全部看完了，请解释一下接触网带电部分和结构体、车体之间的最小净距？

王工程师：好的，这是根据设计标准①，按照本工程的牵引供电电压等级来确定的，其中，因为本工程在高原实施，所以还考虑了一定的高海拔地区的修正系数。

Jones：也考虑了修正系数的计算过程吗？

王工程师：当然，这是必然的计算过程。

procedure for the adoption of JTMH120+CTMH150 wire combination?

Mr Wang: Absolutely. Look, this is the checking calculation data from the aspect of carrying capacity of power supply, and this is the checking calculation data from the relationship between wire's suspension tension and wire's tensile breaking force.

Jones: All right, thanks for your works. Moreover, today I also want to talk about the live part and structural body of OCS, and the minimum clearance between car bodies.

Mr Wang: Fine.

Jones: I've already gone through all the design documents from your company, please give me the explanation about the live part and structural body of OCS, and the minimum clearance between car bodies.

Mr Wang: Ok, this is decided based on the voltage grade of traction power supply for this project as per the design criteria①. Besides, we also considered the correction factor for high attitude area, because this project is carried out on the plateau.

Jones: Have you considered the process for calculating correction factor?

Mr Wang: Definitely. This is an inevitable calculation process.

第一部分　交通工程情景会话

替换单词 Alternative terms

① 规范　　　　　　　　　　　① code
　原则　　　　　　　　　　　　principle

业务情景：中方王工程师汇报设计方案后，外方提问。
Scene: After design proposal presentation, the foreign party is asking Mr Wang some questions.

典型对话 Conversation

王工程师：刚才我已向各位汇报接触网专业的初步设计内容，大家还有何疑问？

Jones：请问您的设计中是否考虑了双重绝缘系统①。

王工程师：从安全上着想，双重绝缘是一定会考虑的。

Jones：您设计的架空地线是否兼有避雷线的作用。

王工程师：是的，架空地线兼作避雷线，其保护范围应满足防雷要求。

Jones：谢谢。请介绍一下设计进度的问题。我们什么时候可以讨论接触网过轨管线的预埋问题。

Mr Wang: That is all about the preliminary design of the OCS discipline, any questions?

Jones: Have you considered double insulation system① in your design?

Mr Wang: For safety, double insulation system should definitely be considered.

Jones: Does overhead ground wire have the role of lightning conductor in your design?

Mr Wang: Yes, and its protection scope should meet the lightning protection requirement.

Jones: Thanks. Please brief us on the design schedule. When can we discuss about the embedding of OCS cross-track pipes and cables?

287

王工程师：关于平面布置，现在我们正在积极沟通正线上变电所的位置，待业主方批复后，我们可以提供具体的里程。

Jones：业主方已经审阅了贵方提交的关于变电所位置的函件，可能会在近期批复，届时，我们再作讨论。

王工程师：好的，谢谢您的提醒。

Mr Wang: As for the layout plan, currently we are communicating with involved parties about the locations of substations on the main line, and going to provide the specific mileage after the approval of the Employer.

Jones: The Employer has already reviewed the letter about the location of substations submitted by your company, and perhaps you can get a reply soon. And then we will discuss it.

Mr Wang: Fine, thanks for your reminding.

替换单词 Alternative terms

① 非双重绝缘系统　　　　　　① non-double insulation system

业务情景：中方王工程师与外方工程师 Jones 讨论进度问题并进行技术交底
Scene: Mr Wang is discussing the work progress with Jones and presenting technical disclosure document.

典型对话 Conversation

王工程师：根据目前的进度，电气化专业的设备型号还没有具体确定，我担心会影响工期建设。

Mr Wang: According to the current progress, the equipment model of the electrification discipline is not determined, so I'm a little concerned that it will affect the construction period.

Jones: 是的，我们已经就此事报告了相关部门，由于该项目是 EPC 项目①，由承包方采购施工，现在正在启动该项工作，请您放心。

王工程师：这是技术交底文件，请审阅。

Jones: 在你们的文件中对接触网支柱施工位置的表述并不是很详细。

王工程师：这是编制的专业性文件，施工人员能够理解。

Jones: 确实是这样，但是还是请贵方对刚才提到的内容再补充详细一点，最好能够附图说明。

王工程师：好的，我们会按贵方意见改进。

Jones: Well, we have reported this to the competent authority. Because this is an EPC project①, the Contractor is responsible for procurement and construction, and right now we are launching this work. Please take it easy.

Mr Wang: This is the technical disclosure document. Please go through it.

Jones: In your documents, the construction location of OCS mast is not so specific.

Mr Wang: This is professional documents, so the constructor can understand it.

Jones: Sure it is. But would you please give us more details about the issue just mentioned and it's better to attach figures for description.

Mr Wang: Ok, we will improve it as you suggest.

替换单词 Alternative terms

① BOT 项目　　　　　　　　　① BOT project
　POT 项目　　　　　　　　　　POT project
　BOO 项目　　　　　　　　　　BOO project
　BTO 项目　　　　　　　　　　BTO project

业务情景：中方王工程师与外方工程师 Jones 讨论一些具体的设计方案。
Scene: Mr Wang is discussing some specific design proposals with Jones.

典型对话 Conversation

Jones：我们对图纸中的接地系统不是很理解，能不能解释一下。

王工程师：好的，接地分为工作接地和安全接地。你所谈到的是安全接地，我们采用架空地线来实现，图纸中有明确的说明。

Jones：好，我们会去查阅。对贵方提到的接触网隔离开关采用柱顶安装的方案，我们建议能否放在路旁。

王工程师：这个方案我们以前考虑过，由于该项目不同于其他轻轨项目，路旁限界有限，不能实现您说的方案，且本工程线路位于公路中间，也不能实现贵方提出的方案。

Jones: We are a little confused about the earthing system in the drawing, would you please explain it?

Mr Wang: Fine. The earthing is divided into working earthing and safety earthing. You are talking about the safety earthing, and we use overhead ground wire. You can find specific descriptions in the drawing.

Jones: Ok, we will check it. You have mentioned that the OCS disconnector will be installed on the top of the mast, while we suggest that it is placed by roadside.

Mr Wang: Previously we have thought about this proposal, but this project is different from other light rail projects, and the roadside clearance is limited. Therefore, your proposal cannot be realized. In addition, this alignment of the project is located in the middle of the highway, so this also constrains to realize your proposal.

Jones: 原来是这样,我们接受贵方的设计。你们在设计中地下段仍采用柔性悬挂,是否可行?

王工程师: 由于本工程只有很短一段隧道,且隧道的净空能够满足要求,接触网并不是制约因素,所以我们采用<u>柔性悬挂</u>①,与地面保持一致性。

Jones: 谢谢你的解释。

Jones: All right, we accept your design. In your design of the underground section, flexible suspension is still being adopted, is that possible?

Mr Wang: In the project there is only one short tunnel, and the tunnel clearance can meet the requirement, the OCS is not the restraining factor, so we adopt the <u>flexible suspension</u>① to keep it consistent with those on the ground.

Jones: Thanks for your explanation.

替换单词 Alternative terms

① 链性悬挂
　简单悬挂

① longitudinal suspension
　simple suspension

第二十章 建筑
Chapter 20　Architecture

业务情景： 中方王工程师与外方工程师 Jones 就工程项目建设进行前期交涉。

Scene: The designer Mr Wang is now negotiating the engineering construction project with Jones, the engineer of the Employer.

典型对话 Conversation

Jones：现在有栋楼想委托给你方设计。

王工程师：请问项目的规模及功能是什么？

Jones：本项目为<u>还建宿舍</u>①，按<u>多层建筑</u>②设计，<u>容积率</u>③控制在0.5。用地范围就在铁路旁边，你们去看后报个方案过来。

王工程师：不好意思，需要甲方提供用地红线及项目所在地的城市规划技术规定作为建筑设计的前提条件。建议先请施工单位现场测量一个围墙界限，我们先开展前期工作。

Jones: Here is a building we want to commission you to design.

Mr Wang: What's the scale and function?

Jones: It's a <u>reconstruction dormitory</u>①, designed as <u>multi-story</u> design②, 0.5 <u>plot ratio</u>③. The land is close to the railway, and you can have a look first and prepare a proposal.

Mr Wang: We need the Employer to provide the boundary line of land, and the technical specifications for urban planning of the city where the project is located, as the reference for architecture design. Meanwhile, it is suggested that construction contractor measure the enclosure boundary first, so we can proceed with the preliminary work.

Jones: 也行。文件中的总图必须要看出<u>用地红线</u>④。现场测量只有相对尺寸及标高数据,放入站场平面图的位置不准确。

王工程师:建议请勘察设计专业进行现场测绘,用地红线按规定需由甲方提供。

Jones: Sure, the general drawing must show the <u>boundary line of land</u>④. The data measured on site are only relative dimensions and elevations; so they can not accurately match the positions indicated in the plan of station and yard.

Mr Wang: We suggest the professional staff to carry out field surveying and mapping. The boundary line of land shall be provided by the Employer according to the provisions.

替换单词 Alternative terms

① 旅客车站　　　　　　　　① passenger station
　 生产用房综合楼　　　　　　 complex building for production
　 调度大楼　　　　　　　　　 dispatching building
　 变配电所　　　　　　　　　 substation and distribution station
　 食堂浴室　　　　　　　　　 dinning hall and bathroom
② 低层建筑　　　　　　　　② low-rise building
　 高层建筑　　　　　　　　　 high-rise building
　 超高层建筑　　　　　　　　 super high-rise building
③ 绿化率　　　　　　　　　③ greening rate
　 覆盖率　　　　　　　　　　 coverage rate
　 建筑密度　　　　　　　　　 density of building
　 总建筑面积　　　　　　　　 overall floorage
　 建筑基底面积　　　　　　　 building area
④ 道路红线　　　　　　　　④ boundary line of roads
　 绿线　　　　　　　　　　　 green line
　 蓝线　　　　　　　　　　　 blue line
　 紫线　　　　　　　　　　　 purple line
　 黄线　　　　　　　　　　　 yellow line

业务情景: 中方王工程师向外方工程师Jones咨询铁路沿线相关资料,并就当地常用建筑材料进行了解。

Scene: Mr Wang is consulting Jones about the information and data regarding the regions along the Line, as well as local building materials.

典型对话 Conversation

王工程师:你好,这条铁路全长多长?
Jones:从A地到B地共308公里。
王工程师:我们需要从A地到B地沿途的气象资料[①]等参数。
Jones:这段线路抗震设防烈度较高,基本风压较高,没有雪压。

王工程师:那全线设计多少个车站呢?我们最为关心这个。

Jones:从A地到B地设计了14个车站,全部是地面车站。

王工程师:你们这里常用的建筑材料是什么呢?
Jones:烧结普通砖[②]。
王工程师:谢谢你们的配合,让我们一次全部收集完了资料。

Jones:好的,我们期待铁路建成。

Mr Wang: Hello, how long is this railway?
Jones: 308km in total from A to B.
Mr Wang: We need such parameters as meteorological data[①] along the line.
Jones: For such section, both seismic fortification intensity and reference wind pressure are relatively high, without snow pressure.
Mr Wang: The number of stations in the whole line is that we are most concerned about.
Jones: There are totally fourteen stations from A to B; and all are ground-level stations.
Mr Wang: What are the building materials commonly used here?
Jones: Fired common brick[②].
Mr Wang: Thank you for your cooperation to help us collect all these information we need.
Jones: Ok, let's expect the completion of this raiway.

第一部分　交通工程情景会话

替换单词 Alternative terms

① 地质资料　　　　　　　　① geological data
　 运量资料　　　　　　　　　 transportation volume
　 抗震设防烈度　　　　　　　 seismic fortification intensity
　 基本风压　　　　　　　　　 reference wind pressure
　 场地类别　　　　　　　　　 site classification
② 烧结空心砖　　　　　　　② fired hollow brick
　 烧结多孔砖　　　　　　　　 fired perforated brick
　 混凝土小型空心砌块　　　　 concrete small hollow block
　 蒸压粉煤灰砖　　　　　　　 autoclaved flyash-lime brick
　 加气混凝土砌块　　　　　　 aerated concrete block

业务情景：中方王工程师就基本设计输入资料向外方工程师Jones进行咨询，了解项目相关法律与建设程序。
Scene: Mr Wang is consulting Jones about the basic design materials, and gets familiar with the relevant laws and construction procedures.

典型对话 Conversation

王工程师：请问该片区是否进行过规划设计？
Jones：没有。我们没有城市规划设计能力。
王工程师：那是否能提供一些基本的设计输入资料，如城市坐标控制网①等？
Jones：这需要你们自己去测量。

Mr Wang: Excuse me, is there any urban planning for this region?
Jones: No, we don't have the capacity for urban planning.
Mr Wang: Could you provide us some basic design information like city coordinate control network①?
Jones: I'm afraid this should be measured by yourself.

295

王工程师：那是否意味着我们只有根据自己的需要自行调查获得各种数据？

Jones：是的。

王工程师：那这里面有没有和建设项目相关的一些法律呢？

Jones：有的，这个可以在法院和档案馆里找到。

王工程师：负责主管建设的部门有哪些呢？

Jones：稍候我们可以去看一看，我再详细给你介绍一下建设程序。

Mr Wang: Does that mean we have to investigate all kinds of data information that we need by ourselves?

Jones: Yes.

Mr Wang: Is there any laws relating to this construction project?

Jones: Yes, you can find them in the local courts and archives.

Mr Wang: Which departments are in charge of construction?

Jones: We can have a visit later, and I will introduce you the procedure in details.

替换单词 Alternative terms

① 高程控制网　　　　　　　　① vertical control network
　百年洪水位　　　　　　　　　 maximum flood level in a century
　水文资料　　　　　　　　　　 hydrologic data
　市政配套设施　　　　　　　　 municipal supporting facilities

业务情景：中方王工程师和外方工程师Jones就建筑整体高度和色彩方案等进行讨论和商榷。
Scene: Mr Wang is discussing with Jones on the overall height of buildings and color scheme.

典型对话 Conversation

王工程师：请先看一下我们这个建筑的外观效果图，整个建筑面宽120m，进

Mr Wang: Please have a look at the appearance design sketch of this building,

深30m,建筑高度18m。建筑高度是按女儿墙①顶点高度计算的。

Jones: 我觉得整体高度偏高,能否降低一些高度,或者局部设置层次错落。

王工程师: 这个我们可以推敲一下,但是高度我们建议不要降低太多,不然比例会失调。

Jones: 好的,另外颜色上稍显平淡,能否增加一些亮色。

王工程师: 好的,我们会再增加两三个色彩方案进行比选。

Jones: 建筑的间距能否再缩小一些。

王工程师: 这是根据防火②等有关规定控制的。

it is 120m in width, 30m in depth and 18m in height. The height is calculated according to the peak of parapet wall①.

Jones: I think it's lightly higher. Can it be lowered or staggered in levels sectionally?

Mr Wang: We can have it discussed, but we suggest that the height is not lowered too much. Otherwise, it will become imbalanced.

Jones: Ok, in addition, the color is a little dull. Some bright color may be better.

Mr Wang: Ok, we will add two or three color schemes for selection.

Jones: Can the distance between buildings be shorter?

Mr Wang: This distance is controlled according to the fire-proof② regulation.

替换单词 Alternative terms

① 楼梯间
   电梯间
   水箱间
   天线
   避雷针
② 日照
   采光
   防视线干扰
   防噪声

① staircase
   elevator room
   water tank room
   antenna
   lightning rod
② sunlight
   daylighting
   anti-interference of sight line
   anti-noise

业务情景： 中方王工程师向外方工程师 Jones 介绍项目概况和一些项目的细节设计。
Scene: Mr Wang is introducing the project overview and some detail design to Jones.

典型对话 Conversation

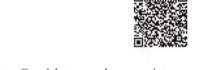

Jones： 请介绍一下项目概况。

王工程师： 该站建筑规模为 2000m²，共一层；站房为<u>线侧平式</u>[①]站房，<u>最高聚集人数</u>[②]为 1500 人。

Jones： 请在总图上指出车站的位置、南北方向，车站附近的交通组织如何考虑的？

王工程师： 根据中国的习惯，图纸一般是上北下南，在车站的正面设置广场，广场的两边分别设置公交车停车场、出租车停车场、社会车停车场和长途汽车停车场，运送旅客进出站区。

Jones： 车站的用水、用电如何解决？

王工程师： 在站区附近打井解决用水；建柴油发电机解决用电。

Jones： 根据该地区的气候特点，如何考虑排水、遮阳？

Jones: Could you please give an introduction about the project overview?

Mr Wang: This station is one-storey <u>lineside</u>[①] building, 2000m² for building area, holding a <u>maximum</u>[②] of 1500 passengers.

Jones: Please point out the position of station and the north-south direction on the general drawing. Besides, what about the traffic control around the station?

Mr Wang: In China, in general, north is at the upside and south is at the downside of the drawing. A square is designed in front of the station. On both sides of the square, parking areas are set separately for buses, taxies, cars and coaches.

Jones: How to solve water and electricity supply within the station?

Mr Wang: Water can be sourced by digging wells nearby, and electricity can be supplied by diesel generator.

Jones: According to climatic characteristics of the region, what's your idea about rain discharging and shade?

王工程师：屋面设置坡屋面③和排水沟④，利用屋面出挑和设置雨棚以达到防水⑤的目的。

Jones：建筑采用什么结构形式？

王工程师：框架结构⑥。

Jones：根据该地区人民的生活习惯，是否有考虑设置祈祷室？

王工程师：是的。

Jones：如何考虑车站附近的商业设置？

王工程师：在站房入口处设置商业区域，在广场上设置多个商业网点。

Jones：如何实现站房的通风采光？

王工程师：用大面积的玻璃幕墙和窗户实现采光，设置通风的防雨百叶实现通风。

Jones：对于车站的无障碍设计是如何考虑的？

王工程师：设置有盲道⑦等方便残疾人旅客的设计。

Jones：窗户是什么开启方式？

Mr Wang: Set sloping roof③ and gutters④ on the roofing and canopy by the roof overhangs to achieve the waterproof⑤ purpose.

Jones: What is the structure form of the building?

Mr Wang: Frame structure⑥.

Jones: Is there any prayer room for local people?

Mr Wang: Yes, there is.

Jones: How about the commercial arrangement near the station?

Mr Wang: Commercial area would be considered at the entrance of the station building, and several commercial positions would be set on the square.

Jones: How to realize ventilation and lighting of the station building?

Mr Wang: We adopt a lot of glass curtain walls and windows for lighting, adopt rainproof shutter for ventilation.

Jones: What about the design on barrier free facilities for stations?

Mr Wang: There are sidewalks for the blind⑦ and other facilities designed for the convenience of disabled passengers.

Jones: What's the open mode of windows?

王工程师：平开窗⑧，选用节能中空玻璃⑨。

Jones：屋面防水做法能介绍一下吗？

王工程师：屋面采用的混凝土屋面⑩，采用刚性防水⑪。

Mr Wang: Casement window⑧, and we choose energy-saving hollow glass⑨.

Jones: Can you introduce the roof waterproofing?

Mr Wang: We adopt concrete roofing⑩ and rigid waterproofing⑪.

替换单词 Alternative terms

① 线侧下式
线侧上式
高架式

② 高峰小时发送量

③ 平屋面
架空屋面
种植屋面
蓄水屋面

④ 天沟
檐沟
雨水口

⑤ 遮阳
保温
隔热

⑥ 砖混结构
框架剪力墙结构
木结构
钢结构
无梁楼盖结构

⑦ 轮椅坡道
无障碍电梯

① line-side lower-type
line side upper-type
overhead-type

② dispatched numbers of passengers at peak hour

③ flat roof
overhead roof
planted roof
water storage roof

④ roof gutter
eaves gutters
gullies

⑤ sunshading
heat preservation
thermal insulation

⑥ brick structure
frame shear wall structure
wood structure
steel structure
non-beam floor structure

⑦ wheelchair ramps
barrier-free elevators

无障碍厕所	barrier-free toilets
低位服务设施	low height service facilities
⑧ 上悬窗	⑧ top-hung window
下悬窗	hopper windows
固定窗	fixed windows
推拉窗	sliding windows
⑨ 吸热玻璃	⑨ heat-absorbing glass
热发射玻璃	thermal emission glass
低辐射玻璃	low-emissivity glass
普通玻璃	ordinary glass
夹胶玻璃	laminated glass
⑩ 压型钢板屋面	⑩ profiled sheet roofing
玻璃采光屋面	lighting glass roofing
瓦屋面	tile roofing
⑪ 涂膜防水	⑪ waterproof coating
卷材防水	waterproof membrane

业务情景：外方工程师 Jones 向中方王工程师咨询国铁、轻轨与机场的换乘及出入口等情况。

Scene: Jones is consulting Mr Wang on the situation of transfer and passageway of railways, light rails and airports.

典型对话 Conversation

Jones: 请大概介绍一下国铁、轻轨与机场的换乘情况。

王工程师: 好的,国铁、轻轨共用站厅层,中间为公共换乘厅,两侧为国铁、轻轨的设备、办公用房。国铁轻轨客流通

Jones: Would you like to introduce us how to transfer between railways, light rails and airports?

Mr Wang: No problem. Railway and light rail will share a concourse, the public transfer concourse will be located

过中间的公共换乘厅直接换乘。公共换乘厅与机场设两条换乘通道,通过换乘通道实现国铁、轻轨、机场三者之间的无缝换乘。

in the middle, equipment rooms and office rooms for railways and light rails will be located on both sides. Passengers can directly transfer between railway and light rail through the public concourse in the middle. Two transfer channels will be built between public concourse and airport for seamless transfer between railway, light rail and airport.

Jones: 有几个出入口出地面呢?

Jones: How many entrances can lead to the ground?

王工程师: 共有三个大的出入口,另外还有几个小的疏散口和风井。

Mr Wang: There are three major entrances, and several small escape exits and air shafts.

Jones: 这些出地面构筑物对航站楼广场的景观影响有多大呢?

Jones: Will these entrances structures affect the scenery of the Terminal Square?

王工程师: 我们尽可能将出入口、风井与地面景观结合起来,使之形成地面景观的一部分,这可以通过造型、绿化等手段来实现。

Mr Wang: We will make the entrances and air shafts harmonious with ground landscape through styling, greening, etc.

Jones: 好的,谢谢!

Jones: Ok, thanks!

业务情景: 中方王工程师向外方工程师 Jones 介绍项目的设计原则及构思。
Scene: Chinese engineer Mr Wang is presenting the design principle and project conception to foreign engineer Jones.

典型对话 Conversation

Jones: 请介绍一下这个项目的设计原则。

Jones: Would you please introduce the design principle of this Project?

王工程师：我们本次设计的原则主要有三项。一是时代性，充分考虑同一个城市不同时期，不同年代的城市特征和建筑风格的差异性，设计必须展示新发展阶段的特色和面貌；二是地域性，建筑所处的地域不同，历史文化有一定的差异，车站应体现地域文化内涵；三是唯一性，每个城市独具特色的历史和发展方向注定其车站是独一无二的。

Mr Wang: We have three major design principles for this project. First,. we give full consideration to the city's epochal character, since architectural styles are different in the different periods. The design must vividly display the characteristics and features of a new development stage; Second, with different territories and varied history and culture, station should embody the local and cultural connotations; Third, Each station is bound to be unique for the unique history of city and orientation of development.

Jones：那在设计上有哪些构思呢？

Jones: What are the ideas on the design?

王工程师：建筑形态上，以本地独具特色的小青瓦[①]搭配白色仿石涂料[②]墙面作为全线的设计母题，同时结合各站的地方特色，在整体的和谐中创造一站一景的效果。设计充分考虑当地的气候环境，多使用空透灵巧的建筑形象，体现旅游岛轻松亲切的休闲度假气质。

Mr Wang: In terms of architectural form, we use unique Chinese-style tiles[①] matched with white stone-like paint[②] wall as the design theme throughout the whole line. Meanwhile, we will integrate local features into a harmonious effect of "one station, one view". Considering the local climate and environment, use more graceful hollow and smart forms to create a relaxed and friendly atmosphere.

Jones：请根据效果图每个站逐一地介绍一下。

Jones: Please introduce each station one by one according to the rendering.

王工程师：好的。

Mr Wang: Ok.

替换单词 Alternative terms

① 混凝土瓦　concrete tile
　平瓦　　　flat tile
　琉璃瓦　　glazed tile
　筒瓦　　　Tongwa
　沥青瓦　　asphalt shingles
② 花岗石　　granite
　文化砖　　culture brick
　轻钢龙骨石膏板　metal frame plasterboard
　GRC 空心墙板　　GRC hollow wall

业务情景：中方王工程师向外方监理工程师 Jones 咨询工程的进度计划。
Scene: Chinese engineer Mr Wang is consulting the Supervisor Jones on the progress plan.

典型对话 Conversation

王工程师：这个项目是 EPC 总承包吗？
Jones：是的。
王工程师：有没有工程进度计划？
Jones：有，4 月底要完成施工图设计。
王工程师：那初步设计已经审查完了吗？
Jones：上周刚刚做完初步设计文件，正在审查，待审查意见一下来，就可以按意见修改进行施工图设计了。

Mr Wang: Is this an EPC project?
Jones: Yes.
Mr Wang: Is there a progress plan?
Jones: Sure, the detailed design will be accomplished at the end of April.
Mr Wang: Has the preliminary design been finished already?
Jones: The preliminary design was accomplished last week and is under examination now. Upon the issue of review comments, we can start with the detailed design.

第一部分　交通工程情景会话

王工程师：那什么时候开放第一版施工图资料呢？
Jones：一周之内。
王工程师：注意开放资料之前必须和设备专业稳定强电间①的大小和位置。

Mr Wang: When will the first edition of detailed design be released?
Jones: Within one week.
Mr Wang: Please confirm the size and the position of high-voltage room① with mechanical discipline before releasing the design.

替换单词 Alternative terms

① 新风井	① new air shaft
排风井	ventilation shaft
烟道	flue
配线间	wiring chamber

业务情景：中方王工程师向外方监理工程师Jones就铁路站房值班室进行双向讨论，确定值班室功能要求及面积的控制。
Scene: Chinese engineer Mr Wang is discussing the duty room of railway station building with the Supervisor Jones, to determine the rooms function and size control.

典型对话 Conversation

王工程师：这份图纸是铁路站房值班室的大样图，连同附属的卫生间一共15m²，请您过目。

Jones：对不起，由于工程预算的原因，业主要求将该值班室压缩为10m²，请对你的平面进行修改。

Mr Wang: This is the detail drawing of railway station duty room, totally 15m²(15 square meters) with the affiliated toilets, please have a look.

Jones: Sorry, the Employer requests to reduce the duty room area to 10m²(10 square meters) due to construction budget, please modify your plan.

305

王工程师：好的，那我取消卫生间，重新调整一次方案。

Jones：对不起，为了我们值班人员的舒适，本着以人为本的原则，卫生间必须保留，而且还要增设一个洗脸盆和淋浴设备。注意值班室的装修要使用地砖地面①，顶棚采用铝合金方板②顶棚。

王工程师：我们建议值班室不设置吊顶③，可以节省部分投资。

Jones：对了，我还要补充一下，这个值班室担负着监控的功能，里面需要布置两个控制柜，你再跟相关人员确认一下。最后还有一点，电力的设备房间面积太紧张，他们的两个开关柜移设到这个值班室里面。

王工程师：我觉得这不太合理。

Mr Wang: Ok, the toilet can be canceled.

Jones: I don't think so. We should insist on the people-oriented principle, so toilet must be reserved for ease of our staff on duty. Furthermore, a washbasin and a shower would be added. Please adopt tile floor① in the duty room, and aluminium alloy square slab② ceiling.

Mr Wang: To save the cost, we suggest not to use ceiling③ in duty room.

Jones: Something more, the duty room also has monitoring function, so two control cabinets should be arranged, please confirm it. The last, two switch cabinets should be moved to this duty room from the narrow electricity room.

Mr Wang: I don't think it's a good idea.

替换单词 Alternative terms

① 采暖地面
　不发火地面
　石材地面
　木质地面
　防静电架空地面
② 铝格栅
　石膏板
　塑料条形扣板
③ 墙裙
　踢脚

① heating floor
　non-sparking floor
　stone floor
　wood floor
　static-free raised floor
② aluminum grating
　gypsum board
　plastic strip pinch
③ dado
　skirting

第一部分 交通工程情景会话

第二十一章 结构
Chapter 21 Structure

业务情景: 中方王工程师与外方工程师 Jones 讨论图纸单位制及分析设计软件问题。

Scene: Chinese engineer Mr Wang is discussing unit system of the drawing and analysis design software with Jones, the foreign engineer Jones.

典型对话 Conversation

Jones: 你们提供的设计图纸[1]将采用什么单位制?

王工程师: 我们设计图纸将采用国际单位制。

Jones: 但我们都是采用英制单位表示。

王工程师: 这样吧,我们在设计图中附上国际制与英制的换算表。

Jones: 这样对施工公司[2]还是不方便,还是全部用英制单位标注吧。

王工程师: 好吧。那你们对于结构分析/设计软件有什么要求吗,能否采用中国的计算软件?

Jones: 这恐怕不行,我们要求采用国际通用的结构计算软件。

Jones: Which unit system will you use in your design drawings[1]?

Mr Wang: We will use international units.

Jones: Oh, but we use the British system.

Mr Wang: Don't worry! We can attach a conversion table between international unit system and British system in the design drawings.

Jones: It's still not convenient for the construction contractor[2], please use British system.

Mr Wang: Ok. What's your opinion on the structural analysis/design software? Can we use Chinese software?

Jones: I'm afraid not. It is required to adopt international analysis software for structure.

307

王工程师：采用 ETABS 或 SAP2000 这样的软件可以吗？

Jones：可以。

王工程师：我知道了，具体采用哪种计算软件我回去考虑一下，还有很多细节问题我们下次再谈。

Jones：好的。

王工程师：另外，能否提供一份计算书的范本给我们。

Jones：可以，稍后我发到你邮箱里。

Mr Wang: What about ETABS or SAP2000?

Jones: That's good.

Mr Wang: I see. I will think on the calculation software, and I suppose there are still many details we'll discuss together next time..

Jones: Ok.

Mr Wang: Besides, can you provide a template of calculation sheets to us?

Jones: Sure, I will email it to you.

替换单词 Alternative terms

① 技术文件
② 监理公司
　　第三方审核公司

① technical documents
② supervision company
　　third-party review company

业务情景：中方王工程师与外方工程师 Jones 讨论图纸中存在的与当地规范不符的问题

Scene: Mr Wang is discussing with Jones the unconformity between some contents in the drawings and local specifications.

典型对话 Conversation

Jones：在你们提供的设计图纸（计算书）中，我们看到有一些与当地规范不相符合的地方。

王工程师：哦，都有哪些问题？

Jones: We found some discrepancies between some contents in your design drawings (calculation sheets) and the local specifications.

Mr Wang: Oh, what're they?

第一部分　交通工程情景会话

Jones：有9处。

王工程师：请把问题的清单和你们做了标记的设计图放在一起，我带回去由工程师们检查一下，尽快把修改后的设计文件再次提交给贵方。

Jones：两个星期后的星期五上午10点你们可以提交吗？

王工程师：可以。

（两个星期以后）

王工程师：我们回去再次核对了一下我们的设计，认为你们提出的问题中有几处需要讨论。

Jones：都有哪几个问题？

王工程师：现在看第一个问题，这是关于建筑物<u>地震作用</u>① 的计算问题。我想知道的是，您提出的问题的关键是什么？

Jones：你们提交的计算书中，关于建筑物底部剪力的计算，钢筋混凝土结构和<u>砌体结构</u>②，剪重比都是一样的，这与我们规范的计算方法不一样。

王工程师：那我们回去再仔细看一下贵国的规范。现在我们来看下一个问题。

Jones：这是关于房屋抗水平力体系的问题。这里我想问的是，为什么在这些没有超过三层的楼房中，全部采用<u>剪力墙</u>③结构体系？

Jones: Totally nine discrepancies.

Mr Wang: So please give me a list, together with the marked drawings. I will bring it back to our engineers. After modification, the latest version will be delivered to you as soon as possible.

Jones: Could you deliver them at 10:00 a.m. on Friday after two weeks?

Mr Wang: I think it should be Ok.

(Two weeks later)

Mr Wang: We have checked our designs, and I'm afraid some of the issues you proposed need to be further discussed.

Jones: What are they?

Mr Wang: Let's see the first one. It's about the calculation of <u>seismic effect</u>① on buildings. I'd like to know your concern on this issue.

Jones: In your calculations, shear-weight ratio of reinforced concrete structure and that of <u>masonry structure</u>② are the same. It's not consistent with the calculation method in our specification.

Mr Wang: Ok. We will study your specification once more. Let's move on to the next.

Jones: It's about horizontal force-resisting system of buildings. Why does the <u>shear wall</u> structure be adopted③ in these low-rise building with not more than three stories?

王工程师：请让我来解释一下，这个问题我们是这样考虑的：虽然不超过三层，但层高高，跨度大，并且平面不规则，竖向也不规则，增加柱断面受限，所以用剪力墙结构体系。

Jones：但是，也可以采用混合的抗水平力结构体系。

王工程师：好，这个问题我们再考虑一下。
王工程师：下一个问题，这个问题我们的确没有考虑周到，我们现在改成这样，请看这张图。
Jones：改成这样是可以的。
王工程师：谢谢！再看下一个问题……
（讨论进行中）
王工程师：看来除了底部剪力之外，其他的问题都解决了。
Jones：对，下次我们就集中讨论底部剪力就可以了。

Mr Wang: Let me explain to you, the shear wall structure is adopted due to the charateristics of the building such as high story height, large span, plane and verticle irregularity and limited increased column section.

Jones: But we think the compounded horizontal force resisting system is also feasible..

Mr Wang: Ok, we will reconsider it.
Mr Wang: Next, we admit we had not considered that thoughtfully, and we modified it, please check this drawing.
Jones: It's Ok.
Mr Wang: Thanks! Let's see the next...
(In discussion)
Mr Wang: So it seems all issues have been solved except for buildings base shear.
Jones: Yes, next time we can focus on it.

替换单词 Alternative terms

① 底部剪力
　地震剪重比
　风荷载
② 木结构
　钢结构
　钢筋混凝土结构
③ 框架
　框架-剪力墙

① base shear
　seismic shear-weight ratio
　wind load
② wood structure
　steel structure
　reinforced concrete structure
③ frame
　frame-shear wall

支撑	bracing
框支剪力墙	frame supported shear wall

业务情景：中方王工程师与外方工程师 Jones 讨论双方建筑抗震设计规范的主要不同点。

Scene: Mr Wang is discussing with Jones the main differences between specifications for seismic design of building used in two counties.

典型对话 Conversation

王工程师： 上次我们谈到建筑物剪重比的计算问题，我回去后对比了两国建筑抗震设计规范，两国规范主要有两个方面的不同。

Jones： 是哪两方面？

王工程师： 第一是我国规范有多遇地震的概念，贵国的抗震设计规范没有这个概念。两国规范关键的不同之处是对于设防地震[①]的折减方法，贵国地震的折减方法是由工程师根据房屋结构材料与结构形式采用不同的折减系数。延性好的结构材料或结构体系，折减系数就大一些，反之，就小些。

Mr Wang: For the calculation of building shear-weight ratio discussed last time, we made a comparison on specifications for seismic design of building used in two countries. The comparison result shows there are two differences between specifications used in two countries.

Jones: Ok, what are they?

Mr Wang: First, we have a concept of frequent earthquake in our specification, which lacks in the design specification of your country. The key difference between the two specifications lies in the reduction method of design earthquake[①]. In your specification, the reduction factor is adopted based on the structural materials and type of building. The better the ductility of structure materials or systems,

Jones:哦,那还是要按我们的规范进行设计吧。
王工程师:好的。
Jones:两国规范第二个不同点是什么?
王工程师:就是关于建筑物在地震作用下侧向位移②的估算问题。

Jones:本国抗震规范中,设防地震作用下建筑物的侧向位移③按等位移假设进行计算。

王工程师:我国规范是以等能量法则为基础计算罕遇地震作用下结构弹塑性位移的。

Jones:哦,同样,在这方面还是要按我们的规范进行设计。不过,您认为,上述两种方法,那一种更为合理一些呢?

王工程师:这个问题理论性较强,一下子无法回答。
Jones:哦,那我们以后再慢慢讨论吧。
王工程师:好。

the larger the reduction coefficient and vise versa.

Jones: I see, any way, please follow our specification?
Mr Wang: Ok.
Jones: What about the other difference?
Mr Wang: It's about the estimation of lateral displacement② of buildings under seismic action.
Jones: In our specification, lateral displacement③ of buildings under design earthquake is based on assumptive equal displacement concept.
Mr Wang: In Chinese specification, the elastic-plastic displacement of structures by severe earthquake is calculated based on equal energy concept.
Jones: Same as before, we insist to follow our specification regarding this matter. However, which method do you think is more reasonable?
Mr Wang: It's too theoretical for me to answer you right now.
Jones: Well, we can discuss it later.
Mr Wang: Ok.

替换单词 Alternative terms

① 设防地震
   罕遇地震

① design/precautionary earthquake
   rare earthquake//maximum considered earthquake (MCD)

众值地震	public value earthquake
② 荷载	② load
恒荷载	dead load
活荷载	live load
风荷载	wind load
③ 层间位移	③ story drift
结构弹塑性位移	elastoplastic displacement

第二十二章　电力
Chapter 22　Electric Power

业务情景: 中方王工程师与埃塞俄比亚国家监理——外方工程师 Tom 就图纸问题进行见面预约。

Scene: Mr Wang, the engineer from Chinese side, is making an appointment with Tom, the supervisor and engineer of Ethiopia, to exchange opinions on drawings.

典型对话 Conversation

王工程师: 你好，Tom 先生，我是 Jim，电力专业的设计者。想跟您谈一下昨天会议上讨论的问题。

Tom: 当然可以，Jim。

王工程师: 我想请您看一下我们 "8.6 公里处扳道房①对其他构筑物的相对距离"，其中包括位置图和详图。

Tom: 你和其他专业的设计者讨论过了吗？

王工程师: 我们已经和其他专业的设计者讨论了这一个问题。其他专业的上述距离经过计算符合规定，我们可以约个时间具体讨论一下这个问题。

Mr Wang: Hello, Tom. I'm Jim, the designer of electric power. Let's proceed with our discussion yesterday.

Tom: Sure, Jim.

Mr Wang: This is the document indicating the relative distance from other structures to the switch control cabin① at the place of 8.6km on the railway line, including site plan and detailed drawing. Please check it out.

Tom: Have you talked about this with designers of other disciplines?

Mr Wang: Yes, we discussed this issue before. Calculation results show that the above-mentioned distance complies with the relevant specification of other disciplines. We may dig into details later.

第一部分　交通工程情景会话

Tom: 可以，请您带着和他们讨论后的新的设计图纸明天 9:30 来开会。

王工程师: 那太好了，非常期待明天的会面，如果您需要改动时间的话，尽管电话联系我。

Tom: No problem. I would like you to bring the newly designed drawings after your discussion to the meeting at 9:30 tomorrow morning.

Mr Wang: That would be great. I'm looking forward to meeting you tomorrow. If you need to change the time, please do not hesitate to let me know.

替换单词 Alternative terms

① 办公楼
　 站房
　 通信站

① office building
　 station building
　 communication station

业务情景：中方王工程师与埃塞俄比亚国家监理——外方工程师 Tom 就图纸问题进行讨论。
Scene: Mr Wang is discussing drawings with Tom.

典型对话 Conversation

王工程师：你好，Tom。这是我们几天前发给您的电力专业设计的 8.6km 扳道房照明①的图纸。您能不能看一下，然后给我一些意见呢？

Tom: 好的，总的说来，这些图纸非常好，就是有一些小问题。

王工程师：请问都有哪些问题。

Tom: 首先，您能不能在洗手间里的洗手盆附近增加一个插座②呢，可能有的人在洗漱的时候会用到。

Mr Wang: Hi, Tom. This is the lighting① drawing of switch control cabin at 8.6km we sent to you a few days ago. Would you please comment on it?

Tom: Generally speaking, it is quite good, but there are still some slight problems.

Mr Wang: So what are the problems?

Tom: Firstly, we recommend installing a socket② near the wash basin inside the wash room for those who may use it.

315

王工程师:没问题。

Tom:然后,因为这个建筑是在轨道的边上,所以我不确定它是否离轨道③太近。

王工程师:结构方面的设计者告诉我距离是足够的。

Tom:你应该需要和其他专业讨论一下这个问题。

王工程师:我稍后将和其他专业的人确认这个问题。

Tom:您可以给我一些能够表明这个情况的图纸吗?

王工程师:当然,我会给你一些图纸。

Tom:从你的图上可以看到,从墙到水平接地体的距离是3m,这是一个很大的范围。

王工程师:3m的距离是根据规范确定的。

Tom:也许水平接地体和接触网支柱会发生冲突,能不能够尽可能地把接地线距墙的距离减至最低呢?

王工程师:因为它是一个小房子,也许我可以通过计算减小那个距离,尽量满足对接触网支柱④的距离要求。

Mr Wang: Ok.

Tom: In addition, since the structure is located next to the track, I'm not quite sure whether it is too close to the track③.

Mr Wang: In the view of the structure designer, the clearance from the structure to track is quite sufficient.

Tom: I think you should further discuss this issue with designers of other disciplines.

Mr Wang: Sure, I will confirm this later.

Tom: May I have some drawings explicitly demonstrating the clearance mentioned above?

Mr Wang: Of course, I will show you some.

Tom: We can see from the drawing that the distance from the horizontal grounding body to wall is 3m, which occupies a relatively large area.

Mr Wang: Distance of 3m is determined in accordance with the specification.

Tom: Is there any possibility to minimize the distance as far as practicable, to avoid location conflict between the horizontal grounding body and OCS mast?

Mr Wang: Since the structure is relatively small, we may reduce the distance by calculation, so as to meet the distance requirements for OCS mast④ to the greatest extent.

第一部分　交通工程情景会话

Tom：那非常好,跟您谈话很开心。如果您完成了刚才所说的改动,我将会给你图纸批复"A"。

Tom: That would be great, nice talking to you. As soon as the modifications we discussed previously are completed, your drawing will be approved with "A".

替换单词 Alternative terms

① 动力　　　　　　　　　　① dynamic
　消防　　　　　　　　　　　 fire protection
　静态标识　　　　　　　　　 static sign
　防雷接地　　　　　　　　　 lightning protection and grounding
② 灯具　　　　　　　　　　② light fixture
　开关　　　　　　　　　　　 switch
③ 接触网支柱　　　　　　　③ OCS mast (pole)
④ 接地　　　　　　　　　　④ grounding

业务情景：中方王工程师到业主那了解车站既有设施的情况。
Scene: Mr Wang is visiting the Employer to get to know the existing facilities in the station.

典型对话 Conversation

王工程师：你好,Tom。前几天我们约定,这次主要是来了解车站既有电力设施的一些情况的。

Mr Wang: Hi, Tom. As arranged, I'd like to get some information on the existing electrical power facilities in this station this time.

Tom：你好,Jim。好的,请问您需要了解哪些情况呢,我将一一为您解答。

Tom: Hi, Jim, no problem. So please tell me what you need to know, I will answer them one by one.

王工程师：请问您这里的中压电压等级[①]是多少?

Mr Wang: Firstly, what's the medium-voltage level[①]?

317

Tom: 中压系统等级为66kV、33kV、15kV。

王工程师: 请问您这站场主要供电负荷点有哪些呢?

Tom: 主要供电负荷点为机辆段、综合维修中心② 以及其他相关配套建筑。

王工程师: 请问您这站场主要供电负荷类型有哪些呢?

Tom: 主要供电负荷类型为信号、通信、信息化③、给排水、暖通及室内外照明等。

王工程师: 请问您这站场电力设计的原则是什么呢?

Tom: 铁路供电设计以安全适用、成熟可靠、经济合理、维护方便为原则。

王工程师: 请问变电设施设在哪里比较合适?

Tom: 变电设施应尽可能设于负荷中心。

王工程师: 对于一级负荷④的供电有哪些要求?

Tom: 对于一级负荷提供两路独立电源供电,低压末端自动切换⑤。

Tom: Medium-voltage level include 66kV, 33kV and 15kV.

Mr Wang: And what are the main power supply points in this station?

Tom: It mainly includes locomotive & rolling stock depot, comprehensive service centre② and other related auxiliary buildings.

Mr Wang: And what's the main type of power load?

Tom: It primarily contains signal, communication, informatisation③, water supply & drainage, heating, ventilation and indoor and outdoor lighting.

Mr Wang: What are the principles you've adopted for electrical power design in the station?

Tom: Railway power supply design shall be carried out based on the principle of safety, applicability, maturity and reliability, economy and maintainability.

Mr Wang: Where is the suitable location for transformation facilities?

Tom: We think it shall be set in the load centre as much as possible.

Mr Wang: What are the requirements for power supply of first level load④?

Tom: Two independent power supply⑤ systems shall be used for first order load and it could switch automatically at low voltage terminal⑤.

王工程师：对于主要电力设备的选用有哪些要求？

Tom：主要电力设备选用成熟可靠、易运营维护的产品，并适合这里的自然环境条件。

王工程师：那我应该根据哪些规范来设计，您有没有具体的要求呢？

Tom：我们做站场电力设计一般参照本国的一些电力规范。

（注：每个国家的规范不一样，请根据具体情况增加规范的名字）

王工程师：好的，我会去了解一下这方面的规范以及本地区的设备。非常感谢你提供了这么多有用的信息给我。

Tom：希望我们今后能有长期的合作。

Mr Wang: What are the requirements for selection of major electrical equipment?

Tom: We think the requirements shall include maturity, reliability, maintainability and environmental adaptability.

Mr Wang: What are the specifications we shall use in the design? What's your requirement?

Tom: Station's electrical design is usually conducted according to some electrical specifications of our country.

(Note: Electrical specification varies with countries, please add the specification name as the case may be.)

Mr Wang: Fine, I will learn about specifications for electrical design and about local equipment. I really appreciate your useful information.

Tom: I wish to establish a long-term cooperation relation with you.

替换单词 Alternative terms

① 低压系统
　频率

② 信号楼
　给水所
　单身宿舍

③ 机务
　车辆
　机械

① low voltage system
　frequency

② signal building
　water supply station
　dormitory

③ locomotive maintenance and repair
　rolling stock
　machinery

④ 二级负荷　　　　　　　　　　④ second level load
　三级负荷　　　　　　　　　　　third level load
⑤ 一路可靠电源供电　　　　　　⑤ one reliable power supply system
　一路电源供电　　　　　　　　　one power supply system

第一部分　交通工程情景会话

第二十三章　暖通
Chapter 23　Heating & Ventilation

业务情景: 中方李工程师和外方工程师 Peter 讨论工程设计范围。
Scene: Mr Li, the engineer from Chinese side, is discussing the engineering design scope, with Peter, the engineer of foreign side.

典型对话 Conversation

李工程师: 你好，Peter，我想讨论一下工程设计范围的问题。

Peter: 好的，请讲。

李工程师: 我们仔细阅读了甲方的招标文件，在业主要求中，供暖不在招标范围之内，是不是我们就不做供暖设计？

Peter: 原则上按招标文件执行设计任务，这个还需要业主进一步明确。

李工程师: 此工程位于严寒地区①，采取供暖措施，才能更好地满足人员舒适和工艺要求，且在初步设计②阶段已经进行了供暖设计，现在进行施工图设计，请你方认真考虑是否配置供暖设施。

Mr Li: Hello, Peter, I want to discuss the issue on design scope of works.

Peter: Ok, please go ahead.

Mr Li: We have carefully read the bidding document of the Owner, and in the Owner's requirements, heating is not included in the bidding scope. Does it mean that we don't need to do the heating design?

Peter: In principle, the design task shall be executed according to bidding document, and be confirmed further by the Owner.

Mr Li: This project is located in severe cold area①; we think heating measures can better meet the requirements of personnel comfort and technological process, and the design of heating has already been carried out in preliminary design② stage, and now we are designing

321

Peter: 初步设计可做参考，但我们应按合同履行职责，如另有要求，会及时通知你。

李工程师: 那请您给书面答复，明确设计内容，好吗？

Peter: 好的，你们制订了明确的设计计划吗？

李工程师: 是的，请尽快回复，以便我们开展设计工作。

Peter: 我们会尽快的。

李工程师: 还有一个问题。

Peter: 请讲。

李工程师: 如不供暖，给排水、消防设计方案是否按无供暖情况做？比如，给水系统采取保温加热措施，消防管网采用干式系统。

Peter: 是的，按无供暖情形进行相关图纸的设计。

李工程师: 好的，期待你的回复。

the construction drawing. Please think over carefully whether to allocate heating facilities or not.

Peter: The preliminary design can be used as reference; however, we should perform duties according to the contract. You will be timely informed if there are any other requirements.

Mr Li: Could you please give a written reply to specify design content?

Peter: Sure. Have you worked out a specified design plan?

Mr Li: Yes, please reply as soon as possible, so that we can immediately carry out the design work.

Peter: We will do it as soon as we can.

Mr Li: One more question.

Peter: Please.

Mr Li: If heating will not be provided, will the design scheme of water supply and drainage as well as fire-fighting be executed based on non-heating condition? For example, water supply system adopts heating and heat insulation measures, and fire-fighting pipe network adopts dry system.

Peter: Yes, relevant drawings are designed as per non-heating condition.

Mr Li: Ok, We are looking forward to your reply.

替换单词 Alternative terms

① 寒冷地区
② 概念设计

① cold area
② concept design

业务情景：中方李工程师和外方工程师 James 讨论现场勘察要求。
Scene: Mr Li is discussing the requirements for field investigation with James, the engineer of foreign side.

典型对话 Conversation

李工程师：上周，我方已提出请求，请贵单位协调我们开展工程勘察，各项工作进展如何？

James：我们已经通知有关部门，在你方收集数据、实地勘察的过程中予以配合。

李工程师：那我们需要什么手续才能得到相关部门的配合？

James：这个需要开具证明①，且你方签字保证此调查数据仅为工程设计所用，不做它用。

李工程师：好的。

James：你还有其他困难吗？

李工程师：许可证明什么时候能办下来呢，我们想尽快开展勘察任务。

Mr Li: Last week, we proposed our request for your collaboration on engineering survey, how is everything progressing?

James: We have already informed relevant departments to provide collaboration for your data collection and on-site survey.

Mr Li: What can help us obtain the collaboration from relevant departments?

James: You shall issue and sign a certificate① that guarantees these investigation data are only used for engineering design, not for other purposes.

Mr Li: Ok.

James: Any other problems?

Mr Li: When can the permit certificate be acquired? We want to carry out the survey task as soon as we can.

James: 暂时还不能确定，因为你方所需数据涉及的运营管理部门较多，我们正在抓紧办理。

李工程师：大概需要多长时间吗？
James: 至少需要 7 个工作日吧。
李工程师：5 个工作日可以吗，因为我们设计工期非常紧张。
James: 我们尽快做好协调工作，派专职人员负责此事。

李工程师：谢谢你对此事的重视，期待你的回复。
James: 应该的。
李工程师：谢谢。

James: Not sure yet, because the data you required is provided by many operating management departments, and we are hurriedly processing now.
Mr Li: How long will it take?
James: At least seven working days.
Mr Li: How about five working days? Because our design period is too tight.
James: We will try our best to provide coordination and arrange a full-time staff to be in charge of this.
Mr Li: Thank you for your help and we are looking forward to your reply.
James: It is my duty.
Mr Li: Thank you.

替换单词 Alternative terms

① 许可证　　　　　　　　　　① permit

业务情景：中方李工程师和外方工程师 Anderson 讨论供暖方案。
Scene: Mr Li is discussing heating scheme with Anderson, the engineer of foreign side.

典型对话 Conversation

Anderson: 你们的概念设计文件我们已经看完了，关于机车车辆检修库的供暖情况需要和你沟通一下。

Anderson: We have already read your concept design document, and we need to discuss with you about heating in locomotive and rolling stock maintenance depot.

第一部分　交通工程情景会话

李工程师：好的，请讲。
Anderson：你方做过机车车辆检修库的供暖必要性分析吗？

李工程师：做过，此工程位于<u>严寒地区</u>[①]，为满足生产工艺和人员舒适性要求，考虑采取集中供暖措施。

Anderson：对于这种建筑面积两万多平方米的库房，你的供暖方案是怎么设计的？
李工程师：针对库房建筑特点，考虑在高大空间设置燃气红外辐射供暖系统，在辅助办公、生活用房设置热水散热器供暖系统。

Anderson：你确定燃气辐射供暖是安全可靠的吗？
李工程师：此系统已广泛应用于实际工程中，且我们在设计中采取了可靠的安全措施。

Anderson：建筑所在地有便利的天然气源吗？

李工程师：有，我们调查过现场，并在燃气公司收集了天然气的基础资料。

Mr Li: Ok, please go ahead.
Anderson: Have you carried out any analysis on the necessity of heating in locomotive and maintenance depot?
Mr Li: Yes, we have. As this project is located in the <u>severe cold area</u>[①], we think concentrated heating measure is necessary to meet the requirement of manufacturing technique and personnel comfort.

Anderson: For the depot with a floor area of over 20000 m^2, what is your design of heating scheme?
Mr Li: Based on architecture features of the depot, gas-fired infrared radiant heating system is considered for high and large space, and hot water radiator heating system is provided for subsidiary offices or living rooms.

Anderson: Are you sure that the gas-fired infrared radiant heating is safe and reliable?
Mr Li: This system has already been widely applied in the practical works, and we also adopt reliable safety measures in the design.

Anderson: Is there any natural gas source at the place where the building is located?
Mr Li: Yes. We have investigated the site and collected basic data of natural gas supply from gas company.

Anderson: 好的,另外,热水供暖系统的热媒温度和供回水温差你是怎么确定的?

李工程师:热媒温度和供回水温差均按相应规范确定,根据工程需要,将会有细微调整。供水温度不大于95℃,供回水温差宜取20℃。

Anderson: 供暖系统的运行调节是怎样实现的?

李工程师:供暖末端②采用恒温控制阀控制室温,热源处采用调节供水水温或水量的方式。

Anderson: 库房值班供暖情况下,设备的运行情况是怎样的?

李工程师:在非工作时间,关闭燃气红外辐射供暖系统,只开启热水供暖系统,且控制室内的温度保持在0℃以上。

Anderson: Alright. Moreover, how to determine the temperature of heating medium and the temperature difference between supply and return water in the hot water radiator heating system?

Mr Li: The temperature of heating medium and the temperature difference between supply and return water are determined as per relevant specifications, and there will be slight adjustments based on the demand of the project. The temperature of supply water is not above 95℃(95 celcius), and the temperature difference between supply and return water will be 20℃(20 celcius).

Anderson: How to realize the operating adjustment of heating system?

Mr Li: Thermostatic control valve is used for control of indoor temperature at the heating terminal② and the supply water temperature or volume adjusting method is adopted at the heat source.

Anderson: How about the operating condition of equipment in the storehouse during on-duty heating?

Mr Li: During the non-working time, gas-fired infrared radiant heating system is shut off and only hot water radiator heating system is opened to keep indoor temperature over 0℃.

Anderson: 鉴于检修库建筑面积大、功能性强的特点,接下来还应该充分讨论该方案的可行性。

李工程师:是的,我们会进一步优化方案,以便开展详细设计。

Anderson:好的。

李工程师:谢谢。

Anderson: Considering that the repair shop is characterized by large floor area and multi-functionality, the feasibility of the scheme shall be further discussed.

Mr Li: Yes. We will further optimize this scheme so as to carry out detailed design.

Anderson: Alright.

Mr Li: Thank you.

替换单词 Alternative terms

① 寒冷地区
② 散热器

① cold area
② radiator

业务情景:中方李工程师和外方工程师 Anderson 讨论通风设计方案。
Scene: Mr Li is discussing the ventilation design scheme with Anderson.

典型对话 Conversation

Anderson: 你们提交的详细设计①文件我们正在审阅,想讨论几个比较关心的问题。

李工程师:好的,请讲。

Anderson: 火车站通风的主要设计原则,请你简单介绍一下。

李工程师:具有自然通风条件的,尽量采用自然通风;在不满足自然通风时,

Anderson: We are reviewing the detailed design① documents you submitted, and we want to discuss several issues concerned.

Mr Li: Ok, please go ahead.

Anderson: Please give me a brief introduction of main design principles of ventilation in railway station.

Mr Li: Natural ventilation mode shall be adopted as much as possible if condition

采用机械通风，这样有利于减少工程投资和运行费用。

Anderson: 在此工程中，哪些房间采用了自然通风，你是怎么考虑的？

李工程师: 有可开启外窗或外门的售票厅及办公用房考虑自然通风，通过优化设计外窗、外门的尺寸和位置，创造良好的自然通风条件。

Anderson: 采用自然通风的房间，室内环境能满足人员舒适及卫生要求吗？

李工程师: 是的，根据自然通风的风压和热压作用原理，我们对室内温度、CO_2浓度进行了<u>数值模拟</u>[②]计算，结果是满足规范要求的。

Anderson: 通风量是怎么确定的，依据是什么？

李工程师: 对于以排除余热为主的设备房间，如电力变电所，根据设备发热量来计算通风量。而对于卫生间、泵房等排除有害气体的房间，我们根据经验数据，按换气次数计算通风量。

permits; otherwise, mechanical ventilation shall be used, which can reduce engineering investment and operation cost.

Anderson: In the project, which rooms adopt natural ventilation, and how do you think of this?

Mr Li: For ticket hall and office room with openable external windows and doors, natural ventilation is considered, through optimization of the dimensions and positions of windows or doors to create a well natural ventilation condition.

Anderson: For the rooms with natural ventilation, can they meet the requirements of personnel comfort and sanitation?

Mr Li: Yes, they can. Based on the theory of wind pressure and thermal pressure of natural ventilation, we carried out <u>numerical simulation calculation</u>[②] on indoor temperature and CO_2 concentration, the result can meet the requirement of specifications.

Anderson: How to determine the ventilation quantity in the room and what is the basis?

Mr Li: The ventilation quantity of equipment rooms, such as power substation, where the main purpose is to discharge the waste heat, will be calculated based on calorific value of equipment. Meanwhile,

第一部分　交通工程情景会话

Anderson: 此火车站候车大厅可以通过自然通风来排除余热余湿③吗？

李工程师: 由于此建筑处于炎热地区，根据热湿负荷特性，若只有自然通风，是不满足夏季人员热舒适要求的，为此，我们设置了空调系统。

Anderson: 好的，机械通风设备的启停、运行状况是否纳入站房的设备监控系统④？

李工程师: 是的，设备都纳入了综合监控系统，方便管理人员及时掌握设备运转情况。

Anderson: 谢谢你详尽的介绍，如果有什么疑问，我们及时沟通。

李工程师: 我会乐意配合的。

the ventilation quantity for other rooms where harmful gas is to be discharged, such as toilet and pumping room, will be calculated as per air exchange rate according to our empirical data.

Anderson: Can the waste heat and humidity③ in waiting hall of the station be discharged through natural ventilation?

Mr Li: As the buildings are located in the hot area, on the basis of load characteristic of heat and humidity, only natural ventilation cannot meet the requirements for personnel comfort in summer; therefore, we set air conditioning system.

Anderson: Ok. Will the start-up, shut-down and operation condition of the mechanical ventilation equipment be incorporated into the equipment's monitor and control system④ of station houses?

Mr Li: Yes, all the equipment is incorporated into the comprehensive monitoring system, so that management staff can timely get to know the operating conditions of the equipment.

Anderson: Thanks for your detailed introduction. If there are more questions, we shall timely communicate with each other.

Mr Li: I will be happy to cooperate.

替换单词 Alternative terms

① 施工设计 　　　　　　　　　① construction design
② 计算流体动力学（CFD） 　　② computational fluid dynamics
③ 热湿负荷 　　　　　　　　　③ heat and humidity load
④ 楼宇自动化系统（BAS） 　　④ building automation system

业务情景：中方李工程师和外方工程师 Anderson 讨论空调方案。
Scene: Mr Li is discussing air conditioning scheme with Anderson.

典型对话 Conversation

Anderson：你好,关于夏季空调设计方案有几个问题请你解释一下。

李工程师：好的,请讲。

Anderson：综合办公楼的空调系统,你是怎么选择的?

李工程师：考虑到建筑体量较大,冷负荷大,办公时间较为集中,本设计考虑采用半集中空调系统。

Anderson：你所指的半集中空调形式是什么?

李工程师：在此办公楼中,半集中空调就是常用的风机盘管加新风系统。

Anderson: Hello. Would you please explain a few issues about the design scheme of summer air-conditioning?

Mr Li: Ok, please go ahead.

Anderson: How do you make your choice on air conditioning system of comprehensive office building?

Mr Li: A semi-central air conditioning system is considered in the design, in consideration of the large size and cooling load and concentrated heavy hours of the building.

Anderson: What does semi-central air conditioning system mean?

Mr Li: For this office building, the semi-central air conditioning system refers to common fan coil unit plus fresh air system.

Anderson：你采用的这种空调系统有什么优势？
李工程师：设备布置紧凑，末端冷量可调，相对于<u>多联空调系统</u>①，有一定的节能优势。

Anderson：人员所需新风量是怎么确定的？
李工程师：根据建筑面积和人员密度，以及规范中规定的最小新风量标准，通过计算求得。

Anderson：新风量的大小直接关系到总冷负荷的大小，新风量占总送风量比例是多少？

李工程师：大概为15%。
Anderson：风机盘管及新风机组的噪声是怎么处理的？
李工程师：新风机组集中放置在空调机房，采取隔振措施；风机盘管选用低噪声设备，并且在安装过程中设置<u>减震设施和吸声材料</u>②。

Anderson：此设计方案通过不断优化，会更加完美。
李工程师：谢谢，我们尽量做得更好。

Anderson: What is the advantage of this air conditioning system?
Mr Li: The layout of equipment is compact, the cooling capacity of terminal is adjustable, and it is more energy efficient than <u>multi-connected air conditioning system</u>①.

Anderson: How to determine the fresh air volume for personnel?
Mr Li: It is acquired by a calculation based on floor area, density of personnel and minimum fresh air volume specified in specifications.

Anderson: The volume of fresh air directly affects the total cooling load. What is the rate of fresh air in the total air output?

Mr Li: It is probably 15%.
Anderson: How to reduce noise from the fan coil unit and fresh air unit?
Mr Li: The fresh air handling unit is arranged centrally in air-conditioner room with vibration isolation measures. Low-noise equipment is selected for the fan coil, and <u>damping facilities and sound absorption materials</u>② are set during installation.

Anderson: The design scheme will be perfect through constant optimization.
Mr Li: Thank you, we will try to do it better.

替换单词 Alternative terms

① 变制冷剂流量空调系统 VRV　　① variable refrigerant volume air conditioning system

② 隔声降噪措施　　② sound insulation and noise reduction measure

第一部分　交通工程情景会话

第二十四章　给排水
Chapter 24　Water Supply & Drainage

业务情景： 中方王工程师与外方 Tom 先生进行设计方案的讨论。
Scene: Mr Wang is discussing the design plans with Tom.

典型对话 Conversation

Tom: 请介绍一下本线上阶段审批意见的主要内容及执行情况。

王工程师: 好，本线除长城站由于位置调整，没有执行审批意见外，其余均按审批意见执行。

Tom: 请介绍一下本线给水站[①]的设置和数量。

王工程师: 全线设有 5 处给水站，除长城站为既有给水站外，其余均为新增，其中长江站为旅客列车给水站，生活供水站、点有黄河站等 10 个。

Tom: 为什么长江站按旅客列车给水站设置？

Tom: We'd like you to describe the main content and the implementation of review comments in the previous phase, please.

Mr Wang: Ok. The whole line was implemented based on review comments except for Changcheng Station owing to its location adjustment.

Tom: And locations and the number of water supply stations[①]?

Mr Wang: There are totally five water supply stations along the line. All stations are newly built except for existing Changcheng Station Changjiang Station serves as the water supply station for passenger trains. There are ten living water supply stations or points including Huanghe Station along the line.

Tom: Why does Changjiang Station serve as the water supply station for passenger trains?

王工程师：根据《铁路给排水设计规范》，旅客列车给水站宜设在区段站、有客整所的车站、有始发终到旅客列车的车站及其他根据行车组织需要上水的车站。长江站为有始发列车的区段站，故按旅客列车给水站设置。

Tom：那本线旅客列车卸污是怎么考虑的？

王工程师：本线长城动车段（所）和长江客车整备所分别采用了固定式卸污和移动式卸污，其中固定式卸污采用真空卸污方式，并配备了移动卸污车两辆。

Tom：各站、点水源方案是什么？

王工程师：长城站自来水距离车站2km，接管点管径为DN100，压力0.3MPa。长江站水源井距离车站1km，井深100m，静水位2m，产水量满足要求，水质<u>铁</u>[②]超标，需进行水处理。

Mr Wang: According to *Specifications on Railway Water Supply & Drainage Design*, water supply station for passenger trains shall be set in section stations, stations with passenger car servicing depot, departure & arrival stations and other stations. Since Changjiang Station is a sectional departure and arrival station, it should serve as the water supply station for passenger trains.

Tom: How about sewage disposal of passenger trains?

Mr Wang: Changcheng EMU depot and Changjiang passenger car servicing depot adopt fixed sewage disposal way and movable sewage disposal way respectively. The former uses vacuum disposal and is equipped with two mobile disposal vehicles.

Tom: And what is water source plans for stations or points?

Mr Wang: Changcheng Station is 2km away from the water supply station with DN100 pipe diameter and 0.3MPa pressure. Changjiang Station is 1km away from Water source well. The well is 100m in depth and 2m in static water level and its water yield can meet relevant requirements. Since <u>the iron</u>[②] content in the water is excessive, it needs to be treated further.

第一部分　交通工程情景会话

Tom: 各站、点分别采用什么供水方式？

王工程师: 长城站采用了<u>变频供水</u>③，长城站在站房设置了直饮水系统。

Tom: 那各站、点消防是怎么设计的？

王工程师: 长城站在城镇消防站保护范围内，采用了低压式消火栓系统，生活、生产及消防合用管道；长江站远离城镇，采用了临时高压系统，消火栓管道单独设置。各站、点消防秒流量分别为30L/s，火灾延续时间为2h。

Tom: 隧道消防是怎么考虑的？

王工程师: 隧道长度大于5km时，考虑在隧道进出两端设置用于客货列车消防降温的消防水池及消火栓设施，并配置一定数量消防器材；隧道长度大于20km时，在紧急救援站设置了消防系统。

Tom: What are water supply modes for stations or points?

Mr Wang: Changcheng Station adopts <u>variable-frequency water supply</u>③ mode and has a drinking water system in the station building.

Tom: And how to design the fire prevention?

Mr Wang: Changcheng Station is located within the protective range of urban fire station. so it is equipped with a low-pressure hydrant system and shared pipeline for living, production and fire prevention. Changjiang Station is far away from urban areas, so it is equipped with a temporary high-pressure system and separate hydrant pipeline. The design flow for fire prevention is 30L/s and the fire life is 2 hours for stations or points.

Tom: And how to consider the fire prevention in tunnels?

Mr Wang: For the tunnels with a length more than 5km, it is planned to install the fire pools and hydrant facilities at entrance and exit ends of tunnels for fire prevention and cooling of both passenger and freight trains, and equip with a certain amount of fire equipment; for the tunnels with a length more than 20km, it is planned to set a fire fighting system in the emergency rescue stations.

Tom: 各站、点排水系统如何设置？

王工程师：沿线各站、点根据污水成分、性质、数量和受纳水体功能区划要求，设置相应的处理工艺，达标排放。有条件的站、点污水排放应尽可能纳入当地城镇排水系统。既有站新增污水排入既有排水系统，对处理能力不足部分进行补强。

Tom: 管材如何选用？

王工程师：明铺给水管道采用给水球墨铸铁管④，埋地给水管道管径小于等于300mm 的采用给水 PE⑤管，管径大于300mm 的采用给水球墨铸铁管。

Tom: 给排水是否设置了自控系统？

王工程师：长城站给水设置了集中监控系统⑥，给水系统监控及自动化设计按铁路自控标准及规程确定的系统等级、监控内容设置。

Tom: How to set drainage systems of stations or points?

Mr Wang: The proper treatment techniques shall be adopted in the stations or points along the line according to gradient, nature, quantity and function division of receiving water to meet the discharge standard. The sewage drainage system shall be incorporated in local urban drainage system if possible. Increased sewage in the existing stations shall be drained into existing drainage system and its system shall be properly enhanced once its capacity fails.

Tom: How to select pipelines?

Mr Wang: The nodular cast-iron pipes④ are used for the ground water supply pipelines and PE⑤ pipes for buried pipes with a diameter of less than or equal to 300mm and nodular cast-iron pipes for buried pipes with a diameter of larger than 300mm.

Tom: Is there any auto-control system for water supply and drainage?

Mr Wang: Changcheng Station adopts a centralized monitoring system⑥ for water supply. The monitoring grade and content setting of water supply system shall be designed according to automatic control standard and regulation for railway.

替换单词 Alternative terms

① 旅客列车给水站   ① water supply station for passenger trains
   动车卸污点   sewage disposal spot for EMU
   生活供水站   living water supply station
   生活供水点   living water supply spot
   桥隧守护供水点   bridge & tunnel water supply spot

② 锰   ② manganese
   细菌   germ
   亚硝酸盐   nitrite
   硬度   hardness

③ 无负压供水   ③ non-negative pressure water supply
   水塔   water tower
   山上水池   pools on mountain area
   钢支架水箱   steel support tank
   屋顶水箱   roof tank

④ 无缝钢管   ④ seamless steel pipe
   镀锌钢管   galvanized steel pipe
   不锈钢管   stainless steel pipe
   铜管   copper pipe
   钢塑复合管   steel plastic composite pipe
   铝塑复合管   aluminum plastic composite pipe

⑤ PVC   ⑤ PVC
   PPR   PPR
   UPVC   UPVC
   玻璃钢   fibreglass

⑥ 自动控制系统   ⑥ automated control system
   自动启停系统   automatic start-stop system
   水泵自动巡检系统   water-pump automatic inspection system

业务情景：外方 Tom 先生询问中方王工程师关于设计工作的安排。
Scene: Tom is asking Mr Wang for design work schedule.

典型对话 Conversation

Tom：外业工作有哪些？需要多久完成？

王工程师：开展设计前，需落实各站、点水源[①]，完成水源勘探、原水水质化验、水源地形测量、管道带状地形测量以及给排水管道迁改调查等外业勘察工作。计划时间为 30 天。

Tom：完成设计需要哪些接口资料？

王工程师：需要站场、房建、暖通及其他有给排水要求的专业互提资料，给排水专业方可开展设计以及向房建、暖通、电力等专业提供资料。

Tom：什么时候能完成？

王工程师：资料齐全后，给排水专业在 30 天内向其他专业收集资料，在 60 天内完成设计[②]文件、图纸及概算。

Tom: What does field work include? How long does it take?

Mr Wang: Prior to the design, field investigation work shall be completed, including water source[①] prospecting, quality examination of raw water, topographic survey of water source, strip topographic survey along pipelines and relocation & reconstruction research for water supply and drainage pipes. It shall take thirty days.

Tom: what is the interface data you need for the design?

Mr Wang: We need station & yard engineers, building engineers, HVAC engineers and other engineers related with water supply and drainage to share their data. And then water supply & drainage engineers can develop their design and provide information to relevant engineers.

Tom: When will it be completed?

Mr Wang: After collecting all necessary data, water supply & drainage engineers will provide information to other engineers in thirty days and complete design[②] documents, drawings and budget estimates in sixty days.

第一部分　交通工程情景会话

替换单词 Alternative terms

① 自来水　　　　　　　　① tap water
　 地表水　　　　　　　　　 surface water
　 地下水　　　　　　　　　 ground water
② 可行性研究　　　　　　② feasibility study
　 初步设计　　　　　　　　 preliminary design
　 施工图　　　　　　　　　 construction drawings

业务情景：中方王工程师向外方 Tom 先生进行技术交底。
Scene: Mr Wang is making technical disclosure to Tom.

典型对话 Conversation

Tom：首先简要地介绍一下各站、点水方案。

王工程师：好，本线主要的设计内容、方案见施工图设计说明。

Tom：施工应注意哪些事项？

王工程师：给排水构筑物①的基坑开挖后，均应复验地基承载力。施工中遇既有管线②，应妥加保护，并及时与有关部门联系会同处理。

Tom: We'd like you to describe water plans for stations or points briefly, please.

Mr Wang: Ok. For main design contents and scheme of this line, please see the design descriptions in the construction drawings.

Tom: What are the precautions in the construction?

Mr Wang: After excavation of foundation of water supply and drainage structures[①], the bearing capacity of foundation shall be rechecked. Existing pipelines[②] shall be properly protected during the construction and dealt together with relevant authorities timely.

替换单词 Alternative terms

① 水塔　　　　　① water tower
　水池　　　　　　 pool
　泵井　　　　　　 pump well
　挡土墙　　　　　 retaining wall
② 石油管道　　　② petroleum pipeline
　天然气管道　　　 natural gas pipeline
　通信电缆　　　　 telecommunication cable
　电力电缆　　　　 power cable

业务情景：中方王工程师与外方 Tom 先生进行咨询方案沟通。
Scene: Mr Wang and Tom are discussing about consulting plans.

典型对话 Conversation

Tom：请提供上阶段设计文件和审查意见纸质文件。

王工程师：好的。我正好带来了，请看。

Tom：请给排水专业设计负责人介绍一下主要设计内容。

王工程师：好的，给排水主要设计内容为以下几个方面……

Tom：接自来水方案有无与自来水公司签订供水协议？

Tom: We'd like you to provide paper documents of design drawings and review comments in previous phase, please.

Mr Wang: Ok, I have these paper documents here.

Tom: We'd like you to describe main design content of water supply and drainage, please.

Mr Wang: It mainly includes following aspects…

Tom: Is there any water supply agreement signed with water supply companies about the water supply plan?

王工程师：已签订了供水协议，自来水接管点压力、管径已落实，见协议内容。

Tom：自来水接管点离车站距离是多少？有无考虑二次消毒？

王工程师：有4km，采用紫外线①进行二次消毒。

Tom：采用无负压供水需取得自来水公司同意，否则不能使用。

王工程师：好，这个我再跟自来水公司落实一下。

Tom：取地下水方案有无地下水勘探报告？

王工程师：每个取地下水的车站，我们均做了详细的水文地质勘探，勘探报告在这里，请看。

Tom：管井产水量能否满足供水要求？请提供水源水质化验单。

王工程师：根据抽水试验及分析，管井产水量及水质满足供水要求。这是卫生防疫站提供的水质化验单，请看。

Mr Wang: Yes, we have entered into an agreement, including water pipe pressure and pipe diameter.

Tom: How far is the connecting point away from the station? Do you consider the secondary sterilization of the water?

Mr Wang: Yes, we do, About 4km. The ultraviolet ray① is used for secondary sterilization at the place of 4km away from the station.

Tom: If you adopt non-negative pressure water supply, you shall get the water company's approval. Or else you are not allowed to use it.

Mr Wang: Alright, we will check that with water supply company.

Tom: Is there any ground water prospecting report for the ground water plan?

Mr Wang: Yes, we have completed detailed hydrogeology prospection for each station intaking ground water. For detailed data, please see relevant reports.

Tom: Can water yield of tube wells satisfy water supply demand? We'd like you to provide testing results of water quality.

Mr Wang: According to pumping test and analysis, both water yield and quality can meet water supply demand. Here is the water quality report given by the sanitation and anti-epidemic office.

Tom: 设计依据的<u>外业资料</u>②应齐全和准确，否则设计方案不成立。

王工程师：好的。

Tom: 消防采用低压、临时高压还是高压系统？依据是什么？

王工程师：由于车站在城镇消防站的保护范围内，所以采用的是低压消防系统。

Tom: 车站污水排放执行什么标准？

王工程师：根据环评报告，车站附近水域环境功能区划为 III 类，污水排放执行一级排放标准。

Tom: Field data② as basis for design shall be complete and accurate, or the design plan shall be invalid.

Mr Wang: Ok.

Tom: What's the basis to use low-pressure, temporary high-pressure or high-pressure system for fire control?

Mr Wang: Since the station is within the range of urban fire station, we use a low-pressure fire prevention system.

Tom: What's the standard for station sewage disposal?

Mr Wang: Based on the EIA report, the functional zoning of water environment is Grade III in vicinity of the station and its sewage disposal shall be completed according to Grade I disposal criteria.

替换单词 Alternative terms

① 二氧化氯　　　　　　　① carbon dioxide
　 液氯　　　　　　　　　　　liquid chlorine
　 次氯酸钠　　　　　　　　　sodium hypochlorite
② 协议　　　　　　　　　② agreement
　 标准　　　　　　　　　　　standard

第二十五章 环评
Chapter 25　Environment Assessment

业务情景：下面是外方 Mike 同中方李工程师的对话，讨论环评工作的法律法规、标准规范、环评机构、主管部门等问题。

Scene: Mike and Mr Li are discussing laws & regulations, criteria & specifications, environment assessment agency, authorities of the environment and so on.

典型对话 Conversation

李工程师：我们希望同贵方讨论几个问题。
Mike：好的，请吧。
李工程师：贵国对环境影响评价是否制定了相应的法律①？
Mike：我国针对环境保护方面，制定了环境保护法和环境影响评价法等法规。
李工程师：那么在环境影响评价的标准②等方面有何要求？
Mike：我们参照国际相关的环境标准，根据本国的实际情况，也制定了相应的标准及规范。
李工程师：对于从事环境影响评价的机构有什么要求？
Mike：依据相关规定，从事环境影响评价的机构需要取得相应资质，从业人员也应该具有相应资格。

Mr Li: We'd like to discuss several questions with you.
Mike: Ok, please go ahead.
Mr Li: Are there any relevant laws① on environmental impact assessment (EIA) in your country?
Mike: Yes, we have laws and regulations on environment protection and EIA.
Mr Li: Are there any requirements on EIA criteria②?
Mike: Yes. We've developed EIA codes and specifications based on international environment standards and local situation.
Mr Li: Any requirements for EIA agencies?
Mike: Yes. An EIA agency shall have relevant qualification and its assessors shall have professional certifications as well.

李工程师：情况与我国基本相同。那请问我们从事环评工作，可以与哪些主管部门沟通？

Mike：你们可以同国家环境部以及地方环境主管部门联系。需要的话，我们也可以帮你们沟通。

Mr Li: In that way, it is quite the same with China. If we'd like to do environment impact assessment in your country, which authorities should we talk to?

Mike: You can talk to, for example, National Environment Department and local environment authorities. We can also help you with that if it's necessary.

替换单词 Alternative terms

① 法规　　　　　　　　　① laws & regulations
　 规定　　　　　　　　　　 regulations
　 规则　　　　　　　　　　 rules
② 规范　　　　　　　　　② specifications
　 导则　　　　　　　　　　 guidelines
　 细则　　　　　　　　　　 detailed rules

业务情景：外方 Mike 同中方李工程师对话，讨论环评工作所需相关资料提供等问题。
Scene: Mike and Mr Li are discussing relevant data necessary for the environment assessment work.

典型对话 Conversation

李工程师：我们希望同贵方讨论几个问题。
Mike：好的，请吧。
李工程师：请问在贵国的环境敏感区①进行施工有无具体要求？

Mr Li: We'd like to discuss several questions with you.
Mike: Ok, please go ahead.
Mr Li: Are there any specific construction restrictions in your country's environmental sensitive areas①?

Mike: 我国依法设立了不同级别和种类的环境敏感区,环境敏感区内生态系统相对脆弱,进行工程建设时应当加强环境保护。

李工程师: 对本工程所涉及的环境敏感区,我们已列出环评工作需要的资料清单并发给贵方,请尽快提供详尽的基本资料。

Mike: 没有问题。也希望你们尽快开展环评工作,保证工程的顺利进行。

李工程师: 在相应资料收集完毕后,我们会依据工程的<u>进度</u>[②],尽早完成环评工作。

Mike: Yes. We have legally-established different levels and types of environment sensitive areas, where the ecosystem is relatively fragile, it shall be protected further during the construction in the areas.

Mr Li: We've sent you the data list necessary for EIA work concerning the areas. We hope to get detailed information as quick as possible.

Mike: No problem. We hope you can carry out your work as soon as possible to guarantee the smooth engineering progress..

Mr Li: After collecting necessary information, we will complete EIA work as soon as possible based on project <u>schedule</u>[②].

替换单词 Alternative terms

① 生态脆弱区
  生态敏感区
② 计划
  安排

① ecologically vulnerable areas
  ecologically sensitive areas
② plan
  schedule

业务情景: 外方 Mike 同中方李工程师对话,讨论环境影响评价报告评审前准备工作。
Scene: Mike and Mr Li are discussing preparation prior to EIA review.

🔊 典型对话 Conversation

Mike: 请对整个环评工作进行简单介绍。

Mike: We'd like you to describe the whole EIA work briefly, please.

345

李工程师：依据贵国环境影响评价相关法律、法规① 及工程设计资料，环评工作小组首先制订出工作方案，然后在现场环境状况调查② 的基础上进行了环境影响预测分析及建设项目环境可行性的评价结论。

李工程师：还有其他需要我们配合的吗？

Mike：由于双方技术、标准体系不同，在环境主管部门进行环评报告评审时，可能会遇见我方难以独立解释的问题及难点，希望能得到帮助。

李工程师：没有问题。我们将全力配合解决相应难点。

Mr Li: The EIA team developed a work plan based on relevant EIA laws, regulations① and engineering design data, and then completed environmental impact prediction analysis and assessment, and environment feasibility for the project according to the field research② .

Mr Li: Is there anything else that we can help with?

Mike: Owing to difference in technology and standardization systems, we may encounter problems and difficulties that cannot be solved independently during EIS review by environment authorities. We need your help on that.

Mr Li: No problem. We will make every effort.

替换单词 Alternative terms

① 法规　　　　　　　　　① laws & regulations
　 标准　　　　　　　　　　 criteria
　 规范　　　　　　　　　　 specifications
② 勘察　　　　　　　　　② survey

第二十六章　环保
Chapter 26　Environment Protection

业务情景: 中方陈工程师与外方 Jack 先生进行设计方案讨论。
Scene: Mr Chen and Jack are discussing design plans.

典型对话 Conversation

Jack: 请介绍一下本线上阶段环保审批意见的主要内容及执行情况。

陈工程师: 对噪声超标的敏感点采取功能置换、设置声屏障①、隔声窗等降噪措施，对沿线城市规划区域，应预留设置声屏障条件。除部分噪声敏感点由于搬迁或拆除原因外，其余均按审批意见执行。

Jack: 请介绍一下本线环境影响评价审批意见的主要内容及执行情况。

陈工程师: 原则同意全线噪声治理设计原则，声屏障长度及高度应细化声学设计。下一阶段应由建设单位组织，对噪声敏感点进行现场核实，进一步优化全线噪声治理措施，除部分噪声敏感点由

Jack: We'd like you to describe main content and implementation of review comments on environment protection in the previous phase, please.

Mr Chen: We adopted noise mitigation measures such as function replacement, sound barrier① and soundproof window at sensitive spots with excessive noise and reserved sound barrier space in urban planning areas along the line. All were implemented according to review comments except certain noise sensitive spots due to removal or demolition.

Jack: Could you introduce main content and implementation of review comments on environmental impact assessment?

Mr Chen: It is basically agreed that the noise control design principles will be applied to the whole line. Length and height of sound barrier shall be further detailed based on acoustic design. In the

于搬迁或拆除原因外,其余均按审批意见执行。

Jack: 本线的噪声功能区是怎么划分的？

陈工程师: 距线路中心线30~60m区域执行Ⅳ类标准,噪声值为昼间70dB,夜间55dB。60m以外区域执行Ⅱ类标准,噪声值为昼间60dB,夜间50dB。

Jack: 本线采用了哪些降噪措施？

陈工程师: 根据本线环境影响评价及上一阶段的审查意见,全线在集中居民区设置声屏障降噪措施,在较为零散的居民区预留隔声窗安装措施。

Jack: 怎么确定本线噪声源强度值？

陈工程师: 根据相关部门的规定确定。

Jack: 请介绍一下本线声屏障设置的规模及结构形式。

next phase, the construction company shall organize field investigation of noise sensitive spots and further optimize noise control measurements. The others are all implemented according to review comments except certain noise sensitive spots due to removal or demolition.

Jack: How are the noise functional areas divided?

Mr Chen: Grade Ⅳ is applied in the area of 30-60m away from the centre line and the noise value is 70dB at daytime and 55dB at night. Grade Ⅱ is applied in the area of 60m and above away from the centre line and the noise value is 60dB at daytime and 50dB at night.

Jack: What noise control measures are used along the line?

Mr Chen: According to environmental impact assessment and review comments in previous phase, it is decided that sound barriers are set in densely-populated residential areas and soundproof windows are reserved in sparsely-populated residential areas.

Jack: And how to determine intensity values of noise sources?

Mr Chen: Based on regulations and rules of relevant authorities.

Jack: We'd like you to describe the scale and pattern of sound barriers, please.

陈工程师：全线共设置声屏障 10000m²，其中路基声屏障 5000m²，桥梁声屏障 5000m²。声屏障分别采用直臂式、弧形和折臂式结构。声屏障的设置高度分别为 2m、3m 和 4m。

Jack：如何计算本线声屏障设计中的自然风荷载和列车风荷载？

陈工程师：本线位于成都地区，自然风荷载按 0.45kN/m² 计列，本线设计时速为 160km/h。

Jack：列车风荷载是怎么考虑的？

陈工程师：由于本线设计时速低于 200 km/h，因此未考虑列车风荷载的影响。

Jack：请问本线桥梁专业设计中是否预留声屏障安装条件？

陈工程师：本线桥梁专业设计中已将声屏障荷载[②]计列。

Jack：声屏障吸隔声板采用什么材料？

陈工程师：城市地段采用金属吸声板，非城市地段采用非金属复合吸声板，上部为通透隔声板。

Mr Chen: There are totally 10000m² sound barriers along line, including 5000m² subgrade sound barriers and 5000m² bridge sound barriers. There are 3 types of sound barriers, i.e. straight-arm shape, arc shape and articulating boom. The sound barriers are respectively 2m, 3m and 4m in height.

Jack: How to calculate natural wind load and wind load in the sound barrier design?

Mr Chen: The line is located in Chengdu region. Thus, its natural wind load is calculated based on 0.45kN/m² and the design speed is 160km/h.

Jack: What about the wind load?

Mr Chen: The wind load is not considered since the design speed is lower than 200km/h.

Jack: Is there any sound barrier space reserved in bridge design?

Mr Chen: Yes, of course. Sound barrier load[②] is considered in the bridge design.

Jack: What is acoustic insulation board of sound barrier made of?

Mr Chen: Metallic acoustic boards are used in urban area and non-metallic compound acoustic boards in non-urban area. Permeable acoustic boards are used for upper structures.

替换单词 Alternative terms

① 隔音屏
　音屏障
　隔声墙
　隔声屏障

① acoustic screen
　sound-absorption barrier
　soundproof wall
　soundproof barrier

② 活荷载

② live load

业务情景：中方王工程师向外方 Jack 先生进行技术交底。
Scene: Mr Wang is making technical disclosure to Jack.

典型对话 Conversation

Jack: 请简要介绍一下本线的降噪措施规模及结构形式等。

陈工程师: 本线共设置声屏障 10000m², 预留隔声窗① 2000m², 声屏障采用插板式结构, 分别采用直臂、弧形和折臂式结构。

Jack: 声屏障工点是如何确定的？

陈工程师: 声屏障工点的确定主要是以上阶段审查意见和项目环评批复意见, 施工图设计②前, 再对噪声敏感点进行现场踏勘, 来确定声屏障的长度和高度。

Jack: We'd like you to describe scale and structures of noise control measures briefly, please.

Mr Chen: There are totally 10000m² sound barriers and 2000m² reserved soundproof windows①. Sound barriers are of plate structure, respectively straight-arm structure, arc-shaped structure and articulating boom structure.

Jack: How to determine sound barrier spots?

Mr Chen: The spots are mainly determined based on review comments in previous phase and review comments on environmental impact assessment. Prior to construction drawing design②, field investigation of

第一部分　交通工程情景会话

noise sensitive spots is implemented to determine length and height of sound barriers.

Jack：施工应注意哪些事项？

Jack: What are the precautions during the construction?

陈工程师：基础施工时应注意避开路基上的各类沟、槽、管、线，防止挖断或损坏管、线，路基声屏障施工造成的路基边沟、边坡损坏部分要及时按照路基有关要求予以恢复。

Mr Chen: Foundation construction shall keep away from trenches, ditches, pipelines and conduits on the subgrade to prevent any damages. Damaged side ditches and side slopes due to sound barrier construction shall be recovered according to relevant requirements.

替换单词 Alternative terms

① 通风式隔声窗
　　中空玻璃隔声窗
② 初步设计

① ventilated-type soundproof window
　　hollow-glass soundproof window
② preliminary design

业务情景：中方陈工程师与外方 Jack 先生进行咨询方案沟通。
Scene: Mr Li and Jack are discussing consulting plans.

典型对话 Conversation

Jack：请提供上阶段设计文件和审查意见纸质文件。

Jack: We'd like you to provide paper documents of design drawings and review comments in previous phase, please.

陈工程师：好的。我正好带来了，请看。

Mr Chen: Ok, I have these paper documents with me.

Jack: 请环保专业设计负责人介绍一下主要设计内容。

陈工程师: 好的,环保专业主要设计内容为全线的降噪工程设计,其中主要为声屏障设计、隔声窗设计和特殊降噪方案设计。

Jack: 噪声敏感点是否进行过现场核对?

陈工程师: 在施工图设计前,对各噪声敏感点进行了逐一核实。

Jack: 与上阶段设计的变化情况如何?

陈工程师: 由于部分居民区发生了拆除或新建,与上阶段相比,声屏障工点共取消 5 处,增加 10 处,声屏障长度共计增加 1000m。

Jack: 是否对典型噪声敏感点进行过声学计算[①]?

陈工程师: 施工图设计前,对具有代表性的噪声敏感点进行过声学计算,采用声屏障降噪措施后,能满足要求。

Jack: 声屏障的降噪效果如何?

Jack: We'd like you to describe main design content of environment protection, please.

Mr Chen: It is mainly about noise reduction engineering design along the whole line, including sound barrier, soundproof window and special noise reduction plans.

Jack: Did you do field check of noise sensitive spots?

Mr Chen: Yes. We checked each spot prior to the construction drawing design.

Jack: Are there any changes compared with those of previous phase?

Mr Chen: Yes, there are. Since some residential areas were demolished or newly built, five sound-barrier spots are cancelled and ten spots added compared with the previous phase. There is an increase in sound barrier length, totally 1000m.

Jack: Did you do acoustic computation[①] of typical noise sensitive spots?

Mr Chen: Yes. We did acoustic computation of typical noise sensitive spots prior to the construction drawing design. The spots can meet relevant requirements after the application of sound-barrier noise reduction measure.

Jack: How does the sound barrier work?

陈工程师：根据声学计算结果和以往类似工程的测量结果，路基声屏障的降噪效果为 8~10dB，桥梁声屏障降噪效果为 6~8dB。

Mr Chen: Based on acoustic computation results and measurement results of previous similar projects, subgrade sound barrier can reduce noise by 8-10dB and bridge sound barrier by 6-8dB.

替换单词 Alternative terms

① 声学设计　　　　　　　　　　① acoustic design
　 噪声预测　　　　　　　　　　　 noise prediction

第二十七章 施预
Chapter 27 Construction Estimate

业务情景：中方王工程师到埃塞尔比亚交通局收集所需资料，Tom先生接待。
Scene: Mr Wang comes to Ethiopian Department of Transportation to collect required data. Tom is receiving him.

典型对话 Conversation

王工程师：我们正在进行埃塞铁路的设计工作，需要收集贵国的劳工政策①规定。

Tom：针对这方面的资料，我们会委派人员开具介绍信陪同你们去劳工部搜集。

王工程师：好的，谢谢。那么请问贵方针对外国劳工的使用有何要求呢？

Tom：本项目的初衷也就是为了创造更多的就业机会，提高本地区的就业率，所以我们要求尽量使用本国劳工。

王工程师：包括专业技术人员吗？

Tom：为了学习更为先进的设计和施工技术，对于国外的高级专业技术人员我

Mr Wang: We need to collect the regulations on labor policy① in your country for design of the Ethiopian railway.

Tom: For this information, we will appoint an officer to issue a reference letter and accompany you to Department of Labor for the information collection.

Mr Wang: Okay, thank you. Then what's your requirement for the employment of foreign workers?

Tom: The original intention of this project is to create more job opportunities and raise the employment rate of the local area, so we require employing native workers as many as possible.

Mr Wang: Are professional and technical personnel included?

Tom: In order to learn advanced design and construction techniques, we positively

们是积极欢迎的。

王工程师：那还请贵方能在将来对于我们技术人员出入境手续的办理方面提供必要的帮助。

Tom：没有问题。

welcome foreign senior professional and technical personnel.

Mr Wang: Then please provide us with necessary assistance in the future for the entry and exit procedures of technical personnel.

Tom: No problem.

替换单词 Alternative terms

① 征地拆迁政策
　关税税收政策

① land acquisition and demolition policy
　duty and tax policy

业务情景：中方王工程师到埃塞尔比亚交通局进行设计方案讨论，Tom 先生接待。
Scene: Mr Wang comes to Ethiopian Department of Transportation to discuss design proposals. Tom is receiving him.

典型对话 Conversation

王工程师：根据目前的调查和研究，我们拟将本项目的建设工期确定为 5 年。

Tom：综合考量该项目将发挥的政治效应和经济效益，我方希望能将本项目的建设工期缩短至 4 年。

王工程师：缩短工期意味着就要增加人力资源、机械设备等的投入，随之就会增加工程投资。

Mr Wang: According to current studies, we intent to determine the construction period of this project as five years.

Tom: Taking comprehensive consideration of the political and economic effects of the project, we hope the construction period can be shortened to four years.

Mr Wang: Shortening construction period implies additional investment in labor resources, machinery and equipment,

Tom:那么请你们向我们提供详细的分析对比数据,以便我们做出评估。

王工程师:好的。我们会向你们提供不同的工期及投资方案,以供选择。

Tom:另外,我国每年都有长达半年的雨季,其对施工质量①都会造成很大的影响。

王工程师:对此我们已经采取了充分的工程措施和施工措施来予以解决。

etc., and the project investment will be increased correspondingly.

Tom: Then please provide us with detailed analysis and comparison among various information to benefit our evaluation.

Mr Wang: All right, we will provide different construction periods and investment plans for your decision.

Tom: In addition, the annual rainy season in our country lasts half a year, which will cause significant impacts on the construction quality①.

Mr Wang: As for that, we will solve it by taking adequate engineering measures or construction measures.

替换单词 Alternative terms

① 施工工期　　　　　　　　　　① construction period

业务情景:中方王工程师到埃塞尔比亚交通局进行设计方案汇报,Tom 先生接待。
Scene: Mr Wang comes to Ethiopian Department of Transportation to report design proposals. Tom is receiving him.

典型对话 Conversation

王工程师:针对本项目的投资额度以及费用条目,贵方有何意见?

Tom:请问计价清单中风险预备金①的计取依据是什么?

Mr Wang: What's your comment on the project investment and cost items?

Tom: Can you explain the basis for risk reserve① in the price list?

王工程师：本项目尚存在工程地质条件、社会环境、工期等不确定性风险，根据国际工程惯例增列了 5% 的风险预备金。

Tom：我方认为不应计列该项费用。因为在 EPCT 银皮书 4.12 条中明确指出：合同价格对任何未预见到的困难和费用不应考虑予以调整。

王工程师：但是在该条以及 5.1 条中也明确指出雇主应对承包商不能核实的部分、数据和资料负责，为了抵御这些不能核实的风险，我方要求必须计列该项费用。

Tom：对于计取比例的确定，我方希望你们提供详细的分析资料。

王工程师：我们可以向你们提供我公司的风险储备金额以及相同地区类似工程项目的风险预留金额，以供你们分析决策。

Mr Wang: As there are such uncertain risks as engineering geological conditions, social environment and construction period in the project, we include an additional 5% risk reserve in according with international engineering practice.

Tom: We don't think such a cost should be included, because it is explicitly specified in Sub-Clause 4.12 of FIDIC EPTC that the contract price shall not be adjusted in case of any unforeseen difficulties or costs.

Mr Wang: However, it is also clearly specified in this sub-clause and Sub-Clause 5.1 that the Employer shall be responsible for items, data and information which cannot be verified by the Contractor. In order to resist these risks, we require this cost must be included.

Tom: In order to determine the reserve ratio, we hope you can provide a detailed analysis.

Mr Wang: We will provide the amounts of risk reserves of our company and similar engineering projects in the same region for your analysis and decision.

替换单词 Alternative terms

① 涨价预备费　　　　　　　　　　① contingencies

第二十八章　城市轨道交通
Chapter 28　Urban Rail Transit

业务情景：中方刘工程师与外方代表David见面，介绍公司情况，与外方建立联系。

Scene: Chinese engineer Mr Liu is meeting David, the representative of foreign side, and introducing the company to him.

典型对话 Conversation

刘工程师：早上好，今天是我公司第一次与贵公司交流，希望通过这次交流，能够将我公司在铁路工程领域的能力及业绩呈现给大家。

David：好的，我们也很荣幸与贵公司进行交流。

刘工程师：中铁二院是中国大型综合甲级勘察设计企业，设有线路、轨道、地质、路基、桥梁①等34个专业，依托铁路，业务拓展到公路、地铁、城市轻轨②等各类工程建设领域。

David：从介绍的情况看，贵公司具有雄厚的实力，能否介绍下贵公司在海外工程的经验。

Mr Liu: Good morning. It is the first time we meet each other and I would like to show our abilities and achievements in the field of railway engineering to you.

David: Fine. It is a great honor to know you.

Mr Liu: CREEC is a large comprehensive Grade I enterprise engaged in survey and design in China, with thirty-four disciplines including route, track, geology, subgrade, bridge①, etc. Relying on railway, the business extends to other fields, like highway, subway and rail transit②, etc.

David: I know your company is very strong through your introduction. Would you please introduce some of your overseas businesses?

第一部分　交通工程情景会话

刘工程师： 我公司承担了委内瑞拉高铁的 EPC 工作、尼日利亚阿布贾城轨的设计工作、埃塞亚的斯亚贝巴轻轨的 EPC 工作及埃塞大铁路的设计工作等。

这次交流的目的除了介绍我公司的情况外，还想针对贵国城轨工程的建设做一些了解，也希望贵公司能给予我方为贵国的发展尽一份力的机会。

David： 好的，城轨工程是我国规划中的一条重要国家铁路，我们也很希望像贵公司这样有经验、有实力的承包商参与其中。关于城轨工程的详细信息，你们可以与我公司的总工程师进行进一步的交流。

Mr Liu: We have undertaken tasks like EPC of high-speed railway in Venezuela, design of Abuja Mass Transit in Nigeria, EPC of light rail in Addis Ababa, capital of Ethiopia, and design of National Railway in Ethiopia.

Besides introducing our company, we want to know something about your rail transit project and wish to have a chance to be involved in the development of your country.

David: No problem. Rail transit is one of the most important national railways under planning, and experienced and substantial contractor like your company is warmly welcomed. You could talk to our chief engineer about the details of the rail transit project.

替换单词 Alternative terms

① 水文
　站场
　给排水
　电气化
② 市政工程
　房地产
　工程监理
　岩土工程施工

① hydrology
　station and yard
　water supply and drainage
　electrification
② municipal works
　real estate
　construction supervision
　geotechnical engineering construction

交通工程情景英语900句

业务情景: 中方刘工程师与外方代表 Henry 举行接洽会谈。
Scene: Chinese engineer Mr Liu and Henry, a representative of the foreign side, are talking over a rail transit project.

典型对话 Conversation

刘工程师: 各位先生早上好,今天我们将针对贵国城轨项目进行一次会谈,希望通过这次会谈,能够了解到贵方的主要需求。

Henry: 此条城轨是我国首都一条重要的城市轨道交通线路,需要承担城市主要城区的乘客运输任务。由于我国在此领域还缺乏建设经验,因此需要有实力的承包商来参与本工程。

刘工程师: 贵国如何解决本工程的资金问题?

Henry: 通过小部分自筹资金,其余部分采用向其他国家银行贷款的方式。

刘工程师: 请问工程建设模式采用何种模式呢?

Henry: 采用 BT 模式[①] 进行建设,在全球范围内进行公开招标。

刘工程师: 如果承包商能够帮助贵国解决资金问题,是否会优先考虑。

Henry: 当然,我们会优先考虑能够解决资金问题的承包商。

Mr Liu: Good morning, gentlemen. Today we are here for the rail transit project. We would like to know your primary concern.

Henry: The rail transit project is an important route in our capital. It will provide transportation for the passengers in the major urban areas. As we lack the construction experience in this field, we hope some capable contractor to get involved.

Mr Liu: How could you raise funds for this project?

Henry: A small part from self-funding, and the rest part from loan of foreign banks.

Mr Liu: Which project construction mode do you prefer?

Henry: BT mode[①]. An open tender will be invited worldwide.

Mr Liu: If the contractor could help with the financial support, will you give him a priority?

Henry: Definitely.

刘工程师：能否将本条城轨的相关资料提供给我方？
Henry：可以，希望你们能提出解决方案。

Mr Liu: Could you give us the related information about the project？
Henry: Sure! We are expecting your solution.

替换单词 Alternative terms

① BOT 模式　　　　　　　　① BOT mode
　 POT 模式　　　　　　　　　 POT mode
　 BOO 模式　　　　　　　　　 BOO mode
　 BTO 模式　　　　　　　　　 BTO mode

业务情景：中方刘工程师到外方收集资料，Miki 先生接待。
Scene: Mr Liu comes to collect the data. Miki is receiving him.

典型对话 Conversation

刘工程师：我公司正在为×××城轨项目进行方案编制工作，希望贵方能提供一些与外部条件相关的资料。
Miki：需要什么资料？
刘工程师：我们需要城市管线资料、城市坐标资料、城市道路规划资料、公共交通资料及地震资料①。
Miki：由于这些资料需要我方协调其他政府部门提供，估计需要一段时间。

刘工程师：十分感谢贵公司的帮助，估计需要多少时间呢？

Mr Liu: We are making a proposal for ××× rail transit project, so could you supply us with some related data?
Miki: What kind of data do you need?
Mr Liu: We need data of urban pipelines, coordinates, road planning and public transport, as well as the seismic data①.
Miki: It might take some time to prepare the data you need, because we shall coordinate other government departments for them.
Mr Liu: Thank you so much. How long do you think it might take?

Miki：一周时间。
刘工程师：谢谢。

Miki: About 1 week.
Mr Liu: Thanks.

替换单词 Alternative terms

① 地质资料

① geological data

业务情景：中方李工程师与咨询方代表 Henok 讨论设计方案。
Scene: Chinese engineer Mr Li is discussing the design proposal with Henok, representative of the Consultant.

典型对话 Conversation

李工程师：今天我们将对本工程信号系统的初步方案设计文件进行讨论，以对主要方案原则和系统总体构成达成一致意见。

Henok：是的，已经收到资料了。

李工程师：下面我将从信号系统开始介绍，在介绍的过程中，如各位有任何的疑问，可以随时打断。可以开始了吗？

Henok：好的，开始吧。

李工程师：本工程信号系统主要包括 CBI 子系统，ATS 子系统，ATP 子系统，ATO 子系统①这四个主要子系统。

Henok：我有一个问题，目前信号系统的构成是否与投标文件一致？

Mr Li: Today we are going to discuss the preliminary design of signal system in order to reach an agreement on principle for the main proposal and system constitution.

Henok: Yes, we have got the data.

Mr Li: I will start the introduction from signal system. If you have any question, please feel free to interrupt me at any time. Shall we start now?

Henok: Ok. Go ahead.

Mr Li: The signal system for this project mainly includes four subsystems, namely, CBI, ATS, ATP, ATO①.

Henok: Sorry, I have a question. Does the constitution of signal system at present accord with it in bidding documents?

李工程师：与投标文件一致，在满足投标文件功能要求的基础上，通过我们的实地调查，对 ATS 子系统的功能进行了扩充，以便将来的运营和维护。

Mr Li: Yes, it does. Based on meeting the functional requirements in bidding documents, the function of ATS subsystem was extended for the convenience of future operation and maintenance, according to our field investigation.

Henok：感谢你们认真、细致的工作。

Henok: Thanks for what you have done.

替换单词 Alternative terms

① DCS 子系统
电源子系统
维护管理子系统

① DCS subsystem
power subsystem
maintenance and management subsystem

业务情景：中方李工程师与咨询方代表 Nados 参与设计方案汇报会。
Scene: Chinese engineer Mr Li and Nados, representative of the Consultant, are participating in design scheme report.

典型对话 Conversation

李工程师：今天由我给业主方、咨询方进行信号系统设计方案汇报。

Mr Li: I will be responsible for the presentation of signal system design to everyone today.

Nados：可以开始汇报。

Nados: Please.

李工程师：信号系统①的情况是……

Mr Li: Signal system① is …

Nados：感谢贵公司的方案汇报，我有几个疑问，请贵方回答。

Nados: Thanks for your presentation. Could you please answer me some questions?

李工程师：请说。

Mr Li: Of course.

Nados: 第一个问题,本次设计方案文件中,并未看到工程数量的内容,请贵方予以解释。

李工程师: 在本阶段的设计过程中,工程数量仅为初步数量,且系统供货商尚未招标,因此,不能提出准确的工程数量。待施工图阶段,将会提出准确的工程数量,且本工程为交钥匙工程,所有设备及材料均为我方采购,贵方应主要审查的是功能是否满足以后贵公司的运营需求。

Nados: 好的,第二个问题,贵方的设计文件中,对运营人员进行了配属,我方认为有不合理之处,应该考虑到我国的国情。

李工程师: 关于文件中运营人员的配属,是我方根据我国运营管理的经验提出的,供贵方参考,贵方可在组建运营部门时,根据需要配置。

Nados: First of all, I don't see anything about the works quantity in your scheme, could you explain it?

Mr Li: For this phase of design, the quantity is just an initial estimation, as the tendering of system suppliers has not been done yet, the exact engineering quantity cannot be put forward. It will be presented when we design the construction drawing. In addition, as it is a turnkey project, it means all the equipment and materials shall be purchased by us; you'd better pay more attention to checking whether the function will satisfy your operational requirement in the future.

Nados: Fine. Secondly, I found out there is something unreasonable in the allocation of the operational staff. I suggest you consider the reality of our country.

Mr Li: The allocation of the operational staff came from our home experience in operational management, is for your reference. You could make the allocation according to your requirement when the operation department is established.

替换单词 Alternative terms

① 通信系统　　　　　　　　　　① communication system
　 售票系统　　　　　　　　　　　　 ticketing system

第一部分 交通工程情景会话

业务情景：中方刘工程师与业主代表 Billy 汇报设计工作安排。
Scene: Chinese engineer Mr Liu is reporting the design progress to Billy, representative of the owner.

典型对话 Conversation

刘工程师：为满足工程进度要求，我将向各位汇报设计工作的安排，主要包括进度安排和还需要业主方协助的问题。

Mr Liu: In order to satisfy the engineering progress, I'm going to present the schedule of design, mainly including the progress and the problems that need assistance from you.

Billy：可以开始汇报。

Billy: You can start.

刘工程师：根据工程进度安排，5月底，我方将提供先期开通段的图纸，以供施工单位按工期计划施工，再过3个月，我方将提供剩余部分的图纸，这样，先期开通段施工与后续施工图设计并行，不会耽误工期。

Mr Liu: On the basis of the engineering scheduling, in late May, we shall supply the drawings of sections that will start early to guarantee the contractor to start the work according to construction schedule of the project. In three months, we shall provide the rest of the drawings, thus the construction of the early section and the design of the subsequent construction drawing are undertaken simultaneously so that the progress will not be delayed.

Billy：有什么问题需要我方协助的？

Billy: What can we do for you?

刘工程师：关于先期开通段，我方建议贵方提前进行预验收，将先期开通段作为本工程<u>示范样本</u>①，同时也有利于后续工程的标准化。

Mr Liu: We suggest you carry out the pre-acceptance for the early section so that this section could be treated as a <u>sample</u>① for the project, it is conducive to the standardization for the subsequent works.

Billy: 这个建议很好，我方同意。

Billy: This idea sounds great, and we totally agree.

替换单词 Alternative terms

① 首件定标

① setting initial criterion

业务情景：中方刘工程师与业主代表 Nick 进行技术交底。
Scene: Chinese engineer Mr Liu is carrying out a technical disclosure with Nick, representative of the owner.

典型对话 Conversation

刘工程师：今天将对施工图进行技术交底，同时也请到了业主代表① Nick 参会。施工单位必须严格按照施工图实施，有任何的疑问必须及时与设计单位联系，不可擅自更改设计图纸。

Mr Liu: Today we are going to have a technical disclosure for the construction drawings and we are pleased to invite Nick, representative of the owners①, to join us. Implementation of construction must be in strictly accordance with the construction drawings, so please contact with the design unit in time when you have any questions, and the design drawings cannot be changed without authorization.

Nick：对的。

Nick: You are right.

刘工程师：施工图中，关于隐蔽工程的实施，需要在业主代表现场监督时实施，不可擅自实施。

Mr Liu: The construction of the concealed works shall be undertaken under the field supervision of the representative of the owner.

Nick：我们将会对此类工程进行现场的监理工作。

Nick: We shall take the supervision on site.

替换单词 Alternative terms

① 监理　　　　　　　　　　① supervisor
　咨询　　　　　　　　　　　 consultant
　现场驻地工程师　　　　　　 resident engineer

业务情景：中方何工程师与业主代表 Nick 讨论配合施工中出现的问题。
Scene: Chinese engineer Mr He is discussing the problems arisen in the cooperated construction with Nick, representative of the owner.

典型对话 Conversation

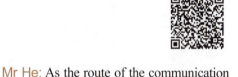

何工程师：本工程通信电缆的路径与当地电信部门通信电缆的路径发生了冲突，今天请业主方的代表 Nick 来到现场，与我方共同解决此问题。

Nick：贵方的设计为什么没有考虑到电信部门的通信电缆？

何工程师：我方在进行设计时，是根据贵方提供的外部管线资料进行相应的设计工作，今天发生冲突的地点，我方已经核实了贵方提供的管线资料，并无通信电缆。

Nick：这份资料是电信部门提供的，我公司将与对方进行核实。

Mr He: As the route of the communication cable for this project clashes with that of the local telecommunication cable, we have invited Mr Nick, representative of the owner, to work it out with us on site.

Nick: Why didn't you consider the local telecommunication cable in your design?

Mr He: Our design is based on the data of the external utility lines provided by your side, and I have checked the data and found out there is no communication cable in the clashed place from your data.

Nick: The data was provided by the department of telecommunication, and we will verify it with them.

何工程师：目前工程工期紧张，根据现场情况，为推进工程，我方将采取迂回敷设①的设计方案，这与施工图不一致，请贵方批准。

Mr He: Considering the tight project schedule and the on-site situations, circuitous laying① of cables shall be adopted to advance the project, but it is inconsistent with the construction drawing, we need your approval.

Nick: 请提交最新的施工图，我方将予以批准。

Nick: Please submit your latest construction drawings and we shall approve them.

替换单词 Alternative terms

① 下穿
  间隔防护

① underneath pass
  interval protection

业务情景：中方何工程师与业主代表 Nick 讨论工程咨询事宜。
Scene: Chinese engineer Mr He is discussing the engineering consultation matters with Nick, representative of the owner.

典型对话 Conversation

Nick：我方对承包商提供的通信、信号及售票系统的初步设计文件进行了审查，现提出咨询意见。

Nick: We have reviewed the preliminary designs of communication, signal and ticketing system provided by the contractor, and we have some consulting opinions.

何工程师：请说。
Nick：在初步设计文件中还需补充设备的规格、型号、参数、材料表、培训计划、维护手册、运营操作要求、质量控制计划、工程实施计划等内容。

Mr He: Please.
Nick: The specification, type, parameters of equipment, material list, training plan, maintenance manual, operational requirement, quality control plan and

engineering implementation plan shall be supplemented in the preliminary design.

何工程师：我方将在<u>详细设计文件</u>[①]中补充上述内容。

Mr He: We will add them in the <u>detailed design documents</u>[①].

替换单词 Alternative terms

① 技术规格书
　 竣工文档
　 系统供货商文件

① technical specification
　 completion document
　 document of system supplier

第二部分

商务旅行情景会话

业务情景： 李工程师到埃塞俄比亚签证，签证官 Bob 受理他的申请。
Scene: Chinese engineer Li is applying for Ethiopian visa and his application is being accepted by visa officer Bob.

典型对话 Conversation

Bob: 先生你好。我能看一下你的票号吗？

李工程师： 当然，给你。这是我的申请表。

Bob: 谢谢，李先生。我是鲍勃.琼斯，我负责处理你的申请。

李工程师： 很高兴见到你，琼斯先生。

Bob: 第一步是要确定你是否有资格申请埃塞俄比亚签证。让我看看……你打算申请<u>商务签证</u>①。其实我认为你办一个旅游签证就可以了，就可以在埃塞俄比亚待上 90 天。

李工程师： 这种签证去开会和公务都可以用吗？

Bob: 当然。你可以持旅游签证在<u>埃塞俄比亚</u>②办理短期业务。如果你打算在埃塞俄比亚开展新业务，就最好办理一个长期签证。

李工程师： 哦，我明白了，我想 90 天足够了。

Bob: 你说你要去参加一个会议，我能看一下你的正式邀请函吗？

Bob: Hello, sir. Can I see your ticket number?

Mr Li: Sure, here you are. And here are my application forms as well.

Bob: Thank you, Mr Li. I am Bob Jones and I will handle your application.

Mr Li: Nice to meet you, Jones.

Bob: The first step is to determine your eligibility for an Ethiopian visa. Let me see…you are applying for a <u>business visa</u>①. I think a visitor visa should suffice. With this visa, you can stay in Ethiopia for up to ninety days.

Mr Li: So I can attend conferences and do business on that visa?

Bob: Yes. You are free to do temporary business with this visa. If you are planning on setting up a new business in <u>Ethiopia</u>②, you might need to apply for a long-term visa.

Mr Li: Oh, I see. I think ninety days are enough.

Bob: You said you planned to attend a conference, may I see your official invitation letter?

李工程师：当然！另外我还有两封我的上司为我写的推荐信。

Bob：好的。我看你的护照里有不少其他国家的签证，你经常去国外出差吗？

李工程师：我是一名工程师。我们公司在很多国家设有办事处，比如埃塞俄比亚、尼日利亚、委内瑞拉。

Mr Li: Of course! I have also attached two recommendation letters from my seniors.

Bob: I see. Your passport has quite a few different visas. You took a lot of business trips, didn't you?

Mr Li: I am an engineer. Our company has offices in different countries, like Ethiopia, Nigeria, and Venezuela.

替换单词 Alternative terms

① 过境签证
② 美国

① transit visa
② America

业务情景：在飞往埃塞俄比亚亚的斯亚贝巴的航班上。
Scene: On the flight to Addis Ababa of Ethiopia.

典型对话 Conversation

空姐：（午饭时间）先生，请问，您要点什么？我们有炸鸡、鱼和牛肉①。

李工程师：请来份鱼。

空姐：饮料要什么，是可乐、橘子汁，还是啤酒呢？

李工程师：你们有茶②吗？

空姐：对不起，我们午饭不供应茶。

李工程师：那么，就来杯可乐③吧。

Stewardess: (At lunch time) What would you like to have, sir? We have fried chicken, fish and beef①.

Mr Li: Fish, please.

Stewardess: How about a drink, coke, orange juice or beer?

Mr Li: Do you have tea②?

Stewardess: Sorry. We don't serve tea at lunch.

Mr Li: Then, coke③, please.

373

空姐：(问坐在李明旁边的张先生) 先生，您呢？
张先生：现在什么都不想要。我有点晕机④。
空姐：我看看能不能给你找点治晕机的药片。请稍等。

张先生：多谢！

Stewardess: (To Mr Zhang, who is sitting next to Mr Li) And you, sir?
Mr Zhang: Nothing right now, I'm feeling a bit airsick④.
Stewardess: I'll see if I can get you some tablets for airsickness. Just a moment, please.
Mr Zhang: Thank you very much.

替换单词 Alternative terms

① 鸡肉汉堡；面包；牛排
② 橘子汁；热水
③ 感冒
④ 晕机

① chicken burger; bread; beef
② orange juice; hot water
③ catch a cold
④ airsick

业务情景：飞行了 15 小时后，飞机在亚的斯亚贝巴国际机场着陆，他们填好入境卡后，持护照排队等待过海关办理入境。
Scene: The plane lands at the International Air Port of Addis Ababa after 15- hour flight. After filling out the entry cards, they are queuing up at the customs with their passports.

典型对话 Conversation

海关官员：请出示护照和入境卡。
李工程师：给您。
海关官员：此行目的？
李工程师：我们来此实施一个工程项目。您看，我们是一起的，大部分人员是工程师和技术员。

C.O.: Passport, landing card, please.
Mr Li: Here you are.
C.O.: What's the purpose of your journey?
Mr Li: Actually, we're going to execute a construction project here. You see, we are a group. Most of us are engineers and technicians.

海关官员：你们计划在<u>埃塞俄比亚</u>①待多久？

李工程师：不超过30天。

海关官员：一切看来都没问题。下一步请到海关。

（在海关柜台）

海关官员：请出示您的申报单。

李工程师：给您。

海关官员：还有什么要申报的吗？

李工程师：我想没有了。

海关官员：这个包中都有些什么？

李工程师：就一些个人物品。

海关官员：好了，检查完了。

C.O.: How long do you plan to stay in <u>Ethiopia</u>①?

Mr Li: No more than thirty days.

C.O.: Everything seems to be Ok. Please proceed to customs next.

(At the customs counter)

C.O: Your declaration form, please.

Mr Li: Here it is.

C.O: Anything else to declare?

Mr Li: I don't think so.

C.O: What's in this bag?

Mr Li: Just some personal belongings.

C.O: Ok. That's all.

替换单词 Alternative terms

① 尼日利亚
委内瑞拉

① Nigeria
Venezuela

业务情景：过海关后，接待人员Jane在机场迎接李工程师一行人员。
Scene: After passing the customs, Mr Li and his co-workers are being greeted by reception clerk Jane at the airport.

典型对话 Conversation

Jane：请问，你是中国来的李先生吗？

李工程师：是的，我是。

Jane：我叫珍，是MAX公司的<u>秘书</u>①。

李工程师：你好，Jane。

Jane: Excuse me! Are you Mr Li from China?

Mr Li: Yes, I am.

Jane: I'm Jane, the <u>secretary</u>① of MAX Corporation.

Mr Li: How do you do, Jane?

375

Jane: 你好,李先生。欢迎来到埃塞俄比亚。

李工程师: 谢谢,你到机场来接我真是太客气了,希望没有让你久等。

Jane: 不客气,一路上很好吧!

李工程师: 很好,谢谢。一路上挺好的。

Jane: 很高兴你这么说,李先生,你是第一次来埃塞吗?

李工程师: 是的,是第一次。

Jane: 希望你在亚的斯亚贝巴② 过得愉快。

李工程师: 谢谢,我相信会的,我想知道我们现在要去哪儿?

Jane: 车在那边,咱们现在就去宾馆。我帮你拿个包吧!

李工程师: 不用,谢谢。我自己能行,我们走吧。

Jane: How do you do, Mr Li. Welcome to Ethiopia.

Mr Li: Thank you. It's very kind of you to come and meet me at the airport, Jane. I hope you haven't been waiting for long.

Jane: No, not at all. I hope you've had an enjoyable trip.

Mr Li: Yes, thank you. It was quite a good trip.

Jane: I'm glad to hear that. Is this your first trip to Ethiopia, Mr Li?

Mr Li: Yes, the very first.

Jane: I hope you will enjoy your stay in Addis Ababa②.

Mr Li: Thanks. I'm sure I will. I would like to know where we are heading now.

Jane: Our car is waiting over there. Let's drive to the hotel. May I help you with one of your bags?

Mr Li: No thanks. I can manage all right. Let' go.

替换单词 Alternative terms

① 行政主管
  翻译
② 阿布贾
  加拉加斯

① manager of admin
  translator
② Abuja
  Caracas

业务情景:李工程师一行人员随 Jane 乘车前往下榻宾馆途中。
Scene: Mr Li and his co-workers, accompanied by Jane, are taking a bus to their hotel.

第二部分　商务旅行情景会话

典型对话 Conversation

李工程师：就我看来，亚的斯亚贝巴真是个漂亮的城市。天空特别的蓝。

珍：是的，的确很美。您可知道"亚的斯亚贝巴"的意思是"新鲜的花朵"？我们现在正在一条主干道上。

李工程师：我住在哪里？

珍：您将下榻卡莱步酒店①。

李工程师：太好了，我喜欢卡莱布饭店。

珍：好。它是本市最好的五星级宾馆之一。我们已经预订了一间带有单独浴室的房间。这个饭店提供24小时客房服务，有很好的餐厅、酒吧和洗衣店。商务中心提供电子邮件、传真、电传和复印等服务。如果您需要组织会议，那儿还可以提供完善的会议服务。

李工程师：听起来很不错，但交通便利吗？

珍：绝对方便！它位于商业区，还有十分钟路程就到了。

（十分钟以后）

珍：李先生，这就是卡莱布酒店。

李工程师：哇！看起来真雄伟。

Jane：李先生，我们到总台登记办理入住手续吧。

Mr Li: Addis Ababa is a really beautiful city from what I see. The sky is exceptionally clear.

Jane: Yes, it is. Do you know "Addis Ababa" means "fresh flowers"? Now we are on one of our main roads.

Mr Li: Where shall I stay?

Jane: You'll stay at Kaleb Hotel①.

Mr Li: Good. I like Kaleb Hotel.

Jane: Yes, among all the five star hotels in this city, it is one of the best. We've reserved a room with a private bathroom. The hotel has 24-hour room service. You'll find a nice restaurant, a bar and a laundry service there. And services such as E-mail, fax, telex and copying are available at the Business Centre. It even has a perfect convention service if you need to organize conferences there.

Mr Li: Sounds great. But is it convenient for travel?

Jane: Absolutely! It is located downtown. We'll get there soon. It's only about ten minutes away.

(ten minutes later)

Jane: This is Kaleb Hotel, Mr Li.

Mr Li: Wow! It looks very grand.

Jane: Shall we go to the reception desk and check in, Mr Li.

377

李工程师：好的，珍，你太客气了，感谢你为我所做的一切。

珍：明天早上九点我到宾馆接你。我们总经理九点三十分在公司见你。下午我们一起去工地现场，你看怎么样？

李工程师：很好。

Mr Li: Sure, Jane. That's very kind of you! Thank you for everything.

Jane: You're welcome! I'll pick you up at the hotel at 9:00 in the morning, and our General Manager will be meeting you at our company at 9:30. In the afternoon, we will have a visit to the construction site, is that all right?

Mr Li: That's fine.

替换单词 Alternative terms

① 希尔顿酒店	① Hilton hotel

业务情景：到达宾馆后稍作休息，李工程师等相继在总台登记入住酒店。
Scene: Having taken a short rest after arrival, Mr Li and his company are checking in at reception desk of the hotel.

典型对话 Conversation

总台：早上好，先生。需要我帮忙吗？

李工程师：早上好！我预订了一间套房/单人房/双床标间房。

总台：能告诉我你的名字吗，先生？

李工程师：李明。

总台：请稍等，先生，我查一下登记表。哦，李先生，有你的预订。请你填一下这张表，我好为你准备钥匙卡。

Receptionist: Good morning, sir. Can I help you?

Mr Li: Good morning! I have a reservation for a suite/single/standard room with twin beds here.

Receptionist: May I have your name, sir, please?

Mr Li: Li Ming.

Receptionist: Just a moment, sir, I will look through our list. Yes, we do have a reservation for you, Mr Li. Would you please fill out this form while I prepare your key card for you?

李工程师:好的,借用一下你的笔,可以吗?

总台:当然可以,给你。

李工程师:房号这一栏我该如何填?

总台:你不填,一会儿我来填。

李工程师:(填表毕)给你。

Mr Li: Yes. Can I borrow your pen for a minute, please?

Receptionist: Sure. Here you are.

Mr Li: What should I fill in under ROOM NUMBER?

Receptionist: You can just skip that. I'll put the room number in later on.

Mr Li: (After he has completed the form) Here you are.

业务情景:李工程师在餐馆点餐。
Scene: Mr Li is ordering food in a restaurant.

典型对话 Conversation

服务员:这里是菜单,现在可以点餐了吗?

李工程师:是的,可以。请先给我来一份例汤,好吗?今日的例汤是什么?

服务员:是意大利蔬菜汤①,可以吗?

李工程师:可以。至于主菜,有什么推荐的吗?

服务员:牛排怎么样?这是我们的招牌菜。

李工程师:嗯,来一份牛排吧。

服务员:你想要几分熟的?

李工程师:五成熟②吧。

服务员:还需要其他什么吗?

李工程师:一份披萨套餐③,一杯柠檬奶昔和水果沙拉。

服务员:好的,汤马上就会上来。

Waiter: Here is the menu. Can I have your order now?

Mr Li: Yes. Could I just have the soup to start please? What is the soup for today?

Waiter: That's minestrone①, is that all right, sir?

Mr Li: Yeah, that's fine, and for the main course, do you have any recommendation?

Waiter: How about the beefsteak? It is our specialty.

Mr Li: Eh, I want a piece of it.

Waiter: How do you like it cooked?

Mr Li: Medium②.

Waiter: What else do you want?

Mr Li: The pizza combo③, a glass of lemon milk shake and the fruit salad, please.

Waiter: All right, I'll bring the soup right away.

替换单词 Alternative terms

① 罗宋汤
② 七成熟
　全熟
③ 意大利面

① borsch
② medium well
　well done
③ spaghetti

业务情景：李工程师要去银行办理相关手续，问路。
Scene: Mr Li has something to do in the bank and he is asking how he could get there.

典型对话 Conversation

李工程师：先生，烦问银行该往哪个方向走？

过路人：在下一拐角处向前直走，你不会错过的。

李工程师：谢谢你。我一定会找到。

李工程师：劳驾，先生，我迷路了。能在地图上指点一下我现在所处的位置吗？

警员：你现在正站在这个地方，就在第五大街的拐角处。

李工程师：国家大剧院①离这里有多远？

警员：不太远，只有十来分钟的路程。走到下一个路口左转，再走三个街区就到了。

李工程师：太感谢了。

Mr Li: Excuse me, sir. Do you happen to know which direction it is to the bank?

Passer-by: Go straight ahead at the next corner. You can't miss it.

Mr Li: Thank you. I'm sure I'll find it.

Mr Li: Pardon me, sir, I'm lost. Could you show me where I am on this map?

Policeman: You are standing at this point, right on the corner of Fifth Street.

Mr Li: How far is it from here to the National Theater①?

Policeman: Not far from here. You can get there in ten minutes. Go to the next corner and turn left. Walk three blocks and there you are.

Mr Li: Thanks a lot.

过路人：劳驾，这条街通哪里？我如何才能到达这个地址？

Passer-by: Pardon me. Where does this street lead to ? And how can I get to this address?

李工程师：对不起，我也是刚到这里的。

Mr Li: I'm sorry. I'm new here.

替换单词 Alternative terms

① 歌剧院
　画廊

① opera house
　gallery

业务情景：张先生和李工程师等工作人员在亚的斯亚贝巴圆满完成此行工作后返回中国，在机场办理登机手续。

Scene: Mr Zhang, Mr Li and their party are going through the boarding formalities after they have successfully accomplished their scheduled tasks in Addis Ababa and prepare to go back to China.

 典型对话 Conversation

（他们在候机大厅正打听办理登记的柜台在哪。）

李工程师：劳驾，请问中国国际航空公司办理登机手续的柜台在哪？

工作人员：沿这条通道走到头，向左拐，你就会在你右方看到牌子。很好找的。

李工程师：多谢。

工作人员：（在办理登机手续的柜台）早上好。请出示机票与护照。

李工程师：早上好。我们是一起的，这些是所有的机票和护照。

(They're are looking for the check-in counter in the airport waiting hall.)

Mr Li: Excuse me, where's the check-in counter of CA Airlines, please?

Staff member: Go down this corridor until the end. Turn left and you'll see the signs on your right. You can't miss it.

Mr Li: Thanks a lot.

Staff member: (at the Check-in counter) Good morning. Your ticket and passport, please.

Mr Li: Good morning. We're in group. Here are all the tickets and passports.

工作人员：你们共有多少人？

李工程师：总共 14 人。
工作人员：对座位有什么要求吗？
李工程师：我叫李明，我和张先生要两个靠窗的座位①，这是我的护照。我问问其他人。

（在询问了他的同事之后）
李工程师：他们没有特别要求。
工作人员：你们准备托运多少件行李？

李工程师：每人两件。顺便问一下，行李限额是多少？
工作人员：每位旅客三十英镑，每件限重二十英镑。把这四个仪器箱放在磅秤上，还有那个行李箱，一件一件地放。

李工程师：希望都没超重。
（在称过所有箱子之后）
工作人员：没有，都没超重。让我给行李系上行李标签。这些是你们的登机卡和护照。祝你们飞行愉快，先生们。

李工程师：谢谢。

Staff member: How many people are there in the group?
Mr Li: Fourteen in all.
Staff member: Any seat preference ?
Mr Li: Two window seats① for Mr Zhang and me. Oh, my name's Li Ming. This passport is mine. For the others, let me ask them about their opinion.
(after enquiring his colleagues)
Mr Li: No preference for them.
Staff member: How many pieces of baggage do you want to check?
Mr Li: Two for each of us. By the way, what's the baggage allowance?
Staff member: Thirty pounds for each passenger and the weight limit for each piece is twenty pounds. Put these four big cartons and that suitcase on the scale then, one by one.
Mr Li: I hope they're not overweight.
(after weighing all the baggage)
Staff member: No, you're Ok. Now, let me put on the baggage tags. Here are your boarding passes and passports. Have a good flight, gentlemen.
Mr Li: Thanks.

替换单词 Alternative terms

① 靠过道座位　　　　　　　　　　① aisle seat

第三部分

常用信息附图附表

一、世界各国应急求救电话号码

国 家 名	电 话 号 码	国 家 名	电 话 号 码
中国(大陆)	报警110	奥地利	133
中国(大陆)	火警119	比利时	101
中国(大陆)	交通事故112	保加利亚	166
中国澳门	000	捷克	333
巴基斯坦	222222	丹麦	112
印度尼西亚	510110	埃及	122
印度	110	芬兰	112
日本	110	法国	17
孟加拉	509922	德国	110
马来西亚	999	英国	999
泰国	191	希腊	171
菲律宾	7575	匈牙利	078668
斯里兰卡	33333	冰岛	11166
新加坡	999	爱尔兰	999
文莱	22333	以色列	100
韩国	112	意大利	113
卢森堡	5860	荷兰	222222
摩洛哥	19	波兰	997
葡萄牙	091	瑞典	112
挪威	112\113		

二、中国与世界各国时差对照表

时间是以 24 小时为单位，+10 算法为北京现在时间加 10 后得出来的就是当地的时间，-10 算法为北京现在时间减 10 后得出来的就是当地的时间。例如：我们要算美国纽约的时间，现在北京时间为 20:00，那就是拿 20-13=7，也就是说中国东八区的晚上八点就是美国纽约的早上七点。

以下表格以各大洲划分区域,大家想要哪个国家直接找相应洲,然后找相应地区即可。

美 洲 国 家

国 家 名	所 属 地 区	与 中 国 时 差
美国	华盛顿 Washington, D.C.	-13
巴拉圭	亚松森 Asuncion	-12
巴西	巴西利亚 Brasilia	-11
哥伦比亚	波哥大 Bogota	-13
阿根廷	布宜诺斯艾利斯 Buenos Aires	-11
委内瑞拉	加拉加斯 Caracas	-12
加拿大	渥太华 Ottawa	-13
巴拿马	巴拿马城 Panama	-13
古巴	哈瓦那 Havana	-13
牙买加	金斯敦 Kingston	-13
玻利维亚	拉巴斯 La Paz	-12
秘鲁	利马 Lima	-13
墨西哥	墨西哥城 Mexico City	-14
乌拉圭	蒙得维的亚 Montevideo	-11
波多黎各	圣胡安 San Juan	-12
智利	圣地亚哥 Santiago	-12

亚 洲 国 家

国 家 名	所 属 地 区	与 中 国 时 差
伊朗	德黑兰 Tehran	-4:30
阿联酋	阿布扎比 Abu Dhabi	-4
也门	亚丁 Aden	-5
约旦	安曼 Amman	-6
土耳其	安卡拉 Ankara	-6

续上表

国 家 名	所 属 地 区	与 中 国 时 差
伊拉克	巴格达 Baghdad	-5
阿塞拜疆	巴库 Baku	-6
文莱	斯里巴加湾港 Bandar Seri Begawan	0
泰国	曼谷 Bangkok	-1
黎巴嫩	贝鲁特 Beirut	-6
印度	新德里 New Delhi	-2:30
斯里兰卡	科伦坡 Colombo	-2:30
叙利亚	大马士革 Damascus	-6
孟加拉	达卡 Dhaka	-2
印度尼西亚	雅加达 Djakart	-1
越南	河内 Hanoi	-1
尼泊尔	加德满都 Katmandu	-2:30
马来西亚	吉隆坡 Kuala Lumpur	0
巴基斯坦	伊斯兰堡 Islamabad	-3
以色列	耶路撒冷 Jerusalem	-6
科威特	科威特 Kuwait	-5
日本	东京 Tokyo	+1
菲律宾	马尼拉 Manila	0
沙特阿拉伯	麦加 Mecca	-5
柬埔寨	金边 Phnom Penh	-1
朝鲜	平壤 Pyongyang	+1
缅甸	仰光 Rangoon	-1:30
韩国	首尔 Seoul	+1
新加坡	新加坡 Singapore	0
蒙古	乌兰巴托 Ulan Bator	0
中国	澳门 Macao	0
中国	香港 Hong Kong	0
中国	台北 Taibei	0

欧 洲 国 家

国 家 名	所 属 地 区	与中国时差
英国	伦敦 London	-8
荷兰	阿姆斯特丹 Amsterdam	-7
比利时	布鲁塞尔 Brussels	-7
罗马尼亚	布加勒斯特 Bucharest	-6
希腊	雅典 Athens	-6
南斯拉夫	贝尔格莱德 Belgrade	-7
德国	柏林 Berlin	-7
丹麦	哥本哈根 Copenhagen	-7
爱尔兰	都柏林 Dublin	-8
波兰	华沙 Warsaw	-7
瑞士	伯尔尼 Bern	-7
意大利	罗马 Rome	-7
芬兰	赫尔辛基 Helsinki	-6
土耳其	伊斯坦布尔 Istanbul	-6
乌克兰	基辅 Kiev	-5
葡萄牙	里斯本 Lisbon	-8
西班牙	马德里 Madrid	-7
俄罗斯	莫斯科 Moscow	-5
挪威	奥斯陆 Oslo	-7
法国	巴黎 Paris	-7
捷克	布拉格 Prague	-7
冰岛	雷克雅未克 Reykjavik	-8
保加利亚	索非亚 Sofia	-6
瑞典	斯德哥尔摩 Stockholm	-7
阿尔巴尼亚	地拉那 Tirana	-7
梵蒂冈	梵蒂冈 Vatican	-7
奥地利	维也纳 Vienna	-7
匈牙利	布达佩斯 Budapest	-7

大洋洲国家

国　家　名	所属地区	与中国时差
关岛	阿加尼亚 Agana	+2
西萨摩亚	阿皮亚 Apia	-19
新西兰	惠灵顿 Wellington	+4
澳大利亚	堪培拉 Canberra	+2
法属新喀里多尼亚	努美阿 Noumea	+3
法属波利尼西亚	帕皮提 Papeete	-18
巴布亚新几内亚	莫尔兹比港 Port Moresby	+2
斐济	苏瓦 Suva	+4
瓦努阿图	维拉港 vila	+3

非洲国家

国　家　名	所属地区	与中国时差
科特迪瓦	阿比让 Abidjan	-8
埃塞俄比亚	亚的斯亚贝巴 Addis Ababa	-5
埃及	开罗 Cairo	-6
阿尔及利亚	阿尔及尔 Algiers	-7
马里	巴马科 Bamako	-8
利比亚	的黎波里 Tripoli	-6
莫桑比克	马普托 Maputo	-6
刚果	布拉柴维尔 Brazzaville	-7
南非	比勒陀利亚 Pretoria	-6
塞内加尔	达喀尔 Dakar	-8
摩洛哥	拉巴特 Rabat	-8
坦桑尼亚	达累斯萨拉姆 Dar es Salaam	-5
吉布提	吉布提 Djibouti	-5
喀麦隆	杜阿拉 Douala	-7
博茨瓦纳	哈博罗内 Gaborone	-6
乌干达	坎帕拉 Kampala	-5
尼日利亚	阿布贾	-7

续上表

国　家　名	所　属　地　区	与　中　国　时　差
苏丹	喀土穆 Khartoum	-6
民主刚果	金沙萨 Kinshasa	-7
加那利群岛	拉斯帕耳马斯 Las Palmas	-8
安哥拉	罗安达 Luanda	-7
赞比亚	卢萨卡 Lusaka	-6
索马里	摩加迪沙 Mogadishu	-5
肯尼亚	内罗毕 Nairobi	-5
利比里亚	蒙罗维亚 Monrovia	-8
乍得	恩贾梅纳 Ndjamena	-7
尼日尔	尼亚美 Niamey	-8
毛里塔尼亚	努瓦克肖特 Nouakchott	-8
毛里求斯	路易港 Port Louis	-4
圣多美和普林西比	圣多美 Sao Tome	-8
马达加斯加	塔那那利佛 Tananarive	-5
突尼斯	突尼斯 Tunis	-7
纳米比亚	温得和克 Windhoek	-6

三、入境海关申报表正面中英对照翻译

中　文	英　文
每一位入境美国的游客或一家之主必须提供以下数据（一个家庭只需申报一份）	Each arriving traveler or head of family must provide the following information (only ONE written declaration per family is required):
1. 姓、名、中间名	Family Name，First(Given)，Middle
2 出生日期：日、月、年	Birth date: Day, Month，Year
3. 与你同行的家庭成员人数	Number of family members traveling with you
4. a.〈在美居住地址（旅馆名称／目的地）b.〈城市〉c.〈州〉	a. U.S. street address (hotel name/destination b. City c. State
5. 发护照国家	Passport issue by (country)

续上表

中　文	英　文
6. 护照号码	Passport number
7. 居住国家	Country of Residence
8. 此次旅游时来美国之前去过的国家	Countries visited on this trip prior to U.S. arrival
9. 航空公司 / 班机号码或船名	Airline/Flight No. or Vessel Name
10. 此次旅程的目的主要是商务 ○ 是 ○ 否	The primary purpose of this trip is BUSINESS ○ YES ○ NO
11. 我（我们）携带 a. 水果、植物、食物或昆虫？是否？b. 肉类、动物或动物 / 野生动物制品？　是否？c. 带病原体、细胞培养或蜗牛？ d. 土壤或你曾经去过美国境外的农场或牧场吗？是否	I am (We are) bringing: a. fruits, vegetables, plants, seeds, food, insects: Yes No. b. meats, animals, animal/wildlife products：Yes No. c. disease agents, cell cultures, snails: Yes No d. soil or have been on a farm/ranch/pasture: Yes No
12. 我有（我们有）靠近（如触碰或接触）牲畜○ 是 ○否？	. I have (We have) been in close proximity of (such as touching or handling) livestock outside: Yes No
13. 你携带现金或财物品，其价值超过一万美金或相当于一万美金的外币吗？ ○是 ○否	I am (We are) carrying currency or monetary instruments over $10,000 U.S. or the foreign equivalent. ○ YES ○ NO
14. 我（我们）有携带商品：（贩卖物品、商业样品或任何不属于个人所有的物品）○是 ○否	I have (We have) commercial merchandise: (article for sale, samples used for soliciting orders, or goods that are not considered personal effects) ○ YES ○ NO
15. 美国居民——我们带入美国所有物品（包含商品及礼品，但不包含邮寄入美国的物品）的总价值为：	Residents-the total value of all good, including commercial merchandise I/We have purchased or acquired abroad, (including gifts for someone else, but not items mailed to the U.S.) and am/are bringing to the U.S. is:
观光客——将留在美国境内的物品价值为（包含商品）：	Visitors-the total value of all article that will remain in the U.S., including commercial merchandise is
请阅读本表背面的说明，请将须申报的物品在空格内列出	Read the instruction on the back of this form. Space is provided to list all the items you must declare.
我已阅读过背面的说明，且已就实申报	I HAVE READ THE IMPORTANT INFORMATION ON THE REVERSE SIDE OF THIS FORM AND HAVE MADE A TRUTHFUL DECLARATION.
签名及日期(日 / 月 / 年)	Signature; Date (day/month/year)